Indian Dialogical Christologies

Interfaith Treasures Uncovered

Under this Series, the Publishers endeavor to focus on Comparative Studies pertaining to Christian Faith & Living in the central matrix and Hinduism, Buddhism, Sikhism, Islam, Judaism, etc., on the peripheral. The Studies shall cover topics like Literature & Poetry, Indigenous Philosophizing, Ethical response towards Agriculture, Health & Healing, Science & Technology, Ecofeminist Theology, Sociological approach towards Human Rights, Law & Politics, Arts, History of Ideas, Ancient Civilizations, Cultural Contiguity, Religious Cosmologies & Mysticism, Footsteps of famous Theologians, World Peace & Harmony, Global Capitalism, Network Marketing, Cybertheology, Population & Demographics, Epigraphic Studies, Contextualized Education, and many others. We welcome a Mss. on any topic/s mentioned, whether they are original works, scholarly monographs, collections of conference papers, revised dissertations, or translations of historical documents. Through the Series, we are striving to put forward published works that may help Institutions, Academic Bodies, Researchers, Scholars and the World at large in furthering their respective knowledge and understanding on the concerned subject. We welcome your comments on our efforts and further suggestions on how we can foster the upcoming books on parallel interfaces between and among Christianity and other religions.

Interfaith Treasures Uncovered - 12

Indian Dialogical Christologies

Recapitulating Advaita Vedanta & Indian Traditions of Swami Vivekananda and Mahatma Gandhi

P. T. Subrahmanyan

CWI

Christian World Imprints™

First Published in 2018 by

Christian World Imprints™
Christian Publishing & Books from India
H-12 Bali Nagar, **New Delhi-110015**
info@christianworldimprints.com
www.ChristianWorldImprints.com
Phone: +91 11 25465925

ISBN 13: 978-93-5148-257-4 ISBN 10: 93-5148-257-X

Cataloging in Publication Data--DK
Courtesy: D.K. Agencies (P) Ltd. <docinfo@dkagencies.com>

Subrahmanyan, P. T., 1978- author.
Indian dialogical Christologies : recapitulating Advaita Vedanta & Indian traditions of Swami Vivekananda and Mahatma Gandhi / Dr. P.T. Subrahmanyan.
pages cm. -- (Interfaith treasures uncovered ; 12)
Includes bibliographical references.
ISBN 935148257X
ISBN 9789351482574

1. Jesus Christ--Person and offices. 2. Christianity and other religions--Hinduism. 3. Hinduism--Relations--Christianity. 4. Advaita. 5. Vedanta. 6. Vivekananda, Swami, 1863-1902. 7. Gandhi, Mahatma, 1869-1948. I. Title. II. Series: Interfaith treasures uncovered ; 12.

LCC BT203.S83 2018 | DDC 232 23

Printed in India

Contents

This work is originally a Ph. D. Thesis submitted to Mahatma Gandhi University, Kottayam, and is published with the written permission. The author is responsible for the title, contents and opinions expressed in it. The original title of the dissertation is 'Metaphysical and Ethical Dimensions of Christ Experience in the Writings of Swami Vivekananda and Mahatma Gandhi – A Critical Analysis'.

Foreword

Appreciation for Dr. P. T. Subrahmanyan's book on 'Indian Dialogical Christologies: Recapitulating Advaita Vedanta & Indian Traditions of Swami Vivekananda and Mahatma Gandhi'.

In Swami Vivekananda's view, there is very little difference between the pure religion of Christ and that of the Vedanda. Jesus was an Advaitin because to the masses who could not conceive of anything higher than a Personal God, he said, 'pray to your Father in heaven'; to others, who could grasp a higher idea, he said, 'I am the vine, ye are the branches', but to his disciples whom he revealed himself more fully, he proclaimed the higher truth, 'I and my Father are One'. We have to realise the kingdom of God which is within us, i.e., we have to realise our spiritual nature that we are immortal spirit, we have to attain perfection through renunciation. Krsna, Buddha, Jesus and Ramakrishna are just few among the many incarnations. Among the incarnated personalities like Zoroaster, Moses, Buddha, Krsna, Jesus, Mohammed, Luther, Ramakrishna, some are called Gods and some prophets. The difference between human person and Christ is a difference in manifestation; but as Absolute Being there is no difference between the two. When intelligence is perfect, we get the Incarnation - the Christ. Jesus was a person who had felt and realised God intensely. Christs are Teachers of teachers; they can transform us into saints. But mere worship of Buddha or Christ will not save a person; God alone can give us freedom. Jesus and others like him are free spirits and hence they took human form, not by the compulsion of their past actions, but just to do good to humankind.

A Christian should retain the essentials of Christianity which according to Swami Vivekananda, are the teachings of Lord Jesus as exemplified in the Sermon on the Mount. Christ shows us the way to become perfect; he shows our true nature which is divine. Christianity considers human person as a sinner, a worm and that is why It could not understand the message of potential divinity implied in his saying, 'I and my father are one'. Human sacrifice was a Jewish idea and to fit the gentle and loving Jesus into Jewish beliefs, the idea of human sacrifice in the form of atonement or as a human scapegoat, by Christianity, was really unfortunate. The problem with Christianity is its idea that religion consists in doctrines. It has the peculiar doctrine of Fall and now there is no way of escape other than belief in Jesus Christ that he died to save us. For the Christians the problem is how to escape the wrath of God. Like the Indians they are unable to see that religion means realization which involves the regaining of the lost selfhood. In the view of Swami Vivekananda, the West has distorted the religion of renunciation and realization of Jesus into a 'shop-keeping religion' of luxury and intolerant superstitious doctrines.

It was the idea of sacrificial suffering in the life of Jesus that appealed most to Mahatma Gandhi, although he rejected traditional doctrines of atonement. The sacrifice of Jesus on the cross was to him a supreme example of self-giving. One such act of perfect sacrifice would suffice for the whole world. Such is held to be Jesus' example. Jesus taught and embodied a pure non-violence. Jesus was non-violence par excellence. Underlying non-violence is love and Jesus' life and death were an expression of pure divine love. 'When I survey the wondrous Cross' was a favourite hymn for Gandhiji.

Gandhiji's attitude to the divinity of Christ is similar to that of Swami Vivekananda. Christ is divine, but not in an exclusive sense. Jesus was for him a supreme satyagrhi. He was a teacher and exemplar of sacrificial love. He was all for the teachings of Jesus contained in the Sermon on the Mount. He has said: It was the New Testament which really awakened me to the value of Passive Resistance. When I read in the Sermon on the Mount such passages as 'resist not him that is evil', 'He that smitteth thee on the right cheek, turn to him the other also' etc. I was overjoyed. The message of Jesus as I understood it is, contained in the Sermon on the Mount, unadulterated and taken as a whole. Jesus belongs not solely to Christianity but to the entire world, to all races and people.

Christians can learn many insights from such Christologies of Swami Vivekananda and Mahatma Gandhi. New dimensions of the meanings of the Gospel of God in Jesus are emerging through these Christologies. We are indeed thankful to God!

K. P. Aleaz
Former Professor of Bishop's College
and NIIPGTS, Kolkata.

Acknowledgments

I am grateful to God who gave me the direction and meaning to my life out of His love. His unfailing mercy and providence helped me to conduct this research.

I would like to place on record my deep and sincere thanks to my *Guru* Dr. K. S. Radhakrishnan, the former Chairman, Kerala Public Service Commission and the former Vice-Chancellor, Sri Sankaracharya University of Sanskrit, Kalady, under whose guidance I could do this research. His thoughtful judgment, compassionate care and scholarly insight helped me to complete this research.

I also express my thanks to teachers of the Department of Philosophy, Maharaja's College, Ernakulam and the library staffs of various libraries for all their services and help towards this research work.

I am especially thankful to Dr. K. P. Aleaz, former Professor of Bishop's College and NIIPGTS, Kolkata for writing a worthy foreword for this book.

I too acknowledge the great effort of my colleague Mr. M. J. Isaac for going through the draft for proof reading and correction.

The publisher Christian World Imprints, New Delhi very well deserves my high appreciation for bringing out this work in book form.

I also express my sincere gratitude to a host of other individuals, whose names are known and unknown, but had contributed much to this project.

Finally, I am much thankful to my beloved wife Tessy and loving children Darsa and Derik, for their patience and constant encouragement for the completion of this work.

Dr. P.T. Subrahmanyan

Preface

Swami Vivekananda and Mahatma Gandhi encountered Christ and Christianity in a colonial context, which seriously questioned the basic values of Indian tradition. The Western civilization they encountered not only affirmed its superiority, but also denigrated the religion and culture of India. Vivekananda and Gandhi responded to this context by rejecting the Western form of Christianity as well as separating Christ from this Western colonial Christianity. They did not accept the customary/dogmatic beliefs of the West on Christ, which was based on the Aristotelian epistemology. On the other, they experienced Christ as an Oriental, and his spirituality as essentially Eastern. This re-definition of Christ-experience was based on *Advaita* epistemology of oneness and equality in Christ. Therefore, Vivekananda's and Gandhi's Christ-experience is metaphysical and ethical in nature in accordance with Indian tradition.

Christ-experience in Indian context is therefore different from the West. It is experiential and mystical in nature, transforming the 'experiencer' into Christ-likeness or into 'another Christ'. This experience cannot be defined into dogmas and doctrines by rationalization as in the Western Aristotelian framework. This understanding of Christ in the context of *Advaita* philosophy and Indian tradition brings a new dimension of Christ-experience. However, this research examines, whether this novel approach is wanting? This research also suggests ways of understanding and dialogical co-existence between Hindus and Christians in contemporary India, from a colonial, confrontational approach of the past.

There are seven chapters in the book. The first chapter is introduction. It deals with the research problem, its significance and the 19th century colonial background and related issues of the study. The second chapter deals with the formation of Vivekananda and Gandhi – the influences that made their personality and philosophical views. The third chapter is about the supremacy of Indian tradition and *Advaita Vedānta* in the writings of Vivekananda and Gandhi. Fourth chapter sees how Vivekananda and Gandhi as *Advaita*

Vedāntins responded to the Christian tradition, plurality of religions and Christ. The fifth chapter analyses the Christ-experience of Vivekananda and Gandhi as metaphysical and ethical, which is quite different from the Western Aristotelian epistemological framework. The sixth chapter is a critical analysis of the *Advaitic* Christ-experience of Vivekananda and Gandhi, as it uses 'comparative method' in the philosophy of religions and the related issues. The sixth chapter also gives observations for the betterment of Hindu-Christian relations in today's post-colonial, secular democratic context of India from the colonial past and its confrontational attitudes. The seventh chapter is the last chapter, which gives the summary and conclusion of the research.

Chapter 1

Introduction

1.1. Introduction

It is a definite fact that the 19th century Western colonial context and its alliance with Christianity had a deep impact upon the views of Swami Vivekananda (1863 –1902) and Mahatma Gandhi (1869-1948), as it is reflected in their writings. Therefore, their writings and reflections on Christ and Christianity have to be seen in the wider context of Indian response to Western cultural invasion, as there was a real encounter of cultures between East and West and between Christianity and Hinduism during the British period.[1] Hence, theirs was an ambiguous context of British colonialism and European Protestant Christianity, which were juxtaposed without much distinguishing marks between them.[2] They experienced negative effects of colonial rule in all realms of Indian life and there was also a subsequent Hindu reaction and response to the same. Therefore their Christ-experience occurred in a political and ideological circumstance of culture, power, and hegemonic influence of the colonizers and the missionaries that affected the lives of the people of India.[3] As such, it is important to study the background of their Christ-experience in a colonial context as they developed their views within these particular cultural and philosophical frameworks.

---

[1] T. V. Philip, "Christianity in India during Western Colonialism: Conflict, Reconciliation or Adjustment," *Indian Church History Review* 21/1 (June, 1987): 24.

[2] *The Complete Works of Swami Vivekananda*, vol. 8 (Kolkata: Advaiata Ashrama, 2009), 160. Hereafter it will be denoted as *CWSV* with different volumes.

[3] Jacob S. Dharmaraj, *Colonialism and Christian Mission: Postcolonial Reflections* (Delhi: ISPCK, 1993), 25.

1.2. The Research Problem

Although, the colonial hegemony and Western form of Christianity with its superior claims and subsequent denunciation of Indian tradition and Hinduism had negative impact on Vivekananda and Gandhi; in spite of all that, they admired and assimilated Christ within Indian context. They separated Christ from Western Christianity and from its doctrinal assertions, and interpreted Christ in terms of Indian *Advaitic* philosophical context. They laid emphasis on the metaphysical and ethical dimensions of Christ-experience, which was totally different from the Western Christian perceptions of Christ, that was dominated by an Aristotelian epistemology which firmly believed in dichotomy and which in turn supported the colonial expansion of Europe and the subjugation of peoples all over the world. Nevertheless, Christ found the foremost place in Vivekananda's and Gandhi's thoughts and the experience of Christ became a part of their heritage, of which, we see a lot of references in their writings. This research, therefore, focuses on the critical analysis of the metaphysical and ethical dimensions of their Christ-experience in their writings. Some of the pertinent questions that guide this research are: Why Vivekananda and Gandhi differ in their Christ-experience from that of Christianity? What are the differences of Aristotelian and *Advaitic* philosophical methodology in Christ-experience? What are the defects they found in the Western epistemological conceptions of Christ? What are the 'pros' and 'cons' of their Christ-experience? How can we overcome the past mistakes and the comparative approach in Hindu-Christian relations? What are the ways of mutual reconciliation? How can it contribute to religious harmony and secular tradition of Indian culture?

1.3. Significance of the Research

Vivekananda and Gandhi responded to a Western colonial Christianity and its wider context, which questioned the validity of Hindu religion and denigrated the Indian tradition. Therefore theirs were a reactionary response which affirmed the supremacy of Indian tradition over the British colonialism and Western Christianity, which were associated to each other. However, even in such a context, they did not criticize Christ, but separated Christ from the 'distorted' form of Western Christianity, and encountered, admired and assimilated Him as part of Indian tradition. Hence, as exponents of Indian tradition, they viewed Christ from an Oriental and *Advaitic* perspective and thus their responses to Christ attain philosophical significance. They rejected the colonial epistemology and dogmas of Western Christianity, rather affirmed the direct-experience (*anubhava*) of Christ within Indian tradition, without being converted to, or accepting the so called doctrines of 'orthodox' Christianity. So, their Christ-experience is from an Indian *Advaitic* philosophical framework, which is different from the 'Christ' of Western dogmatic and philosophical affirmations rooted in the epistemology of Aristotle.[4] This research, thus, focuses on the shift of philosophical framework from Aristotelian to *Advaita* in the Christ-experience of Swami Vivekananda and Mahatma Gandhi.

Further, this research tries to critically analyse and bring a mutual understanding and philosophical reconciliation between Hinduism and Christianity in the post-colonial, secular, democratic context of India, from the conflicting and confrontational relations of the colonial past. The superior-colonial approach of Western Christianity and the comparative-reductive approach of the *Advaita Vedānta* in a competitive manner to prove the superiority of each over the 'other' have to be corrected today for a fruitful dialogical relationship. Instead of asserting superior claims and refutation of the faith of the 'other,' it is time to accept the equality of all religions. Hence, this research attempts at inter-religious understanding, peace, harmony and unity in present day pluralistic context of India. It can reduce the tensions between the majority Hindu community and the minority Christian community by opening windows of understanding, love and co-operation.

1.4. The Colonial Background and Issues of Hindu-Christian Encounter

Colonialism was exploitative, despotic, racist and repressive.[5] Because the Europeans had intrudingly roamed the world, as if they were its masters and invaded, enslaved, brutally assaulted and even eliminated large groups of people in their unscrupulous pursuit of wealth and power. [6] India was also plundered externally and shattered internally under the British domination.[7] Hence, Vivekananda says that British administration was "insolent" and "despotic,"[8] which led to poverty and frequent famines in India resulting in "terrible gloom."[9] Gandhi too was against this superior attitude of the colonizers and fought against the racial and colour discrimination in South Africa and resisted non-violently the British-raj in India. His *satyāgraha* movements in South Africa and in India aimed at achieving human equality,

---

[4] K. V. Paul Pillai, *India's Search for the Unknown Christ* (New Delhi: Fazl Publishers, 1978), 245.

[5] Bhikhu Parekh, *Colonialism, Tradition and Reform: An Analysis of Gandhi's Political Discourse* (New Delhi: Sage Publications, 1989), 56.

[6] Ibid., 36.

[7] Pravrajika Vrajaprana, "What Do Hindus *Do?*—The Role of the Vedanta Societies in North America," *Cross Currents* 47/1 (Spring, 1997): 72.

[8] *CWSV*. 8: 160.

[9] *CWSV*. 8: 476.

religious harmony and political freedom.[10] He thus says: "...fundamentally the whole position of the British in India was wrong...."[11]

Thus in the 19th century, for Indians, colonialism was undoubtedly the White racial superiority in everything - politics, religion and culture, and subsequent exploitation and denigration of Indian resources, tradition, religion and culture. Hence, Norman R. Adams notes that, "...Indians were rudely shaken in the eighteenth and nineteenth centuries by the apparent superiority of Western invaders."[12] Because Britain was looked upon as an advanced and progressive civilization, while India was condemned as backward, barbarous and superstitious.[13] Moreover, the Westerners claimed their superiority as "an inalienable divine right"[14] and colonizing was carried as if, it is their "divine vocation and right."[15] This belief in the racial and cultural superiority of the West in everything also promoted the view, that the inferior culture and superstitious religion of India should be replaced by superior Western culture and Christianity.[16] Moreover this belief in the superiority of Western civilization was also used to justify the colonial rule in India, as it would displace and transform the culturally inferior India on the model of West; because the colonial theory affirmed that the European life, culture and religious beliefs were better than the Indian ways of life, religion and culture.[17] However, Vivekananda rejected such assumptions and affirmed the superiority of Indian tradition. He says: "The traditions of India were all true."[18] Therefore, he admonished the Indians that,

> Everything that comes from India take as true, until you find cogent reasons for disbelieving it. Everything that comes from Europe take as false, until you find cogent reasons for believing it. Do not be carried away by European fooleries.[19]

---

[10] Nirmal Minz, *Mahatma Gandhi and Hindu-Christian Dialogue* (Madras: Christian Literature Society, 1970), 12.

[11] *Harijan*, 17.04.1937.

[12] Norman R. Adams, "Background of Some Hindu Influences in America – The Ramakrishna Movement," *Journal of Ecumenical Studies* 9/2 (Spring, 1972): 319.

[13] T. V. Philip, "Christianity in India during Western Colonialism: Conflict, Reconciliation or Adjustment," op.cit., 19.

[14] Santhosh Thomas, *Christianity and Culture* (New Delhi: Mittal Publications, 2005), 299.

[15] Ibid., 15.

[16] *Harijan*, 13.03.1937.

[17] M. Stephen, *Introducing Post Modernism and Post Colonialism* (New Delhi: Concept Publishing Company, 2013), 48.

[18] *CWSV*. 4: 426.

[19] *CWSV*. 6:123.

Because colonial attitude supposed that, the East should be conquered, civilized and converted. [20] To such an attitude, Vivekananda responded, "Indian nation cannot be killed. Deathless it stands...."[21] Gandhi also did not accept this inferior view of Asia by the Westerners.[22] Instead, Gandhi praised Indian tradition while blaming the Western civilization.[23]

1.4.1. Missionary Attitude and Attack of Hinduism

Along with colonizers, the European missionaries also came to India with a pre-determined notion of the darkness of the Indian world and they took a negative approach to Hindu culture and religion.[24] Vivekananda thus says about this missionary attitude:

> In the beginning of the present century, when Western influence began to pour into India, when Western conquerors, sword in hand, came to demonstrate to the children of the sages that they were mere barbarians, a race of dreamers, that their religion was but mythology, and god and soul everything they had been struggling for were mere words without meaning, that the thousands of years of struggle, the thousands of years of endless renunciation, had all been in vain.[25]

Gandhi also commented about this missionary attitude, that

> Up till now they have come as teachers and preachers with queer notions about India and India's great religions. We have been described as a nation of superstitious heathens, knowing nothing, denying God. We are a brood of Satan....To me this is a negation of the spirit of Christ.[26]

He thus says that the European missionaries had the belief that, "... Hinduism is an error and that Christianity as they believe it is the only true religion."[27]

---

[20] Jacob S. Dharmaraj, op.cit., 74.

[21] *CWSV*. 4: 160.

[22] *Young India*, 21.03.1928.

[23] *The Collected Works of Mahatma Gandhi*, vol. 10 (New Delhi: Publication Division, Ministry of Broadcasting, Government of India, 1956 – 1994), 189. Hereafter it will be denoted as *CWMG* with different volumes.

[24] T. V. Philip, "Christianity in India during Western Colonialism: Conflict, Reconciliation or Adjustment," op.cit., 20.

[25] *CWSV*. 4: 158.

[26] *Harijan*, 07.01.1939.

[27] *Harijan*, 13.03.1937.

Hence, the missionaries upheld the colonial supremacy of the West over the East, as B. R. Nanda, says, "...the missionaries saw the West robed in light, and the East clothed in darkness."[28] The basis of this assumption was their theological conviction that Western culture was a real preparation for the Gospel of Christ.[29] As a result, they shared in the colonial educational project of teaching European knowledge through the English language with a view of disrupting Indian tradition[30] and undermining the faith of the students in Hinduism[31] thus leading them to Christianity. The total displacement of Hindu culture and religion and their substitution by Western culture and Christian religion was the goal of the early educational missionaries.[32] As a result, many Christian missionaries in India sincerely believed that within a few generations, the whole of India would become Christian.[33] They believed that Hinduism would perish with the introduction of Western civilization and its various innovations such as railways, scientific medicines and widespread literacy, etc.[34] In contrast to Hinduism, the missionaries thus presented Christianity as the only true religion, universally valid, perfectly rational and scientific, and absolutely moral. Moreover, the all-round progress of the West, and even the British rule in India were interpreted as the clear proofs of the truth and greatness of Christianity by the West and attributed these to the acceptance of Christianity[35]. Hinduism was ridiculed and condemned as idolatrous and polytheistic[36] and made responsible for the pathetic and degrading conditions of India.[37] Thus with its superior truth claims, the Western colonial Christianity constantly attacked the Hindu religion and culture in the 19th century. This is clearly portrayed by B. R. Nanda. He says: "Throughout the nineteenth century Hinduism had been on the defensive, as the principal target of the missionaries' assault was Hinduism, hence the Hindu society felt threatened,

---

[28] B. R. Nanda, *In Search of Gandhi Essays and Reflections* (New Delhi: Oxford University Press, 2002), 233.

[29] M. M. Thomas, *The Acknowledged Christ of the Indian Renaissance* (Madras: CLS, 1991), 248.

[30] T. V. Philip, "Christianity in India during Western Colonialism: Conflict, Reconciliation or Adjustment," op.cit., 20.

[31] Ibid., 21.

[32] M. M. Thomas, op.cit., 250.

[33] P. S. Daniel, *Hindu Response to Religious Pluralism* (Delhi: Kant Publications, 2000), 164-165.

[34] Ibid.

[35] Ibid.

[36] Anantanand Rambachan, *The Limits of Scripture Vivekananda's Reinterpretation of the Vedas* (Delhi: Sri Satguru Publications, 1995), 13.

[37] P. S. Daniel, op.cit., 164-165.

as Christianity was making converts at its expense."[38] About this situation Vivekananda also commented that, "We do not believe in Christianity, but we are forced to call ourselves Christians."[39] Thus the arrogance, aggressiveness and confrontational mood of these missionary threats and attacks on Hinduism are evident in Vivekananda's and Gandhi's response to Christ and Christianity.

In fact, missionary preaching wounded both Vivekananda and Gandhi. About which Vivekananda says: "Platform speeches have been made by the thousand, denunciations in volumes have been hurled upon the devoted head of the Hindu race, and its civilization...."[40] Further he says: "You train and educate and clothe and pay men to do what? To come over to my country to curse and abuse all my forefathers, my religion, and everything. They walk near a temple and say, "You idolaters, you will go to hell."[41] According to Tapan Raychaudhuri these criticisms of missionaries by Vivekananda reflected "anti-European feelings," and "echoed his anti-colonial sentiments" and his anger at the starving condition of the society under British rule.[42]

Gandhi too was pained by such missionary preaching.[43] For example, he recalls his Rajkot experience:

> In those days Christian missionaries used to stand in a corner near the high school and hold forth, pouring abuse on Hindus and their gods. I could not endure this. I must have stood there to hear them once only, but that was enough to dissuade me from repeating the experiment. About the same time, I heard of a well-known Hindu having been converted to Christianity. It was the talk of the town that, when he was baptized, he had to eat beef and drink liquor; that he also had to change his clothes, and that thenceforth he began to go about in European costume including a hat. These things got on my nerves. Surely, thought I, a religion that compelled one to eat beef, drink liquor, and change one's own clothes did not deserve the name. I also heard that the new convert had already begun abusing the religion of his ancestors, their customs and their country. All these things created in me a dislike for Christianity.[44]

---

[38] B. R. Nanda, op.cit., 65.

[39] *CWSV*. 8: 215.

[40] *CWSV*. 3:194-195.

[41] *CWSV*. 8:211-212.

[42] Cited by Abraham Stephen, *The Social Philosophy of Swami Vivekananda: Its Relevance to Modern India* (Delhi: ISPCK, 2005), 23-24.

[43] *Young India*, 04.03.1926.

[44] M. K. Gandhi, *An Autobiography OR The Story of My Experiments with Truth* (Ahmedabad: Navajivan Publishing House, First Edition - 1927, Reprint, 2011), 31. Hereafter it will be denoted as *An Autobiography*.

Besides these, through literature also missionaries abused Hindu religion as Gandhi says:

> I have read several missionary publications, and they are able to see only the dark side and paint it darker still.... I was favoured with some literature even at the Yervada prison by well-meaning missionaries which seemed to be written as merely to belittle Hinduism.[45]

However, Vivekananda rejected missionaries' views and protected the Hindu religion by suggesting its superiority to Christianity. [46] Hence, most of his extraordinary claims about *Advaita Vedāntic* Hinduism were clearly counter-attacks on his part against the onslaught of the missionary activities. And almost all the claims he made for Hinduism and India were clearly against the claims the missionaries made for Christianity.[47] Therefore to the missionaries' thesis that 'Christianity is the only true universal religion;' Vivekananda put the anti-thesis that '*Advaita Vedānta* as the only universal religion.'[48] Gandhi too affirmed the glory of Hinduism, to defend against the claims made for Christianity by the missionaries. He says: "Hinduism with its message of ahimsa is to me the most glorious religion in the world."[49]

1.4.2. Alliance between Christianity and Colonialism

Besides these criticisms of Indian culture and religion during the 19th century, Christian missionaries had deep alliance with colonial power and were very active in India,[50] as India was one of the major areas of missionary attention.[51] And many of the European missionaries believed that 'colonization of India was the divine providence.'[52] In fact, the missionary theology of this period featured that colonialism was willed by God, for the salvation of India.[53] Therefore in a way, Christianity of this period justified the European colonial exploitation of the countries of the East. Hence there was an alliance of imperial, commercial

---

[45] *Young India*, 04.03.1926.

[46] Abraham Stephen, op.cit., 236.

[47] *CWSV*. 3:182.

[48] *CWSV*. 3: 182.

[49] *Young India*, 19.01.1928.

[50] Abraham Stephen, op.cit., 22.

[51] Linda Keller Brown, "Mission, A Cultural Confrontation: Swami Vivekananda and The American Missionary Movement," *Journal of Dharma* 6/2 (April-June, 1981): 171.

[52] Jacob S. Dharmaraj, op.cit., xvi.

[53] T. V. Philip, *Reflections on Christian Mission in Asia* (Delhi: ISPCK/CSS, 2000), 53.

and missionary interests.[54] In fact, missionaries and colonizers favoured and helped each other.[55] For example, the Christian missionaries were convinced that the European presence would civilize the people, which will eventually lead them to embrace Christianity,[56] and the colonizers thought that converted natives would be loyal to the British Empire,[57] thereby strengthening the British raj, to the extent of its permanent rule in India. English education, administration, railways, and modern communication were introduced by the British government, in order to displace the national culture,[58] which in turn would help the spread of Christian religion and Western civilization.[59] However, this alliance between British colonialism and Christianity had in many ways influenced the nature of the encounter between Christianity and Indian cultural and religious traditions.[60] For example, the educated class in India did not consider Christianity as a substitute for Hinduism,[61] rather they became anti-Christian and anti-Western[62] and thereby began to view Christianity suspiciously as 'Whiteman's religion', 'the religion of the colonizer', 'a strange instrument' and as 'an agent in the cultural conquest of India by the West,'[63] which contributed to the humiliation of the East.[64] Therefore for many renascent thinkers like Vivekananda and Gandhi in the nineteenth century, the acceptance of Christianity was the last surrender to colonialism. [65] Thus with the development of Indian nationalism towards the end of the 19th century, many national leaders including Vivekananda and Gandhi saw Western Christianity as an entrapment to lure the Indians away from their own religious and cultural traditions leading to denationalization and acculturation of Indians.[66]

---

[54] T. V. Philip, "Christianity in India during Western Colonialism: Conflict, Reconciliation or Adjustment," op.cit., 21.

[55] Jacob S. Dharmaraj, op.cit., xix.

[56] Ibid., 49.

[57] Ibid., 24.

[58] Ibid., 21.

[59] Jacob S. Dharmaraj, op.cit., xvi.

[60] T. V. Philip, *Reflections on Christian Mission in Asia*, op.cit., 94.

[61] Ibid., 68.

[62] Ibid.

[63] C. E. Abraham, "The Rise and Growth of Christianity in India", in *The Religions*, vol. 4, *The Cultural Heritage of India*, edited by Haridas Bhattacharyya (Calcutta: The Rama Krishna Mission Institute of Culture, 2001), 569.

[64] Santhosh Thomas, op.cit., 301.

[65] T. V. Philip, *Reflections on Christian Mission in Asia*, op.cit., 44.

[66] T. V. Philip, "Christianity in India during Western Colonialism: Conflict, Reconciliation or Adjustment," op.cit., 23.

Hence, both Vivekananda and Gandhi reacted against this alliance between Colonialism and Christianity. Vivekananda said: "... the conquest of India by England is not a conquest by Jesus or the Bible as we are often asked to believe... behind all these, there is always the virtual presence of England."[67] Gandhi too commented about this nexus between colonialism and Christianity. First of all, he considered that the sending of missionaries to India was "part of imperialist exploitation."[68] He says, "Christian missionaries come to India under the shadow... under the protection of a temporal power...."[69] He again made it explicit that this 'shadow' or 'temporal power' is the British Empire. He says,

> Unfortunately, Christianity in India has been inextricably mixed up for the last one hundred and fifty years with the British rule. It appears to us as synonymous with materialistic civilization and imperialistic exploitation by the stronger white races of the weaker races of the world. Its contribution to India has been, therefore, largely of a negative character.[70]

Hence "... when Christianity and Western Civilization came to be associated, the Hindus began to look upon that religion with disfavour."[71]

1.4.3. Western Challenge and Reactionary Response

Thus, colonialism tried to displace the national culture as it destroyed the will-power and self-respect of the natives.[72] Hence, there was a widespread feeling among Indians that, this Western invasion was in fact an aggression, an insult, and an attack on Indian life[73] - that Western culture as inimical to India's best interest. It thus inflicted Indians with many deep injuries.[74] This sense of frustration and humiliation caused by the foreign conquest became the context of Vivekananda's and Gandhi's response to Western Christianity and Christ, which came to Asian countries as part of the Western conquest of Asia.[75] This Political subjugation and the resultant misery and humiliation

---

[67] *CWSV*. 4: 452.

[68] *CWMG*. 73:29.

[69] *Young India*, 06.08.1925.

[70] *Young India*, 21.03.1929.

[71] *Indian Opinion*, 15.04.1905.

[72] Jacob S. Dharmaraj, op.cit., 21.

[73] Santhosh Thomas, op.cit., 17.

[74] Ibid., 8.

[75] T. V. Philip, *Reflections on Christian Mission in Asia*, op.cit., 66.

led them to search for a self-identity in India's past history.[76] They did not like these continuous 'inferiorization' and biased definition of Indian tradition by the colonizers and missionaries, and having no other way to counter it, they provided an alternative self-definition,[77] which affirmed the glory, value and pride in Indian tradition. Hence the rediscovery of India's past cultural heritage gave them a sense of pride in their religion and national culture, which provided a powerful incentive for the growth of renascent movements as well as religious and political nationalism.[78] Thus, in a sense, this 'reactive nationalism' and self assertion of Indians was caused by the Western contact.[79] The basic motif of this Indian resurgence was the defence of Indian religion and culture against Western colonial supremacy and threats from Christian missionaries.[80] In this context, the defence of Hinduism was but a defence of Indian culture.[81] Hindus began to adopt the 'exclusive' and 'superior' language of Christianity to fight against Christianity.[82] The Hindus even utilized the gifts of English education in opposing missionaries. For example, the rational criticism and historical analysis which the missionaries themselves employed to dislodge Hinduism was adopted by Vivekananda to defend his religion and criticize the doctrines of Christianity.[83] As a result, many modern exponents of Hinduism, including Vivekananda and Gandhi began to affirm the superiority of Hinduism in its *Advaitic form*,[84] to counter the superior truth claims of Western Christianity. They used the 'comparative approach' in the philosophy of religions and projected Hindu spirituality as superior and above externalist, historicist, rational and doctrine-oriented Western religiosity. An interesting feature of this cultural defence and religious nationalism is a belief that India is essentially spiritual and Europe is materialistic in attitude.[85]

Hence, Vivekananda taught his people to believe in themselves and to be confident of the superiority of Indian culture over Western.[86] Moreover his reaction is even reflected in his Chicago speeches, in which he actually

---

[76] T. V. Philip, "Christianity in India during Western Colonialism: Conflict, Reconciliation or Adjustment," op.cit., 26.

[77] Bhikhu Parekh, op.cit., 34-35.

[78] T. V. Philip, *Reflections on Christian Mission in Asia*, op.cit., 65.

[79] Santhosh Thomas, op.cit., 151.

[80] T. V. Philip, *Reflections on Christian Mission in Asia*, op.cit., 66.

[81] Sisir Kumar Das, *The Shadow of the Cross Christianity and Hinduism in a Colonial Situation* (New Delhi: Munshiram Manoharlal Publishers, 1974), 37.

[82] Ibid., 61.

[83] T. V. Philip, "Christianity in India during Western Colonialism: Conflict, Reconciliation or Adjustment," op.cit., 26.

[84] P. S. Daniel, op.cit., 57.

[85] Sisir Kumar Das, op.cit., 130.

[86] Norman R. Adams, op.cit., 320.

challenged the Christian superior claims of the West (both the civilisational and the religious superiority through Christianity) and presented the glorious, inclusive and universal nature of Indian tradition and Hinduism through *Advaita Vedānta*. It was the validity of the Westerner's knowledge of India that Vivekananda had challenged. [87]

In reaction, Gandhi too thought that the Indian civilisation is superior.[88] Hence he considered Indian tradition as the 'ancient and best civilization' the world has ever seen and compared it with the "Kingdom of God" and he called Western civilization 'modern' which represented the "Kingdom of Satan."[89] Further Gandhi's reaction is also reflected in his *swaraj* (self-rule) and *swadeshi* (indigenous) movements, which called for the rejection of Western colonialism,[90] and condemnation of missionaries and their message.[91] Moreover, in *Hind Swaraj* (1909) Gandhi's intense patriotism is reflected by his admiration for the civilization of his country and criticisms of British colonialism in India. He intended the demolition of modern Western civilization in India (*e.g.*, industrialization, railways) and tried to expel the British from India through non-violent means. The concept of *swadeshi* in religion also meant that people should retain their ancestral religion, which was in contrast to the missionaries' concept of conversion to Christianity.

1.4.4. Objections to Christian Superiority and Doctrinal Claims

Further Hindu objections also continued against Christianity on account of its superior claims and doctrines as well as against conversion and related issues.[92] For example, Vivekananda said, "I cannot go with you when you shut out, when you deny," that "There is no other true religion, there is no other revelation of God."[93] Gandhi too strongly opposed the superior and exclusive dogmatism of Western Christianity. He did not have any respect for the exclusive views of the Church concerning the person and work of Christ, because for Gandhi, Indian civilisation was essentially plural and non-dogmatic. From the very beginning it had been realised that the ultimate reality was infinite and inexhaustible and that different individuals grasped different aspects of it. None was wholly wrong and none wholly right. Everyone was therefore

[87] Linda Keller Brown, op.cit., 168.

[88] Bhikhu Parekh, op.cit., 82.

[89] *CWMG*. 10:189.

[90] Santhosh Thomas, op.cit., 149.

[91] John A. Maynard, "Christian Theology and Hindu Religious Thinking," *Anglican Theological Review* 1/2 (1918): 184.

[92] Lowell D. Streiker, "The Hindu Attitude toward Other Religions," *The Journal of Religious Thought* 23/1 (1966-1967): 86.

[93] *CWSV*. 6:138.

left free, even encouraged, to live out the truth as he saw it and to discover for himself its limits and possibilities. That's why, in Gandhi's view, Hinduism allowed its adherents full freedom of choice between different religious texts, conceptions of God and forms of worship.[94] However, this plural, inclusive and non-dogmatic Indian tradition was challenged by the exclusive, dogmatic and aggressive Western Christian tradition, which proclaimed itself as the 'only true religion', denigrating all other religions as false and non-valid. Such superior and exclusive claims of missionaries were called by Gandhi as "super-arrogation".[95] Gandhi thus rejected the Christian dogma that "Christ is the one and only Saviour and Lord."[96] He being a staunch Hindu, on the other hand, found the spiritual succour, he needed, in the faith of his fathers.[97] He consequently said: "My quarrel with missionaries is that they think no religion other than Christianity is true." [98] Hence he declared, "It was impossible for me to regard Christianity as a perfect religion or the greatest of all religions."[99] And "It was impossible for me to believe that I could go to heaven or attain salvation only by becoming a Christian."[100] Because according to Gandhi, "God's grace and revelation are the monopoly of no race or nation. They descend equally upon all who wait upon God"[101] because God has no partiality.

1.4.5. Objections to Conversion and Denationalization

The Indian reaction also expressed disapproval of conversion from Hinduism to Christianity,[102] because for Hindus, conversion to Christianity meant rejection of Indian culture and denationalization of the individuals.[103] For example, Vivekananda wrote a letter to the Rev. R. A. Hume, the director of a mission in India on March 29, 1894 expressing his view against religious conversion that, "India can never be converted to Christianity."[104] Because during his time, systematized British education with its concomitant cultural and religious indoctrination and conversion to Western Christianity made

[94] Bhikhu Parekh, op.cit., 75.

[95] *Harijan*, 13.01.1940.

[96] Vern Middleton, "Caste Issues in the Minds of McGavran and Gandhi," *Missiology: An International Review* 13/2 (April, 1985): 165.

[97] Cited by I. Jesudasan, "Gandhian Perspectives on Missiology," *Indian Church History Review* 4/1 (June, 1970): 63.

[98] *Harijan*, 17.02.1939.

[99] *An Autobiography*, 126.

[100] Ibid.

[101] *CWMG*. 25: 479.

[102] P. D. Devanandan, "The Modern Hindu Attitude Toward Christian Evangelism," *Union Seminary Quarterly Review* 12/ 3 (March, 1957): 65.

[103] P. S. Daniel, op.cit., 261.

[104] *CWSV*. 7: 460.

the younger Indian generation to question its previously held religious and social traditions. Inevitably, a large number of India's intelligentsia became Westernized to a lesser or greater degree, Vivekananda being one among them.[105] Being influenced by Western colonial education and Western philosophy, he "dismissed the larger portion of his Hindu heritage as childish superstition".[106] About which he says: "Instead of throwing away superstition and making a real search after truth, the test of truth became, 'What does the West say?' The priests must go, the Vedas must be burned, because the West has said so."[107] However, later Vivekananda became convinced of the validity of the ancient Indian tradition through Sri Ramakrishna.[108] Actually he was for Western scepticism and philosophy, but has realised its folly through the touch of Sri Ramakrishna and thereby the lofty ideals of *Advaita Vedānta*. Hence, he came to know the supremacy of Indian tradition and *Advaita* through Sri Ramakrishna, his Master. Thus,

> As Vivekananda became more assured of Hinduism's essential vitality and its validity for human concerns, he became increasingly disenchanted with what the West could offer the world in terms of viable answers to both social and existential problems. India's Westernization, he felt, had done much more harm than good.[109]

Gandhi also resented against conversion to Christianity and the subsequent denationalization, which destructed the Indian tradition. He thus declared, "The great faiths held by people of India are adequate for her people. India stands in no need of conversion from one faith to another."[110] According to him conversion was the violation of the fundamental principle of the equality of all religions. Moreover, in conversion, he saw an attempt "to root out traditions, effects of heredity, climate and other surroundings," which "is not only bound to fail but a sacrilege."[111] For Gandhi, conversion also destroys the stability of the age-old social superstructure of Indian villages.[112] Further Gandhi found "Christianity synonymous with denationalization and Europeanization",[113] and feared the disintegration of Indian tradition through denationalization

---

[105] Pravrajika Vrajaprana, op.cit., 72.

[106] Ibid.

[107] *CWSV*. 4: 158.

[108] Pravrajika Vrajaprana, op.cit., 73.

[109] Ibid., 75.

[110] *CWMG*. 46:28.

[111] *Young India*, 25.09.1925.

[112] *Harijan*, 28.09.1935.

[113] *Young India*, 11.08.1927.

and Westernization as a result of conversion to Christianity.[114] Hence he said: "Conversion must not mean denationalization."[115]

1.5. Chapterisation

There are seven chapters in the study. The first chapter is introduction. It deals with the research problem, its significance and the 19th century colonial background and related issues of the study. The second chapter deals with the formation of Vivekananda and Gandhi – the influences that made their personality and philosophical views. The third chapter is about the supremacy of Indian tradition and *Advaita Vedānta* in the writings of Vivekananda and Gandhi. Fourth chapter sees how Vivekananda and Gandhi as *Advaita Vedāntins* responded to the Christian tradition, plurality of religions and Christ. The fifth chapter analyses the Christ-experience of Vivekananda and Gandhi as metaphysical and ethical, which is quite different from the Western Aristotelian epistemological framework. The sixth chapter is a critical analysis of the *Advaitic* Christ-experience of Vivekananda and Gandhi, as it uses 'comparative method' in the philosophy of religions and the related issues. The sixth chapter also gives observations for the betterment of Hindu-Christian relations in today's post-colonial, secular democratic context of India from the colonial past and its confrontational attitudes. The seventh chapter, the last one gives the summary and conclusion of the research.

---

[114] M. M. Thomas, op.cit., 231.

[115] *Young India*, 20.08.1925.

Chapter 2

The Making of Swami Vivekananda and Mahatma Gandhi

2.1. Introduction

This chapter deals with the 'making' of Vivekananda and Gandhi. Different sources of influence, both Indian and Western that went into the making of Vivekananda and Gandhi are analysed, as these influences are instrumental in forming their metaphysical and ethical response to Christ. Nevertheless, it should be noted that their lives and ideologies were formulated under the colonial rule during the nineteenth century.

2.2. The Making of Swami Vivekananda

Swami Vivekananda was a multiple-genius. Almost all sides of his personality were well developed and his disciples admired his personality thus:

> This preacher of religious harmony and toleration, who was Sankara in wisdom, Buddha in love and sympathy to all beings, Christ in humanity, Mahavira in faith and loyalty to his Lord, Narada in Bhakti, Arjuna in courage, and Karma-Yoga, Vyasa in the knowledge of the Sastras, Suka in purity. [1]

However, he was primarily a man of religion and spirituality.[2] Various sources, circumstances and influences caused the making of his mind and

---

[1] Cited by Dev Raj Bali, *Modern Indian Thought from Rammohun Roy to Jayaprakash Narayan* (New Delhi: Sterling Publishers, 1996), 55-56.

[2] N. Lekshmikutty, *Swami Vivekananda on Indian Reconstruction* (Vadakara: Malabar Institute for Research and Development, 2009), 86.

philosophy. Nevertheless, only the major ones which played a vital role that made the 'transformation of Narendranath into Swami Vivekananda'[3] are discussed here.

2.2.1. Influence of Family

It is a common fact that family background during the early childhood influences in the character formation of a man. So also Swami Vivekananda's moral principles and religious ethos were derived from his parents.[4] Both the mother's and father's influence are evident in Vivekananda's personality. Hindu religiosity was imbibed by him from his mother Bhuvaneswari Devi during his early childhood. Her great contribution was the passing down of the Indian heritage through the stories of *Rāmāyaṇa* and *Mahābhārata*.[5] He acknowledges his mother's contribution as follows: "The love which my mother gave to me has made me what I am, and I owe a debt to her that I can never repay."[6] His father's liberal approach, discussions with visitors in the house, importance given to rationality, Western ideas and English education – all these had an impact in the mental makeup of Vivekananda.[7] For example, the traces of first Christian influence on him could be found from his father Visvanath Datta himself; it was his father who gave him the Bible and thereby the knowledge of Jesus.[8] Hence at home, he became the heir of two different cultures, the Eastern and Western.[9] Another influence which came from family was through his grand-father – Durga Charan Datta, who renounced the world and became a monk. Vivekananda heard this example in his early childhood

---

[3] Santi L. Mukherji, *The Philosophy of Man-Making: A Study in Social and Political Ideas of Swami Vivekananda* (Kolkata: New Central Book Agency, 2008), 84.

[4] K. S. Bharati, *Encyclopaedia of Eminent Thinkers: The Political Thought of Vivekananda*, vol. 8 (New Delhi: Concept Publishing Company, 1998), 27.

[5] Eastern and Western Disciples, *The Life of Swami Vivekananda*, vol. 1 (Kolkata: Advaita Ashrama, Tenth Impression, 2010), 9, 14, 101. Hereafter it will be denoted as *The Life* with different volumes. *The Life*.

[6] *CWSV*. 9:203.

[7] Asim Chaudhuri, *Swami Vivekananda in Chicago: New Findings* (Kolkata: Advaita Ashrama, 2005), 28; V.K.R.V. Rao, *Swami Vivekananda: The Prophet of Vedantic Socialism*, (New Delhi: Publications Division, Ministry of Information and Broadcasting, Government of India, 1979), 8; V. R. Karandikar, *Ramakrishna and Vivekananda* (Bombay: Bharatiya Vidya Bhavan, 1991), 15, 474-497, 499.

[8] Sailendra Nath Dhar, *A Comprehensive Biography of Swami Vivekananda*, Part-1, (Chennai: Vivekananda Kendra Prakashan, Third Edition, 2005), 7-8; Marie Louise Burke, *Swami Vivekananda in the West New Discoveries*, vol. 2 (Calcutta: Advaita Ashrama, 1st edition, 1986), 202. Hereafter it will be denoted as *New Discoveries* with different volumes.

[9] A. V. Rathna Reddy, *The Political Philosophy of Swami Vivekananda* (New Delhi: Sterling Publishers, 1984), 2.

and this might have influenced him to renounce the world and to choose the life of a monk.[10]

2.2.2. Impact of Renascent Context of Bengal

Vivekananda was a product of nineteenth century Bengal,[11] as the socio-religious, political and cultural renaissance of nineteenth century Bengal was crucial in his making.[12] As V.K.R.V. Rao opines, he was born and brought up in the "...environment of compendium of religion, reform and patriotism."[13] Thus the twin factors that affected his formation were the British impact on India and the Indian renaissance movement.[14] So his mental development was related to the intellectual aspects of Bengali renaissance of nineteenth century, which was a reactionary response to British colonialism and Western Christianity.[15]

2.2.3. Influence of Hinduism

Despite the modern renascent context, Vivekananda was deeply rooted in his ancient Indian tradition and Hindu religion. As Thomas Mannumel notes, "Orthodox Hinduism was evidently the earliest influence in his intellectual and emotional make-up."[16] His proficiency in Sanskrit enabled him to study the original Hindu text books, [17] and to get firsthand knowledge of Hindu literature such as *Vedas*, *Upaniṣads*, *Gītā*, etc. and to quote them aptly in his lectures. By '*Veda*' he meant *Vedānta*,[18] and held *Advaita Vedāntic* views firmly[19] as he committed himself to *Advaita Vedānta* as the supreme one.[20] He was also highly influenced by the *Upaniṣads*.[21]

---

[10] *CWSV*. 9:490; Ajeet Jawed, *Swami Vivekananda: An Iconoclastic Ascetic* (New Delhi: Ane Books India, 2007), 3.

[11] Bhupendranath Datta, *Swami Vivekananda Patriot-Prophet: A Study* (Calcutta: Navabharat Publishers, 1954), 102.

[12] Abraham Stephen, op.cit., 1.

[13] V.K.R.V. Rao, *Builders of Modern India, Swami Vivekananda* (New Delhi: Publications Division, Ministry of Information and Broadcasting, Government of India, 1979), 7.

[14] Swami Ranganathananda, *Eternal Values for a Changing Society* (Bombay: Bharatiya Vidya Bhavan, 1971), 317.

[15] Thomas Mannumel, *The Advaita of Vivekananda: A Philosophical Appraisal* (Madras: T. R. / Satya Nilayam Publications, 1991), 12.

[16] Ibid., 11.

[17] V.K.R.V. Rao, *Builders of Modern India, Swami Vivekananda*, op.cit., 16.

[18] *CWSV*. 1: 357.

[19] *CWSV*. 6:229.

[20] Basant Kumar Lal, *Contemporary Indian Philosophy* (Delhi: Motilal Banarsidass, 1995), 2; Sister Nivedita, *The Master As I Saw Him* (Calcutta: Udbodhan Office, Sixth Edition, 1948), 163.

[21] *CWSV*. 3: 225.

2.2.4. English Education - College and Western Philosophy

It is said: "Narendranath received the best of western education as was possible to obtain in Calcutta of those days."[22] As an excellent student and reader, he had a keen and enquiring mind and renowned himself in different branches of knowledge during his college days.[23] In fact, he was very much influenced by colonial educational policy, as he studied mostly in Western Christian Institutions such as Metropolitan Institute, Presidency College and Scottish Church College and obtained B.A. degree in philosophy. His main interaction was with modern Western philosophers and writers such as Descartes, Comte, Hume, Spinoza, Spencer, Mill, Kant, Hegel, Darwin, Schopenhauer, and Huxley.[24] Herbert Spencer and John Stuart Mill seem to have influenced him the most.[25] Hence Western ideas of agnosticism, scepticism, atheism and rationalism influenced him to a great extent, especially in his inquiry on the concept of God, that he even doubted the very existence of God and loosed his childhood faith in God, which he inherited as part of his Indian tradition and became a sceptic and agnostic.[26] About this, a senior student of him, Dr. Brojendra Nath Seal says:

> This was the beginning of a critical period in his mental history, during which he awoke to self-consciousness, and laid the foundations of his future personality. John Stuart Mill's *Three Essays on Religion* had upset his first boyish theism and easy optimism which he had imbibed from the outer circles of the Brahmo Samaj. The arguments from causality and design were for him broken reeds to lean upon, and he was haunted by the problem of the Evil in Nature and Man which he, by no means, could reconcile with the goodness of an All-wise and All-powerful Creator. A friend introduced him to the study of Hume's Scepticism and Herbert Spencer's doctrine of the Unknowable, and his unbelief gradually assumed the form of a settled philosophical scepticism.[27]

Thus, modern Western philosophy and its absoluteness of reason and critical approach made him an 'unbeliever;' it gave a sort of immediate

---

[22] Binoy K. Roy, *Socio-Political Views of Vivekananda* (New Delhi: People's Publishing House, Third Reprint, 1983), 4.

[23] V. R. Karandikar, op.cit., 125.

[24] Ibid; V.K.R.V. Rao, *Builders of Modern India, Swami Vivekananda*, op.cit., 16.

[25] D. S. Sarma, *Hinduism through the Ages* (Mumbai: Bharatiya Vidya Bhavan, 2000), 145.

[26] *The Life*. 1:102.

[27] Brojendra Nath Seal, "An Early Stage of Vivekananda's Mental Development," *Prabuddha Bharata*, (April, 1907), cited by R. C. Majumdar, *Swami Vivekananda: A Historical Review* (Kolkata: Advaita Ashrama, 2004), 153-154.

satisfaction, but not the lasting peace.[28] It confused him and made him intellectually restless.[29] About which, he himself says: "I myself had tremendous difficulty, being educated in Western philosophy in my boyhood."[30] However, later when he met Sri Ramakrishna, he relocated his faith from Western philosophy to the Indian tradition of *Advaita Vedānta*. Therefore he was only a "temporary disciple" of the West.[31]

The study of Western philosophy also had its positive impact on Vivekananda. It widened his mental outlook, strengthened his reasoning power to analyse deeply and made him liberal.[32] He did not swallow superstitions and half-truths. He questioned before he believed; tested before he accepted.[33] He insisted that whatever was to be considered real could not be contradicted by reason, and further, that truth or reality could and should be tested.[34] He even adopted a rational and liberal attitude towards the *Vedas*.[35] Then he used Western scientific tools and methods in his interpretation and presentation of Indian tradition and *Advaita Vedānta* in a rational way, against the Western denigration.[36]

2.2.5. Influence of Buddha and Buddhism

Vivekananda is also influenced by Buddhism.[37] He was particularly attracted to the life of Buddha and his renunciation of the world for the removal of the sufferings of humanity with love and compassion.[38] The order of *sannyāsa* he started, is influenced by the Buddhist monastic life, as it attracted his mind. However, as an *Advaita Vedāntin*, Buddha's teachings may not have much appeal to him.[39]

---

[28] *The Life*. 1:109; Bhupendranath Datta, op.cit., 19.

[29] R. K. Dasgupta, *Swami Vivekananda on Indian Philosophy and Literature* (Calcutta: The Ramakrishna Mission Institute of Culture, 1996), 170.

[30] *CWSV*. 2:444.

[31] Christopher Iserwood, *Ramakrishna and His Disciples* (Calcutta: Advaita Ashrama, 1986), 192.

[32] Abraham Stephen, op.cit., 67; A. V. Rathna Reddy, op.cit., 24.

[33] B. Prasannakumary, "Vedanta Philosophy and Religion of Swami Vivekananda" (Ph. D Thesis, University of Kerala, 1990).

[34] Ibid.

[35] A. V. Rathna Reddy, op.cit., 24.

[36] *The Life*. 1:102-103.

[37] Basant Kumar Lal, op.cit., 2.

[38] Swami Vivekananda, *Practical Vedanta*, Part – 4 (Calcutta: Advaita Ashrama, 1958), 105, cited by Dev Raj Bali, op.cit., 34-35.

[39] *CWSV*. 8:103.

2.2.6. Impact of Christ and Christianity

The Christian influence in him, was started from his home, through his father. His father's presentation of the Bible to Vivekananda can be considered as the starting point of his contacts with Christianity and thereby the knowledge of Jesus.[40] He had a good knowledge of the Bible and quoted it often.[41] Especially he drew great inspiration from the Gospels.[42] He realized the truth of the great teaching of Jesus that, "Blessed are the pure in heart, for they shall see God."[43] Thus "Life of Jesus influenced him greatly."[44] Despite the Christian missionaries' criticisms of Hindu religion and the propagating of negative image of his character in America, he was able to love Christ and fascinated by the Christ – ideal.[45] He considered Christ as an idealist who sacrificed himself for the benefit of humanity.[46] Hence, before taking *dīkṣā* – an oath for *saṇnyāsi* life – he asked his fellow monks to live like Christ.[47] So, the monastic order of Sri Ramakrishna was started by Swami Vivekananda on a Christmas Eve[48] with a meditation on the life story of Jesus Christ.[49] Thus, Christ is linked up in a unique way with the order of Sri Ramakrishna.[50] It was Sri Ramakrishna, his Master, who contributed to the development of such a reverential attitude towards Christ. It may be mentioned, in this connection that, Sri Ramakrishna looked upon Christ as a great incarnation of God.[51]

Thomas A Kempis' *The Imitation of Christ*, which is actually a critic of Western Christendom, was another chief source of Christian influence on Vivekananda. It was his travelling companion and he even translated parts of it into Bengali.[52] He thus said: "It is a wonderful book. One is astonished to find

---

[40] Sailendra Nath Dhar, op.cit., 7-8; *New Discoveries*. 2:202.

[41] Rajagopal Chattopadhyaya, *Swami Vivekananda in the West* (Calcutta: K. P. Bagchi & Company, 1994), 33-34.

[42] K. P. Aleaz, *Jesus in Neo-Vedanta: A Meeting of Hinduism and Christianity* (Delhi: Kant Publications, 1995), 188.

[43] Gospel of Mathew. 5:8; *The Life*. 1:57-58.

[44] K. S. Bharati, *Encyclopaedia of Eminent Thinkers, The Political Thought of Vivekananda,* vol. 8, op.cit., 32.

[45] *CWSV*. 3: 210-211; *cf.* 8: 211-212.

[46] *CWSV*. 2: 50, 174.

[47] K. S. Bharati, *Encyclopaedia of Eminent Thinkers, The Political Thought of Vivekananda*, vol. 8, op.cit., 32.

[48] Swami Nikhilananda, *Vivekananda: A Biography* (New York: Ramakrishna-Vivekananda Center, 1953), 215.

[49] P. S. Daniel, op.cit., 169.

[50] K. P. Aleaz, *Jesus in Neo-Vedanta*, op.cit., 203.

[51] Ibid., 208.

[52] Ibid., 188; R. S. Ramabadran, *Vivekananda Divinity on Earth* (Madras: Vivekananda Literature Society, 1991), 55.

that such renunciation, Vairagya and Dasya Bhakti have existed even among the Christians."[53] Further, visits and the experiences there in the Western Christian lands made him more familiar with Christianity, to gain first-hand knowledge about it. Hence, he had deep and original views on Christ and Christianity.[54]

2.2.7. Influence of Brahmo Samaj

Brahmo Samaj was another influence in the making of Swami Vivekananda's personality.[55] During his student days, due to Western influence, he joined Brahmo Samaj, because it followed a rational method of the West.[56] For a time the intellectual atmosphere of the Brahmo Samaj satisfied him[57] and he became an active member and accepted its creeds.[58] It influenced him in developing his reforming attitude to religion and society.[59] However, it did not fully satisfy his spiritual needs.[60] Very particularly Brahmo Samaj leaders could not answer his quest for God - 'Sir, have you seen God?' So as described by A. V. Ratna Reddy, "... he found no solace in the intellectual dryness of the Samaj and marched into the spiritual abode of Sri Ramakrishna."[61]

2.2.8. Quest for God and Meeting of Sri Ramakrishna

It was from his Principal Hastie that Narendranath heard about Sri Ramakrishna[62] for the first time, and his first meeting with him took place in 1881. This meeting was an important one in the lives of both.[63] The result of this contact (of Narendranath with Sri Ramakrishna) was Swami Vivekananda.[64] It was actually his quest for the existence of God, led him to Sri Ramakrishna. While he was in Brahmo Samaj he asked its prominent leader, Devendranath Tagore, 'Sir, have you seen God?' But Brahma Samaj could not answer his question satisfactorily. This question came out of his contact with Western sceptical ideas, which actually stimulated such a restless rational quest in him.

---

[53] *CWSV*. 6: 209; *cf.* 8: 160.

[54] *The Life*. 1:319.

[55] Santi L. Mukherji, op.cit., 90.

[56] A. V. Rathna Reddy, op.cit., 2.

[57] *The Life*. 1:59.

[58] K. S. Bharati, *Encyclopaedia of Eminent Thinkers, The Political Thought of Vivekananda*, vol. 8, op.cit., 30.

[59] V. R. Karandikar, op.cit., 499.

[60] B. Prasannakumary, op.cit.

[61] A. V. Rathna Reddy, op.cit., 2.

[62] Sri Ramakrishna Paramahamsa (1836–1886) was born in a Bengali village in 1836. He had become a priest at the *Kāḷi* temple at Dakshineswar near Calcutta. But he was given to obsessive God-intoxication and frequent *samādhis* (trance).

[63] Swami Nikhilananda, op.cit., 14.

[64] *The Life*. 1:75.

But Sri Ramakrishna answered his question – "Yes, I see Him just as I see you here, only in a much intense sense."[65] Sri Ramakrishna represented traditional India, with its spiritual perspective, asceticism and realizations – the India of the *Upaniṣads*.[66] As Vivekananda was influenced by Western rationalism and scepticism, at first, he did not accept Sri Ramakrishna as his *Guru*. Of their six years – relationship, only in the fifth year that, he accepted Sri Ramakrishna as his *Guru,*[67] for he says: "I fought my Master for six years...."[68] Thus, Naren discarding his Western sceptic outlook, finally accepted Sri Ramakrishna as his *Guru*. So Sri Ramakrishna's and Vivekananda's six years' (1881-1886) *Guru-Śiṣya* relationship is famous and has been compared to that of Socrates and Plato; even deeper than that.[69] About this he says: "A mass of reading does not make men; those who were real men were made so by personal contact."[70] Hence, "Of all the influences that moulded Vivekananda, the foremost was of his Master Sri Ramakrishna."[71] Therefore, Vivekananda was the creation of his master Sri Ramakrishna Paramahamsa.[72] The story of his life cannot be completed without the story of the life of Sri Ramakrishna, because the two lives formed, as it were, one whole.[73]

The peculiarity of Sri Ramakrishna was spiritual experience and realization; he was considered as a realised soul, an experienced *Advaita Vedāntin*. So Sri Ramakrishna realised the spiritual capacity[74] of Vivekananda and initiated him into *Advaita* consciousness (non-dual experience) from his Western sceptic and Brahmo Samaj's rational mentality[75] and proclaimed him as his spiritual heir by transmitting all his spiritual energy.[76] Vivekananda thus got cured of his Western scepticism by experiencing the *nirvikalpa samādhi* from the mystical powers of Sri Ramakrishna.[77] So it was Sri Ramakrishna,

---

[65] *The Life*. 1:77. *cf. CWSV*. 3:345-346.

[66] *The Life*. 1:75.

[67] Makarand Paranjape, ed., *The Penguin Swami Vivekananda Reader* (New Delhi: Penguin Books, 2005), 9.

[68] *CWSV*. 9:411.

[69] S. S. Mital, *The Social and Political Ideas of Swami Vivekananda* (New Delhi: Metropolitan Book, 1979), 24; V. R. Karandikar, op.cit., 1.

[70] *CWSV*. 5:284.

[71] A. V. Rathna Reddy, op.cit., 18.

[72] V. R. Karandikar, op.cit., 3.

[73] *New Discoveries*. 1:4.

[74] V. R. Karandikar, op.cit., 110, 500-501.

[75] N. Lekshmikutty, op.cit., 94; K. S. Bharati, *Encyclopaedia of Eminent Thinkers, The Political Thought of Vivekananda,* vol. 8, op.cit., 33.

[76] P. Parameswaran, *Marx and Vivekananda: A Comparative Study* (New Delhi: Sterling Publishers, 1987), 22; K. S. Bharati, Ibid., 20-21.

[77] Sailendra Nath Dhar, op.cit., 576.

through whom Vivekananda was freed from the Western skepticism and realized the glory of Indian tradition and *Advaita Vedānta.* Therefore Vivekananda is highly indebted to Sri Ramakrishna for his own philosophy as he learned *Advaita Vedānta* not from books, but from the realisations, life and experiences of Sri Ramakrishna, the ascetic mystic.[78] For example, Swami Nikhilananda observes: "It was his Master who had taught him the divinity of the soul, non-duality of God-head, the unity of existence and one more, a greater thing that is the universality or harmony of all different religions."[79] Therefore the seed of many of the thoughts and achievements of Vivekananda can be traced to the teachings of Sri Ramakrishna.[80] He repeatedly acknowledged his *Guru* as: "My teacher, my master, my hero, my ideal, my God in life – Shri Ramakrishna Paramahamsa."[81] "I am a disciple of Shri Ramakrishna Paramahamsa, a perfect Sannyasin whose influence and ideas I fell under."[82] "At whose feet I have learnt everything...."[83] "If there has ever been a word of truth, a word of spirituality, that I have spoken anywhere in the world, I owe it to my Master; only the mistakes are mine."[84] Nevertheless, these aspects of Sri Ramakrishna's philosophy were further cultivated along the same line by Vivekananda and carried over a long distance.[85] Hence, there are many new and original ideas developed by him which were not found in Sri Ramakrishna,[86] as Sri Ramakrishna provided only seeds, but it was Vivekananda who developed Sri Ramakrishna's philosophy into "Practical *Vedānta*," as a highly developed and universal form.

2.2.9. As a Wandering Monk

Another source of Vivekananda's formation was his wandering experiences. His *parivrājaka* years lasted nearly for six years (1886-1893); it started with the *samādhi* of his master and ended at Chicago World Parliament of Religions.[87] It provided him with wandering experience and knowledge throughout the

---

[78] *The Complete Works of Sister Nivedita*, vol. 1 (Kolkata: Advaita Ashrama, Fifth Impression, 2006), 10.

[79] Swami Nikhilananda, op.cit., 53. Vivekananda's concept of religion and relation between religions are entirely from Sri Ramakrishna as he learned about the plurality, harmony and equality of religions from the life and teachings of Sri Ramakrishna as Sri Ramakrishna held very positive and liberal views towards all religions. *CWSV*. 7:115; 6:469.

[80] V. R. Karandikar, op.cit., 3.

[81] *CWSV*. 3:312.

[82] *CWSV*. 5:190.

[83] *CWSV*. 3:313.

[84] *CWSV*. 4:186-187.

[85] V. R. Karandikar, op.cit., 358.

[86] Ibid., 500-501.

[87] Thomas Mannumel, op.cit., 17.

length and breadth of India, to get a closer outlook of India.[88] The wandering life was of great educational value to him. It gave him opportunities for first-hand observation and original thought.[89] He, thus came to know the Indian realities – the condition of masses, extent of poverty and caste, being the guest of kings as well as untouchables. This broadened his awareness of India and hence he became a patriot and prophet of India.[90] So his 'Practical *Vedānta*' took its proper shape and form during his wanderings in India,[91] as his "... philosophy arises from the awareness of the social, religious and economic conditions of the Indian masses."[92]

2.2.10. Role of Chicago and Parliament of Religions

Vivekananda went to the United States, and delivered an impressive speech in the World Parliament of Religions[93] at Chicago in 1893. He became famous with this single speech.[94] He was considered as the 'greatest figure'[95] in the Parliament and Chicago became an 'opening'[96] for him to the West. Hence, Chicago made him influential in the rest of his life and acceptable in both East and West.[97] Thus at Chicago, he became world famous, with the message of harmony of religions, which he learned basically from his Master Sri Ramakrishna.

2.2.11. Journey and Mission to the 'West'

Formation of Vivekananda was not completed at Dakshineswar or with Sri Ramakrishna – but he went a long way even to West for the same. With Dakshineswar ends the first phase of his life but the second phase, which witnessed his emergence as a world teacher begins thereafter.[98] He thus had

---

[88] *CWSV*. 1: xvi-xvii.

[89] *The Life*. 1: 357.

[90] Swami Nikhilananda, op.cit., 52.

[91] Santi L. Mukherji, op.cit., 101.

[92] Basant Kumar Lal, op.cit., 2.

[93] The Parliament of Religions was held in Chicago from 11 – 27 September, 1893 as a part of the World fair. This meeting was held in conjunction with the World's Columbian Exposition to mark the 400th anniversary of Columbus' discovery of America. The Parliament was organized by leaders of various Christian denominations to show a new tolerance towards other faiths and probably to demonstrate the ultimate superiority of Christianity. Swami Vivekananda gave six talks at the Parliament and made a deep impression upon the seven thousand people attended it. In these speeches he glorified the traditions of India.

[94] V. R. Karandikar, op.cit., 367.

[95] *CWSV*. 8: 327.

[96] *CWSV*. 3:310.

[97] Asim Chaudhuri, op.cit., front page.

[98] Santi L. Mukherji, op.cit., 107.

travelled to America, England and Europe, and his work spread over three continents.[99] In relation to Chicago, he spent almost five years in the West and almost all of his lectures were delivered in the West. Consequently, he took up the mission of propagating Hinduism in the West, especially in America and Europe. This he did, by interpreting Hindu scriptures and philosophy and the Hindu way of life and institutions to the Western people in an idiom which they could understand. He was, thus, able to change the 'dark picture' of India in the West, as propagated by the colonial missionaries, to a brighten one. He made the Western people realize that they had to learn much from Indian spirituality for their own well-being. He showed that, in spite of her poverty and backwardness, India had a great contribution to make the world culture. He based this on Practical *Vedānta* and Universal Religion.

2.2.12. Founding of Ramakrishna Mission – Organizing Hinduism in a 'New' Perspective

Traditionally, Hinduism lacked a central authority or an organized institutional structure, but after his visit to the Christian West, Vivekananda realized the power of organization in religious life.[100] So, he wanted to work on an organized and systematic basis in order to give practical application of his Master's philosophy. Thus Swami founded the monastic order, Ramakrishna Math and Mission in 1897.[101] He proposed an integration of educational, philanthropic, and religious activities in the Mission and also combined contemplation and social service. The Mission was "first of its kind in the long history of Hinduism,"[102] "the concept was revolutionary," and "involved changes and innovations,"[103] that in it Vivekananda combined Indian spirituality, Western organization and social service. Hence,

> The intense activity of the West was to be combined with the deep meditation of the East. Asceticism and retirement were to be supplemented by work and service to others. From the merging of these two currents came the new Hinduism ...."[104]

[99] V. R. Karandikar, op.cit., 604.

[100] K. P. Aleaz, *Jesus in Neo-Vedanta*, op.cit., 204.

[101] N. Lekshmikutty, op.cit., 96. Founding of Ramakrishna Mission was a unique step in organizing Hinduism in a new perspective. Vivekananda founded it after the name of his Guru Sri Ramakrishna, in order to keep the bands of the monks together.

[102] Thomas Mannumel, op.cit., 18-19.

[103] *New Discoveries*. 6:237.

[104] *The Life*. 1:75. The 'new' thing Vivekananda brought into Hinduism was 'organization' and 'institutionalization' for 'propagation and service'. Traditional Hinduism lacked a central organizational system, but he tried to organize and institutionalize Hinduism for the first time for systematizing his work, which was earlier unknown to Hindu religion. This can be

It gave "...a new shape, a new purpose, and a new meaning to Indian monasticism."[105] Through this, he desired to propagate *Advaita Vedānta*, so to make 'Hinduism active, aggressive, and a missionary faith.'[106] He thus said: "Shankara left this Advaita philosophy in the hills and forests, while I have come to bring it out of those places and scatter it broadcast before the workaday world and society."[107]

In this mission, Vivekananda philosophically and practically connected service of humanity with service of God. This is done within an *Advaita* framework through the concept of "Daridra Narayana."[108] Christian concept and emphasis on social service also influenced him to form this combination.[109] Further as an *Advaita Vedāntin*, service of God and service of man were not two, as there is no distinction between man and God, in *Advaita*. He thus elevated social service as divine service through his *mānavadvaitavāda* (humanistic monism). Hence, by giving adequate concern for the poor and making *Advaita Vedānta* a socially relevant one in everyday life,[110] he stood for 'Man-making religion'[111] and aimed at construction of a better society. As a result his 'Practical *Vedānta*' has played a great role in the shaping of modern India.[112] Therefore V.K.R.V. Rao calls him as the "Prophet of Vedantic Socialism."[113] In this 'New Hinduism' he repudiated "don't-touch-ism" and untouchability and suggested 'root and branch reform'[114] for the regeneration of religion.

To sum up, Vivekananda was a spiritual personality. There were a number of influences and experiences behind his intellectual personality ranging from his parents to the resources of the West. For example, he mastered the *Upaniṣads*, *Mahābhārata*, *Rāmāyaṇa*, *Bhagavadgītā*, and Bible and also Western philosophy. He also had high admiration for *Vedic* and *Advaita Vedāntic* tradition and was impressed by the life and teachings of Gautama

---

understood as part of his 'reaction' and 'defence' of Hindu religion in the context of colonialism and missionary threats.

[105] *The Life*. 1:535.

[106] *CWSV*. 9:390; Sister Nivedita, op.cit., 159, 236.

[107] *CWSV*. 7:162. *cf.* 3:245.

[108] *CWSV*. 7: 245.

[109] P. T. Raju, *The Philosophical Traditions of India* (London: George Allen & Unwin Ltd., 1971), 230; Basant Kumar Lal, op.cit., 3; Abraham Stephen, op.cit., 26.

[110] V. R. Karandikar, op.cit., 474-493.

[111] *CWSV*. 3:224.

[112] V.K.R.V. Rao, *Builders of Modern India, Swami Vivekananda*, op.cit., 246-247.

[113] V.K.R.V. Rao, *Swami Vivekananda: The Prophet of Vedantic Socialism*, op.cit., The very 'title' of this book.

[114] *CWSV*. 3:213.

Buddha and Jesus Christ,[115] above all, by his Master Sri Ramakrishna. Hence as an *Advaitist*, he was able to integrate every influence in his personality and became a synthesis of the finest and foremost heritage of East and West. Thomas Mannumel's observation is also worth noting in this regard: "Both East and West went into the making of the Swami. As a matter of fact the different influences moulding the mind of Vivekananda could be reduced to two great currents. One was the Western education and philosophy, which formed the intellectual 'bread and butter' of an anglicised Calcutta; the other, much deeper and more profound, the Upanishadic Hinduism seen and felt through the singular life and contact with the sage of Dakshineswar."[116] However, one can note that, the English education and Western philosophy gripped him at the early stage of his mind, but later he realized the glory of Indian tradition of *Advaita Vedānta* and made a fine defence of the same against the Western attack.

2.3. The Making of Mahatma Gandhi

Mahatma Gandhi's formation of personality and thought took a long process and a number of experiences and influences. Dhananjay Keer rightly says: "The making of a superman is not a one-sided development. It is a long, hard process. It is the result of action and reaction between man and his destiny."[117] Thus a variety of influences shaped Gandhi's personality and thought.[118] His thought "…carries on it the stamp of a number of influences."[119] For example, Gandhi himself says: "My young mind tried to unify the teaching of the *Gita*, the *Light of Asia* and the Sermon on the Mount."[120] Among these, only the major ones from both Indian and Western sources are described here.

2.3.1. Influence of Heredity and Family

The following words of Gandhi reveal the impact of heredity and family on his life: "Children inherit the quality of parents no less than the physical features. Environment does play an important part, but the original capital on which a child starts life is inherited from its ancestors."[121] His family in Gujarat followed *Vaiṣṇavism*, which believed in the efficacy of vows, fasts and devotional practices. Hence, Gandhi's several qualities as a person were born and nour-

---

[115] V.K.R.V. Rao, *Swami Vivekananda: The Prophet of Vedantic Socialism*, op.cit., 141.

[116] Thomas Mannumel, op.cit., 19.

[117] Dhananjay Keer, *Mahatma Gandhi* (Bombay: Popular Prakashan, 1973), 9.

[118] D. M. Dutta, *The Philosophy of Mahatma Gandhi* (Madison: The University of Wisconsin Press, 1953), 3.

[119] Basant Kumar Lal, op.cit., 92.

[120] *An Autobiography,* 64.

[121] Ibid., 286.

ished in this family atmosphere. His father Kaba Gandhi's life of uprightness and ideas cast a considerable influence on Gandhi, especially in his early life. The harmonious coexistence of several religions in Kathiawad and his father's interest in discussions with members of different religions gave Gandhi an early initiation to religious toleration and to the concept of equality of all religions. His mother Putlibai was a saintly, puritan and religious woman. The love for saintliness, for hard vows and an unflinching adherence to them even in the midst of severe trials, in other words, a heroic devotion to high ideals, were all apparently imbibed by Gandhi from the example of his mother's life. He states: "The outstanding impression my mother has left on my memory is that of saintliness.... She would take the hardest vows and keep them without flinching."[122] Hence, this resulted in Gandhi taking a pledge before he started on a voyage for studies in England to keep his mother's wish–to eschew wine, women and meat eating.[123] This vow to mother actually helped him to be away from the evils of Western civilization.

Gandhi was also influenced by his family nurse Rambha who inculcated in him the idea of reciting the name of *Rāma* in moments of difficulty. He used to be afraid of ghosts and spirits. That is why Rambha suggested to him '*Rāmanāma*' to be a sovereign remedy for all evils. Hence, Gandhi says: "I think it is due to the seed sown by that good woman Rambha that today Ramanama is an infallible remedy for me."[124] Hindu stories of '*Shravana*'[125] and '*Harishchandra*'[126] which he came to know as part of his heredity also had a great impact on Gandhi to lead a truthful and sincere life.

2.3.2. Jainism

Jainism had a deep influence in the Kathiawad area of Gujarat and from his childhood onwards Gandhi had been familiar with Jainism and its teachings.

---

[122] Ibid., 4.

[123] Ibid., 36. Nirmal Kumar Bose, *My Days with Gandhi* (New Delhi: Orient Longman, 1987), 165-166.

[124] M. K. Gandhi, *My Religion* (Ahmedabad: Navajivan Publishing House, 1958), 6.

[125] *Shravana's* is of sacrificial devotion to his blind parents. *An Autobiography*, 6-7.

[126] It is a story of a king of rare goodness called *Harishchandra*. The gods wanting to test him, sent a Brahmin to him. The Brahmin asked for alms and would not be satisfied until the king gave him all he had including his kingdom. *Harishchandra*, true to his dharma, parted with all his possessions, became a slave and was put in charge of the cremation grounds. His wife left him after taking their son with her. After a while, when the son died the wife brought the corpse to *Harishchandra* for cremation. But, he insisted on the customary fee which the woman was unable to pay. The gods, pleased with the truthfulness of *Harishchandra*, intervened to restore the kingdom to him. *An Autobiography*, 7.

Hence, Jainism cast a deep impression on the ethical and religious life of Gandhi.[127] He says:

> Jainism was strong in Gujarat, and its influence was felt everywhere and on all occasions. The opposition to and abhorrence of meat-eating that existed in Gujarat among the Jains and *Vaiṣṇavas* were to be seen nowhere else in India or outside in such strength.[128]

Pyarelal writes about three things in Jainism which influenced Gandhi the most: "...*Ahimsa* on the religious side, *anekantavad* or *syadvad* on the philosophical side, and institutions of vows on the ethical side."[129] For example, the five vows prescribed for right conduct by Jainism was accepted by Gandhi such as *ahiṃsā* (non-violence), *satya* (truth-speaking), *asteya* (non-stealing), *aparigrahāḥ* (non-possession), and *brahmacarya* (chastity).[130] Moreover, he adopted these vows as part of his personal life and made it as a code of conduct to the inmates of his *ashram*.[131]

2.3.3. Christian Contacts and Christianity

Gandhi's first impressions of Christianity were received as a schoolboy in Rajkot, Gujarat, which left him with a negative image. About which he says:

> In those days missionaries used to stand in a corner near the high school and hold forth, pouring abuse on Hindus and their gods. I could not endure this. I must have stood there to hear them once only, but that was enough…[132]

He also heard that a prominent Hindu convert was required to eat beef, drink liquor, and wear European clothing.

> Surely, thought I, a religion that compelled one to eat beef, drink liquor, and change one's own clothes did not deserve the name. I also heard that the new convert had already begun abusing the

---

[127] Jaladhar Pal, *The Moral Philosophy of Gandhi* (New Delhi: Gyan Publishing House, 1998), 33.

[128] *An Autobiography*, 19-20.

[129] Pyarelal, *Mahatma Gandhi: The Early Phase*, vol. 1 (Ahmedabad: Navajivan Publishing House, 1965), 276.

[130] M. K. Gandhi, *From Yervada Mandir* (Ahmedabad: Navajivan Publishing House, 2011), 3-17.

[131] Ibid., Preface.

[132] *An Autobiography*, 31.

religion of his ancestors, their customs and their country. All these things created in me a dislike for Christianity.[133]

Although this initial experience was negative, he continued to develop friendship with Christians while being in London and it continued later in South Africa and after coming back to India too. Concerning Christian contacts Gandhi says, "My acquaintance …with so many missionaries is by no means a new thing."[134] "I have come under the influence of noted Christian missionaries belonging to different denominations. And I enjoy to this day the privilege of friendship with some of them."[135] Among Christians C. F. Andrews was his close friend.[136] These Christian contacts were instrumental in moulding him. As K.C. Chacko states, "...but for the Christian contact, Gandhi would not have been moulded as he was."[137]

Thus among world religions, although Gandhi hated the Western form of Christianity introduced to him, he was influenced by Christianity, in shaping many aspects of his life and ideas. Several of the core aspects of his life and thoughts were influenced by Christianity. For example, Evangelical Christianity influenced him in areas of prayer, devotion, divine guidance and inner voice. He was particularly moulded by the Christian principles in the Sermon on the Mount.[138] Hence, Rama Shanker Srivastava rightly states: "If any religion has touched and pervaded the very being of Mahatma Gandhi, it was Christianity."[139] However, "...by Christianity is meant the life of Jesus Christ and his teachings as enumerated in the Sermon on the Mount, and not any brand of (orthodox) Christianity or Christian theology."[140]

'1893' was crucial in Gandhi's life as he encountered deeply and intensely with Evangelical Christians in South Africa. About which he says: "In the year 1893, I came into close contact with some Christian gentleman in South Africa."[141] They were Baker, Coates and Polak - missionaries who tried to persuade Gandhi to embrace Christianity. Hence, from June to

---

[133] Ibid.

[134] *CWMG.* 27:434.

[135] *CWMG.* 13:220.

[136] Mahatma Gandhi, *The Spirit of Hinduism* (New Delhi: Pankaj Publications, 1980), 29.

[137] K. C. Chacko, *Metaphysical Implications of Gandhian Thought* (Delhi: Mittal Publications, 1986), 44.

[138] E. Stanley Jones, *Mahatma Gandhi: An Interpretation* (New York: Abingdon-Cokesbury Press, 1948), 60.

[139] Rama Shanker Srivastava, *Contemporary Indian Philosophy* (New Delhi: Munshiram Manoharlal Publishers, second edition, 1983), 170.

[140] M. P. Mathai, *Mahatma Gandhi's World-View* (New Delhi: Gandhi Peace Foundation, 2000), 39.

[141] *CWMG.* 32:4.

October 1893, Gandhi underwent five months' of intense Christianization in South Africa.[142] They gave him books, took him to services, argued with him and tried their best to convert him, even to make him waver between Hinduism and Christianity. Books given by Christian missionaries, Christian services like Wellington Convention and the doctrine of 'only begotten Son' etc. did not impress Gandhi, but it awakened in him a religious quest.[143] The influence was so strong that, he confesses, there was a time when his mind was "wavering between Hinduism and Christianity."[144] For example, he says, "…I do not know where I am, and what is and what should be my belief."[145] Thus Gandhi was not able to stand with Christian missionaries by himself and was wavering, so he sought the help from Raychandbhai. His correspondence with Raychandbhai was in 1894; as a result he regained his faith in Hinduism and Indian tradition from these Western missionary influences.

Hence Gandhi was not attracted to Evangelical Christianity, but to Esoteric Christianity[146] as expounded in the writings of Maitland and Kingsford.[147] He found in Esoteric Christianity, an alternative form of Christian interpretation, without 'arrogant claim of dogmatic superiority' and also was close to *Advaita Vedāntic* ideas. Thus, Gandhi carried on a correspondence with Maitland which had a specific and lasting influence on his making. Gandhi read Maitland's books – *The Perfect Way* and *The New Gospel of Interpretation*. These works interpreted the incarnation and resurrection of Christ as allegories of the inward development of soul.[148] Gandhi became a member of this union and promoted this view.[149] The subtitle of *The Perfect Way* was "The Finding of Christ," and it suggested that Christ was to be found within the person, "neither a person merely historical nor one supernatural; but the type of the highest possibilities of humanity."[150] After reading Maitland's books Gandhi wrote: "I liked both. They seemed to support Hinduism."[151] Because Gandhi accepted the Christian ideas, which were in conformity with Indian tradition and Hinduism. Hence about the interaction of Gandhi with Esoteric Christian Union, James D. Hunt

---

[142] James D. Hunt, *Gandhi and Nonconformists Encounters in South Africa* (New Delhi: Promilla & Co., Publishers, 1986), 36.

[143] *An Autobiography*, 128.

[144] *CWMG*. 19:571.

[145] *An Autobiography*, 242.

[146] 'Esoteric Christian Union' was a tiny offshoot of theosophy and it was based on the writings of its founder Edward Maitland (1824-1897), who was a former theosophist.

[147] Raghavan N. Iyer, *The Moral and Political Thought of Mahatma Gandhi* (Delhi: Oxford University Press, 1973), 20.

[148] James D. Hunt, op.cit., 40.

[149] Ibid.

[150] Cited by Ibid.

[151] *An Autobiography*, 127.

remarks that, it 'provided a new religious identity for Gandhi'[152] and 'helped… to reconcile the Bible with Hinduism.'[153] Thus, Maitland's writings helped Gandhi to give a reasoned presentation of some of the basic tenets of Hinduism like the doctrines of rebirth, the essential identity of God and the individual soul, and the salvation from the possibility of fall by realising the Supreme.[154]

Another notable Christian contact of Gandhi was with Plymouth Brethren[155] in South Africa.[156] Plymouth Brothers were of the teaching that since Christ redeemed the sins of those who accepted Him, after embracing Christianity the person who accepted it is free to do anything he liked, since Christ redeemed the sins of those who accepted him.[157] Hence, they believed once a person was saved, no crime or sin could cause him to lose his salvation. This Gandhi considered as a distortion of Christianity by pride and moral insensitivity.[158] Gandhi thus opposed the teaching of salvation and its eternal security by Plymouth Brethren. It, for him, did not put any moral responsibility to persons who accepted Christ.

Quakers were another Christian sect, which stood near to the true form of Christianity in Gandhian conception. He considered it as 'the nearest representation of…the Christian life in the Gospels.'[159] He liked their corporate life and importance given to the guidance of the Spirit. Of all these Christian denominations, Gandhi was not attracted to the Orthodox/Evangelical Christianity of missionaries or to Plymouth Brethren, but accepted a form of Christianity, which was compatible with Hinduism – for example, esoteric Christianity of Maitland, Tolstoyan Christianity and Quaker Christianity– in all these, inner experience/inwardness was emphasized as that of Indian tradition of *Advaita*. Hence Gandhi accepted a 'form' of Christianity, which is in agreement with Indian tradition and rejected the imperial claims and Western forms of Christianity, which tried to subjugate and denounce the Indian tradition and Hinduism.

---

[152] James D. Hunt, op.cit., 7.

[153] Ibid., 40.

[154] Gummadi Veerraju, *Gandhian Philosophy Its Relevance Today* (New Delhi: Decent Books, 1999), 17.

[155] The Plymouth Brethren are a conservative Protestant evangelical sect which began in the 1820s in England.

[156] *CWMG*. 72:298.

[157] *CWMG*. 86:95.

[158] James D. Hunt, op.cit., 18.

[159] Ibid., 19.

2.3.4. Influence of Raychandbhai

In 1891 Gandhi got introduced to Raychandbhai.[160] Gandhi got a guiding relationship with Raychandbhai, which he calls as a 'living contact.'[161] Gandhi was struck by his 'simplicity and independence of judgment,' and considered him 'refuge' in moments of spiritual crises and religious doubts.[162] When missionaries troubled him in South Africa and tried their best to convert him to Christianity, even to the point of 'wavering' between Hinduism and Christianity, Gandhi entered into correspondence with Raychandbhai during 1894.[163] He asked twenty-six questions on religious, philosophical, and ethical subjects, some of them reflecting his struggles with the missionaries. For example – 'If a claim is put forward that a particular religion is the best, may we not ask the claimant for proof?', 'The Christians hold that the Bible is divinely inspired and that Christ was an incarnation of God, being his son. Was He?', 'Were all the Old Testament prophecies fulfilled in Christ?'[164] Raychandbhai answered these questions and gave a general criterion for evaluating religions: "That religion alone is the best and is truly strong, which is most helpful in destroying the bondage of worldly life and can establish us in the state which is our essence."[165] He also sent a number of books, which were, for Gandhi 'highest solace,'[166] and 'the most satisfying'[167] that helped him to resolve his doubts about Hinduism. The result was that he gained peace of mind, and felt reassured that Hinduism and Indian tradition could give him what he needed.[168] Thus Raychandbhai's advice made Gandhi firmer in Hinduism and in his belief that no need to change one's religion for spiritual progress.[169] As a result, Christian missionaries' effort to convert Gandhi became unsuccessful. Hence, Christian missionaries confused Gandhi about the validity of Indian tradition and Hinduism, but it was Rajchandra, who restored Gandhi's faith in Hinduism and Indian tradition from the Western colonial Christian missionary influences, and helped to give a sense of direction to Gandhi's religious quest.[170]

---

[160] *CWMG*. 32:5. Raychandbhai was a Jain jeweller and a religious poet and a philosopher.

[161] *An Autobiography*, 83.

[162] *An Autobiography*, 83.

[163] *CWMG*. 32:4; 100:136.

[164] *CWMG*. 1:128 f., 32:1-13, 593-602.

[165] *CWMG*. 32:598.

[166] *CWMG*. 9:213.

[167] *CWMG*. 9: 242.

[168] *CWMG*. 32:4.

[169] *CWMG*. 32:13.

[170] B. R. Nanda, op.cit., 68.

2.3.5. Influence of Christ, Bible and Sermon on the Mount

Gandhi had the chance to read the Bible during his stay in London through his Christian contacts.[171] Gandhi thus said on the influence of Bible in his life: "...there have been many times when I did not know which way to turn. But I have gone to the Bible and particularly the New Testament, and have drawn strength from its message."[172] In the New Testament, the 'Sermon on the Mount' had a significant role in the transformation of Gandhi's personality. He says, "But when I came to the New Testament and the Sermon on the Mount, I began to understand the Christian teaching, and the teaching of the Sermon on the Mount echoed something I had learnt in childhood and something which seemed to be part of my being ...."[173] Part of this appeal of the Sermon was its resemblance to Shamal Bhatt's Gujarati stanza[174] known and loved from childhood.[175] Further he says: "…the Sermon on the Mount …went straight to my heart."[176] "*The Sermon on the Mount* left a deep impression on my mind when I read it."[177] The teaching of Jesus, particularly 'resist not evil' impressed him. He often quoted from the Gospel of Mathew 5:39, which reads as,

> Love your enemies, do good to those who hate you. Bless those who curse you and pray for those who treat you badly. To the one who strikes you on the cheek, turn the other cheek; to the one who takes your coat, give also your shirt.

He therefore says, "The message of Jesus, as I understand it, is contained in his Sermon on the Mount unadulterated and taken as a whole...."[178] And for Gandhi, "...the Sermon on the Mount was the whole of Christianity...."[179] And "It is that Sermon which has endeared Jesus to me."[180] Further he asserted, "If then I had to face only the Sermon on the Mount and my own interpretation of it, I should not hesitate to say, 'Oh yes, I am a Christian.'"[181]

---

[171] *An Autobiography*, 63.

[172] *CWMG*. 16: 496.

[173] *Young India*, 31.12.1931. Cited by Robert Ellsberg, *Gandhi on Christianity* (New York: Orbis Books, 1991), 21.

[174] *An Autobiography*, 64.

[175] Marjorie Sykes, "East Wind, West Wind," in *Facets of Mahatma Gandhi*, vol. 4, edited by Subrata Mukherjee and Sushila Ramaswamy (New Delhi: Deep & Deep Publications, 1994), 168.

[176] *An Autobiography*, 63.

[177] *CWMG*. 15:305.

[178] *CWMG*. 35:248.

[179] *CWMG*. 48:438.

[180] *Young India*, 31.12.1931.

[181] *CWMG*. 35:248.

Because of this deep impact, Jesus and his teachings are an important source of Gandhi's philosophy of *satyāgraha*. Gandhi says that, the revelation of passive resistance came to him after reading the Sermon on the Mount in 1893.[182] Hence Gandhi, like Christ, preached the brotherhood of all men. Jesus' compassion for the poor and the dispossessed is reflected in Gandhi's love for the poor and the outcastes. He said "...I can say that Jesus occupies in my heart the place of one of the great teachers who have had a considerable influence on my life."[183] He also added, "Though I cannot claim to be Christian in the sectarian sense, the example of Jesus' suffering is a factor in the composition of my undying faith in non-violence which rules all my actions, worldly and temporal."[184]

Gandhi also compared Sermon on the Mount with *Gītā*.[185] He found practically no "difference between the Sermon on the Mount and the Bhagavad Gita…."[186] On the other hand, he found a meeting ground between the Sermon and the ***Gītā*** and saw them as mutually complementary.[187] "What the Sermon describes in a graphic manner, the *Bhagavad Gita* reduces to scientific formula."[188] He thus stated: "The spirit of the Sermon on the Mount competes almost on equal terms with the *Bhagavad Gita* for the domination of my heart."[189] Gandhi therefore perceives essential unity in the teachings of ***Gītā*** and Sermon and both become '*giri-gītā*' in Gandhi.

2.3.6. Vegetarianism

During his stay in London, another influence was his reading of Henry Salt's *A Plea for Vegetarianism* (1886) and of the writings of the other members of the group such as Howard William, Anna Kingsford and Dr. Thomas Allinson, which introduced Gandhi to the morality of vegetarianism.[190] As a result, he had become a convinced vegetarian.[191] It was an intellectual conversion from the simple vow to his mother. Hence as a vegetarian, the sense of the sacredness

---

[182] *Young India*, 25.02.1920.

[183] Gandhi, *The Spirit of Hinduism*, op.cit., 29.

[184] *Harijan*, 07.01.1939.

[185] *An Autobiography*, 63.

[186] *Young India*, 22.12.1927.

[187] K. C. Chacko, op.cit., 44.

[188] *Young India*, 22.12.1927.

[189] *CWMG*. 13:220.

[190] Rama Jha, "Gandhi's Encounter with Western Thought," *Gandhi Marg* 5/4 (July, 1983): 210.

[191] K. S. Bharati, *Thoughts of Mahatma*, vol. 1 (Nagpur: Dattsons, 1995), 81.

of all life was a deep religious principle with Gandhi.[192] This was contrary to the 'beef eating' practice of Western Christianity.

2.3.7. Theosophy

Gandhi came in contact with two members of the London Theosophical Society in 1889. They gave him Edwin Arnold's *The Song Celestial* and *Light of Asia*. He also read its founder Blavatsky's *The Key to Theosophy*. About which he says: "This book [*The Key to Theosophy*] stimulated in me the desire to read books on Hinduism."[193] Hence, contact with Theosophy was instrumental in 'awakening of interest in his heritage'[194] and to have a more positive conception of Hinduism.[195] Rama Jha considers 'vegetarianism to theosophy' as the next stage in the evolution of Gandhi's thought.[196]

2.3.8. Hinduism

Gandhi was born in a Hindu *Vaiṣṇava* family and claimed himself to be a "… staunch *sanatani* Hindu."[197] However, while he was in England and later in South Africa that he came into closer and deeper study of Hinduism.[198] He was introduced to the intellectual and spiritual heritage of his own country through Theosophy.[199] He thus acquired knowledge of Hinduism through secondary sources and translations as he read translations of *Gītā* while in England and translations of *Upaniṣads* while in South Africa.[200] For he says: "I have not read the Vedas in the original."[201]

On the contrary, his life and thoughts were immensely shaped by Hindu religion and culture.[202] For he said: "Hinduism as I know it entirely satisfies my soul, fills my whole being."[203] He also stated: "My notions were an outcome

---

[192] C. F. Andrews, *Mahatma Gandhi's Ideas* (New York: The Macmillan Company, 1930), 67.

[193] *An Autobiography*, 63.

[194] James D. Hunt, op.cit., 6.

[195] Joseph J. Doke, *M. K. Gandhi: An Indian Patriot in South Africa* (New Delhi: n.p., 1967), 137.

[196] Rama Jha, op.cit., 212.

[197] *CWMG*. 31:351; *cf.* 89:193.

[198] Daniel Mangalath, *A Challenge and a Promise Mahatma Gandhi's Philosophy of Man and Life* (Trivandrum: M S Publications, 1996), 27.

[199] Rama Jha, op.cit., 212.

[200] S. K. Kim argues that, Gandhi read Max Muller's translation of the *Upaniṣads* for the first time somewhere in 1894-1896 in South Africa. Recitation of some of the verses of the *Upaniṣads* was part of Gandhi's daily prayers. S. K. Kim, *The Philosophical Thoughts of Mahatma Gandhi* (New Delhi: Vikas Publishing House, 1996), 197.

[201] *CWMG*. 34:261.

[202] M. P. Mathai, op.cit., 38.

[203] *Young India*. 06.08.1925.

of a study of the Gita, Ramayana, Mahabharata, Upanishads, etc."[204] Thus Gandhi is the efflorescence of Hindu tradition and culture.[205]

Gītā and *Rāmāyaṇa* of Tulsidās were more influential texts in Gandhi.[206] He says: "Nothing elates me so much as the music of the 'Gita' or the 'Ramayana' by Tulsidas, the only two books in Hinduism I may be said to know."[207] Philosophically he belonged to the *Advaita Vedānta* school of Hindu religion and explicitly declared: "I am an *Advaitist...*"[208] Further he says: "I believe in the Advaita, I believe in the essential unity of man and for that matter of all that lives."[209] He also believed truth and non-violence as the cardinal virtues of Hinduism and said: "I believe that the essence of Hinduism is truth and non-violence."[210]

Gandhi also explained the characteristic features of Hinduism:

> On examination, I have found it to be the most tolerant of all religions known to me. Its freedom from dogma makes a forcible appeal to me in as much as it gives the votary the largest scope for self-expression. Not being an exclusive religion, it enables the followers of that faith not merely to respect all the other religions, but it also enables them to admire and assimilate whatever may be good in the other faiths.[211]

Thus Gandhi continually emphasized the broad,[212] inclusive and assimilative character of Hinduism and its tolerance and respect for other faiths.[213] He confessed his Hindu religion is not 'exclusive'[214], 'narrow'[215] or 'sectarian.'[216] In other words, his Hinduism is 'all-embracing'[217] and included all that is best in Islam, Christianity, Buddhism and Zoroastrianism.[218] For

---

[204] *Harijan*, 03.10.1936.

[205] Kasthuri Vasudev, "The Metaphysical Basis of Gandhian Political Philosophy," *Indian Philosophical Annual*, vol. 5 (University of Madras, 1969, T.M.P. Mahadevan, ed.): 189.

[206] M. K. Gandhi, *Hindu Dharma* (New Delhi: Diamond Books, 2009), 11.

[207] Ibid.

[208] M. K. Gandhi, *God is Truth* (Mumbai: Bharatiya Vidya Bhavan, 1998), 9.

[209] *Young India*, 04.12.1924.

[210] *CWMG*. 19: 328.

[211] *CWMG*. 100: 152.

[212] *CWMG*. 35:254-255.

[213] *Harijan*, 30.11.1947.

[214] Gandhi, *The Spirit of Hinduism*, op.cit., 19.

[215] *CWMG*. 88: 468.

[216] *CWMG*. 67: 37.

[217] *CWMG*. 54: 132

[218] *CWMG*. 67: 37.

example, he said: "There is in Hinduism room ... for Jesus...."[219] Hence for Gandhi, "to be a true Hindu meant also to be a true Christian or Muslim."[220] Thus he was able to say, "It was through the Hindu religion that I learnt to respect Christianity and Islam."[221] Hence, such a broad conception of Hinduism made Gandhi to develop his concept of *sarva-dharma-samānatva* – equality of all religions.

Gandhi also stood for the reformation of Hinduism. However, Gandhi was not a radical reformer, for he said: "I am a reformer through and through. But my zeal never takes me to the rejection of any of the essential things of Hinduism."[222] He thus distinguished between essentials and non-essentials through his interpretation and tried to purify it of its excrescences.[223] He did not agree with *manusmṛiti*, untouchability, child-marriage, prohibition of foreign travel, etc. He very particularly attacked 'untouchability' and said: "I hold that untouchability is no part of Hinduism. On the contrary, it is a serious blot on it."[224]

2.3.9. Influence of *Bhagavadgītā*

Among the books that influenced Gandhi's thoughts and ideas, *Gītā* can be ranked first. It has become his 'infallible guide of conduct' and the 'dictionary of daily reference.'[225] He says: "My life has been full of external tragedies, and if they have not left any visible and indelible effect on me, I owe it to the teachings of the Bhagavad Gita."[226] He first read it, when he was studying in England.[227] He says: "My first acquaintance with the Gita was in 1889, when I was almost twenty."[228] He got Sir Edwin Arnold's *Gītā* translation – the *Song Celestial* through Theosophists. Later he referred *Gītā* as his 'mother'[229] which had become his key to the scriptures of the world.[230] He admitted that the central teaching of the *Gītā* was *anāsakti* or 'selfless action', the the most excellent way to attain self-realization. K. C. Chacko is of the opinion that

[219] *Harijan*, 30.01.1937.

[220] *Harijan*, 27.04.1947.

[221] *CWMG*. 14: 74.

[222] *Young India*, 06.10.1921.

[223] P.S. Daniel, op.cit., 222.

[224] *Young India*, 24.04.1924; *CWMG*. 23: 485.

[225] *An Autobiography*, 244.

[226] Cited by C. F. Andrews, op.cit., 73.

[227] *An Autobiography*, 62. Gandhi himself admits that he had not read the *Gitā* before going to England.

[228] *Young India*, 12.11.1925.

[229] *Harijan*, 24. 08.1939.

[230] *CWMG*. 62:334.

Gandhi derived almost all his concepts of religious, moral, social and political philosophy from the *Gītā*.[231] Gandhi also found the 'Sermon' and the *Gītā* as mutually complementary; between them he found a meeting ground.[232]

2.3.10. Buddhism

Buddhism started influencing him while he was in England. Edwin Arnold's *Light of Asia* which influenced him a great deal[233] was the first book he read on Buddha.[234] The Buddha's life of renunciation and his doctrine of compassion and toleration had influenced Gandhi to some extent.[235] He thus said: "I owe a great deal to the inspiration that I have derived from the life of the Enlightened one."[236] P. T. Raju also suggests: "Gandhi's ideas that religion lies in the service of humanity may be traced to the Buddha."[237]

2.3.11. Islam

Gandhi read Thomas Carlyle's *Heroes and Hero-worship* and learned about the life of the prophet.[238] He also read *The Life of Mahomet and His Successors* by Washington Irving. Hence, he regarded Islam as a religion of peace in the same sense in which Christianity, Buddhism and Hinduism are.[239] The chief contribution of Islam according to Gandhi was the brotherhood of man. The message of Prophet Mohammed was essentially a message of kindness, consideration, peace, love and non-violence as a means of conquering evil.[240]

2.3.12. Influence of Modern Thinkers

Although Gandhi was an Indian, he owed indebtedness to the modern thinkers, who were from outside India. Although he opposed, Western colonialism and superiority, he did not think that everything Western had to be rejected. On the other hand, he learnt about *ahiṃsā* from the Western tradition also.[241] Thus Gandhi was deeply influenced by some of the modern Western and Russian thinkers and writers while he was in South Africa. However, he 'was quite selective' as he followed only the writings of daring Christian moralists and

---

[231] K. C. Chacko, op.cit., 39.

[232] Ibid., 44.

[233] S. K. Kim, op.cit., 29.

[234] K. C. Chacko, op.cit., 32.

[235] Daniel Mangalath, op.cit., 29.

[236] M. K. Gandhi, *All Religions Are True* (Bombay: Pearl Publications, 1962), 196.

[237] P. T. Raju, op.cit., 224-225.

[238] *An Autobiography*, 64.

[239] K. S. Bharati, *Thoughts of Mahatma*, vol. 1, op.cit., 85.

[240] Ibid.

[241] *Young India*, 11.10.1928.

humanist thinkers of the nineteenth century such as Ruskin, Thoreau and Tolstoy who criticised modern industrial civilization, use of violence and colonialism.[242] Therefore Ruskin and Thoreau from the West and Tolstoy from Russia are not well accepted in the West. Their ideas do not have many followers in the West and their thoughts are not well recognized in the mainstream Western philosophy. But Gandhi said: "...I have but endeavoured humbly to follow Tolstoy, Ruskin, Thoreau... besides the masters of Indian philosophy."[243] So Ruskin, Thoreau and Tolstoy exerted a powerful influence in confirming Gandhi's views and ways.[244]

2.3.12.1. Ruskin

John Ruskin (1819-1900) had a great part in shaping Gandhi's thinking. Ruskin's book, *Unto This Last*[245] made an instant change on the whole priorities of Gandhian life and outlook.[246] He calls the whole incident as 'the magic spell of a book.'[247] He thus says:

> ...the book that affected me more than any other was Unto This Last by Ruskin. I was living in South Africa then. It was the reading of Unto This Last on a railway journey to Durban in 1904 when I was thirty-five, that made me decide to change my whole outward life. There is no other word for it, Ruskin's words captivated me. I read the book in one go and lay awake all the following night and I there and then decided to change my whole plan of life.[248]

He further continues:

---

[242] Rama Jha, op.cit., 211. Gandhi accepted the 'alternative forms of thoughts' from West. He did not embrace the Western ideologies as it is but adapted them to Indian situation. Ruskin, Thoreau and Tolstoy - all represent a critique of Western civilization itself. Hence, the main streams of Western tradition undergo a change in Gandhi. He marginalised the mainstream Western thinkers but elevated the marginalised thoughts of the West.

[243] *CWMG*. 10:189.

[244] *CWMG*. 100: 37.

[245] *Unto This Last* is a collection of Ruskin's humanistic essays on political economy published in 1862. The title of the book is taken from the New Testament parable of workmen in the vineyard (Gospel of Mathew. 20:1-16). The labourer who was recruited 'last' was also given wages equal to that of the others who were recruited earlier in the day.

[246] Lizy Paul, *Dynamics of Personality Development A Study based on Mahatma Gandhi's Life and Writings* (Bangalore: Dharmaram Publication, 1997), 82. "If any single book made a revolutionary impact on Gandhi's mind overnight, it was Ruskin's *Unto This Last* which he read in 1904 in South Africa." Rama Jha, op.cit., 216.

[247] *An Autobiography*, 273-275.

[248] *CWMG*. 48:180.

> The book was impossible to lay aside, once I had begun it. It gripped me. I could not get any sleep that night. I determined to change my life in accordance with the ideals of that book....I believe that I discovered some of my deepest convictions reflected in this great book of Ruskin, and that is why it so captured me and made me transform my life.[249]

The transforming impact of this book thus made Gandhi to renounce property and privileges, to establish socialist communities and to think in terms of *Sarvodaya*.[250] R. R. Diwakar also thinks that the "seed of the whole concept of Gandhi's Sarvodaya ideal lies in the teaching of Ruskin."[251] Other lessons that Gandhi learned from Ruskin include - the dignity of all labour, absence of concentration of wealth and economic power and equality and social justice.[252]

2.3.12.2. Thoreau

Another Western thinker who influenced Gandhi was Henry David Thoreau (1817-1862) with his essay *Civil Disobedience*. He says: "My first introduction to Thoreau's writings was I think in 1907....It left a deep impression upon me."[253] Gandhi read Thoreau during a crucial stage of his life when he was fighting in South Africa. He wrote that Thoreau's essays contained "the essence of his political philosophy not only as India's struggle related to the British but as to his own views of the relation of citizens to government."[254] Hence Gandhi owed his concept of 'Civil Disobedience' to Thoreau. Thoreau's was political philosophy. If the government is wrong, no need to pay tax, co-operate or show obedience to the State by the citizens. Injustices of the State is not accepted; State is not the highest, but conscience. Hence, Thoreau's essay encouraged Gandhi in developing his *satyāgraha* or civil-disobedience/ resistance in the political/colonial context of South Africa and India.[255] Thus to his American friends Gandhi said: "You have given me a teacher in Thoreau,

---

[249] *An Autobiography*, 274-275.

[250] K. S. Bharati, *Thoughts of Mahatma*, vol. 2, op.cit., 42-43. 'Unto This Last' was translated by Gandhi into Gujarati under the heading *Sarvodaya*, which literally means 'Welfare of All.'

[251] Cited by Daniel Mangalath, op.cit., 32.

[252] K. S. Bharati, *Thoughts of Mahatma*, vol. 1, op.cit., 99.

[253] Cited by Raghvan Iyer, ed., *The Essential Writings of Mahatma Gandhi* (Delhi: Oxford University Press, 1994), 71. However, K. C. Chacko states that, Gandhi did not become acquainted with the works of Thoreau till 1909. K.C. Chacko, op.cit., 48.

[254] G. Ramachandran and T. K. Mahadevan, eds., *Quest for Gandhi* (New Delhi: Gandhi Peace Foundation, 1970), 173.

[255] R. R. Diwaker, *Gandhi's Life, Thought and Philosophy* (Bombay: Bharatiya Vidya Bhavan, 1963), 47-48.

who furnished me through his essay 'On the Duty of Civil Disobedience' scientific confirmation of what I was doing in South Africa."[256]

2.3.12.3. Tolstoy

Leo Tolstoy (1828-1910) was a Russian Christian. However, he totally rejected the organised Christianity and was ex-communicated by the Russian Orthodox Church.[257] For Tolstoy, love, self-denial and returning good for evil was the essence of Christianity.[258] From 1908 onwards Gandhi had been influenced by Tolstoy as he studied Tolstoy's books while in the prison of South Africa (1909-1910) and entered into correspondence with him. [259] So, these years were memorable for Gandhi's correspondence with Tolstoy.[260] Gandhi himself testifies about Tolstoyan impact on his life: "Tolstoy has been one of my teachers for a number of years."[261] And "He affected the inner being."[262] Tolstoy's book *The Kingdom of God Is within You* impressed him the most - the profound morality, truthfulness and independent thinking of which overwhelmed him and left an abiding impression on his mind.[263] In *The Kingdom of God is within You,* Tolstoy forcefully reclaims the idea that non-violence is central to the teaching of Jesus. In rejecting that truth through centuries in favour of nationalism, war, and imperialism, Christianity lost its way.[264] Hence, its reading made Gandhi a "firm believer in *ahimsa*"[265] as he learned *ahiṃsā* from Tolstoy.[266] Thus Gandhi followed the Christianity presented by Tolstoy, which was contrary to the beliefs and practices of colonial Christianity, he encountered with. Gandhi was also influenced by Tolstoy in developing his concept of 'bread labour'[267] and the 'vow of celibacy.'[268]

---

[256] *CWMG*. 76:358.

[257] Hugh Tinker, "Nonviolence as a Political Strategy: Gandhi and Western Thinkers," *Gandhi Marg* 2/5 (August, 1980): 245.

[258] Prem Kumari, *Comparative Ethics of Gandhi and Kant* (New Delhi: Classical Publishing Company, 1996), 5.

[259] S. K. Kim, op.cit., 137.

[260] Margaret Chatterjee, *Gandhi's Religious Thought* (London: The Macmillan Press, 1983), 50.

[261] *CWMG*. 10:189.

[262] *CWMG*. 48:180.

[263] *An Autobiography*, 127.

[264] Terrence J. Rynne, *Gandhi and Jesus The Saving Power of Non-violence* (Bangalore: Asian Trading Corporation, 2009), 29.

[265] *CWMG*. 38:260.

[266] *CWMG*. 37:262.

[267] *CWMG*. 50: 214.

[268] *CWMG*. 37: 240.

2.4. Conclusion

"The correct judgement of a great man like Gandhi is a difficult, and perhaps an impossible task."[269] Because such was Mahatma, the sort of man who made his advent in the world only once in many generations.[270] In his *Autobiography,* Gandhi acknowledges the roots and the influences which gave shape and form to his thought, which in fact contributed to the development and evolution of his mind and ideas. He was not influenced by a single source alone, but many sources, ancient and modern; both Indian and Western were instrumental in making him, his life and thought. It is difficult to determine the most influential in forming his world-view. But there was some influence from all these sources as he was a 'multiple genius' and integrated / assimilated in himself, ideas and values from several sources. On the other hand, all what he had read did not influence him; as he had blind faith in none, but he tested everything with his inner voice, heart and reason.[271] Thus he was quite selective and critical and learned to distinguish between essential and non-essential.[272] Because Gandhi said: "...at every step, I have carried out the process of acceptance and rejection and acted accordingly."[273] Moreover, he shared the views, Oriental and Occidental, in his own way. As he was an ardent and ceaseless experimenter with truth, his eclectic yet sceptic mind tested all views which he came across in the hard grindstone of his own experience; and modified, changed, enriched, sometimes abandoned, ideas in the light of experience and surroundings.[274] In this process, Gandhi fused the āstika and *nāstika* systems of Indian philosophy in his integrated system and represented the essence of the religious-philosophical traditions of India. Above all, he declared himself as an *Advaitin* and perceived the essential oneness and unity of everything. Christ and Christian tradition as represented by Esotericism, Quakers, Sermon on the Mount, Ruskin, Thoreau and Tolstoy was also a major source of influence on Gandhi, which prompted him to fight against the distorted Western colonial Christianity. Nevertheless, Gandhi was more than the sum total of the influences that made their impact on him.[275]

Thus the making of both Vivekananda and Gandhi were a long process. Different sources, persons, ideas, religions and circumstances were

---

[269] Jaladhar Pal, op.cit., 307.

[270] Suniti Kumar Chatterji, "Reminiscences," in *Mahatma Gandhi 100 Years*, edited by S. Radhakrishnan (New Delhi: Gandhi Peace Foundation, 2009), 43.

[271] Pratap Chandra Chunder, *On Understanding Gandhiji* (Mumbai: Bharatiya Vidya Bhavan, 2003), 32.

[272] K. S. Bharati, *Thoughts of Mahatma*, vol. 1, op.cit., 82.

[273] *An Autobiography*, xiii.

[274] Jaladhar Pal, op.cit., 36.

[275] Lizy Paul, op.cit., 91.

influential in the formation of their personality and the development of their philosophical views. However, one can sense a greater commitment in them to defend the Indian tradition and the *Advaitic* form of Hinduism in all these circumstances, against the onslaught of colonialism and Western Christianity, which questioned and attacked everything 'Indian'. Hence, this wider context of European colonial domination had an over-arching effect in their making and response, especially in relation to their Christ-experience.

Chapter 3

The Pre-dominance of Indian Tradition and *Advaita Vedānta* in the Writings of Swami Vivekananda and Mahatma Gandhi

3.1. Introduction

Against the Western colonial philosophy of distinctions and separation, which became the basis of inequality, superiority, exploitation and oppression, Vivekananda and Gandhi affirmed the *Advaitic* culture of unity, oneness, sacredness and equality of all life, thus love of the entire universe. Therefore there is a pre-dominance of Indian tradition and *Advaita* in their writings. This is actually a philosophical defence of Indian thought and the rejection of colonial philosophy of superiority and domination founded on Aristotle's thought. *Advaita* philosophy of oneness of all creation and unity of all life is thus the background of their life and work and the social movements headed by them. This chapter, thus, explores the predominance of Indian tradition and *Advaita* in their writings, which is in fact, was an attempt to uphold the supremacy of Indian *Advaitic* tradition against the tide of Western colonialism and Christian missionary denigration of Indian religion and culture.

3.2. Swami Vivekananda and Indian Tradition

Swami Vivekananda as a renascent thinker aimed at the regeneration of Indian culture, and comprehensively presented the glory, unity and continuity of Indian tradition.[1] His presentation of the glory of Indian tradition was in the context of colonial onslaught of Indian nation as well as in reaction to the European missionary attack and denunciation of Hindu religion.

---

[1] R. K. Dasgupta, op.cit., 320; Dev Raj Bali, op.cit., 37.

In contrast to modern Western civilization, Vivekananda considered India, as a very old nation,[2] as it is founded upon ages and ages of experience.[3] He traced the sources of Indian tradition to Sanskrit literature such as *Vedas* and *Upaniṣads*.[4] He said: "The Upanishads are the Bible of India."[5]

Moreover, against the missionary notion of the 'darkness' and 'inferiority' of Indian civilization, Vivekananda was proud of India and considered it as the 'ideal civilization.'[6] Therefore love of motherland, and patriotism was present in him in a much intense sense.[7] For example, he called India as '*Punya Bhumi*'[8] and '*Tirtha*.'[9] He also said: "I am not ashamed of my race or my birth or nationality."[10] Because, "The soil of India is my highest heaven, the good of India is my good."[11] The glorification of Indian tradition was therefore a prominent feature of Vivekananda. Through his Chicago address he brought before the world the essentiality of Indian tradition for world's existence. Hence, he created value and respect for India in the West.[12]

Against the colonial and Oriental approach, Vivekananda took a nationalist approach towards the history of India. He said: "It is for Indians to write Indian history."[13] According to him, Western scholars were prejudiced to Indian history to fix latter dates.[14] On the other hand, for him, *Vedas* are the Aryan literature and oldest in the world.[15] It is eternal and revelation to *ṛṣis* (seers).[16] Its date cannot be fixed.[17] So he did not agree with the dates assigned to Indian history by Western scholars.[18] Rather he tries to push back Indian antiquity towards farthest B.C. claiming seniority to India than any nations.[19]

---

[2] *CWSV*. 5: 509.

[3] *CWSV*. 8: 71.

[4] Dev Raj Bali, op.cit., 34; *The Life*. 2:6.

[5] *CWSV*. 1:446.

[6] *CWSV*. 4: 100-101.

[7] *CWSV*. 4: 312; 3:381; *The Life*. 2: 560.

[8] Swami Nirvedananda, comp., *Swami Vivekananda on India and Her Problems* (Almora: Advaita Ashrama, 4th edition, 1946), 1.

[9] *CWSV*. 3: 309.

[10] *CWSV*. 8: 523.

[11] *CWSV*. 4: 480.

[12] *CWSV*. 5: 121-122; V. R. Karandikar, op.cit., 426.

[13] *The Life*. 1: 272.

[14] *CWSV*. 3: 457-458; 9: 251.

[15] *CWSV*. 6: 47.

[16] *CWSV*. 3: 118; 8: 232.

[17] *CWSV*. 3: 118.

[18] *CWSV*. 6: 508.

[19] *CWSV*. 7: 366.

Vivekananda believed in the continuity of Indian tradition and considered it as a living civilization.[20] For him, longevity and continuity is the uniqueness of India which is not claimed by other civilizations.[21] Indian tradition is self-renewing,[22] incomparable, stable and developed through trial and experimentation process of thousands of years.[23] It is based on non-resistance therefore it is immortal and eternal and cannot be killed.[24] He was thus responding to the colonial view of 'replacing' Indian culture. On the other hand, he reminded them that, India has survived so many troubles and tribulations.[25] So many invasions and wars could not destroy India or make it into a wilderness; it is firmer than rocks and still lives strongly.[26] On the contrary, old civilizations like Greece and Rome were dead and gone,[27] however he says: "India is still living; who says she is dead?"[28] Nevertheless, as a reformer, he pointed out and opposed some of the defects and degradation of Indian culture of his times, such as untouchability and 'don't-touch-ism'[29] and suggested, "root-and-branch reform."[30] All these reformatory attempts were "to regain the lost Selfhood"[31] of India.

Further, Vivekananda understood civilization in terms of spirituality and said: "Civilization is the manifestation of that divinity in man."[32] Hence R. K. Dasgupta observes that: "...Swami Vivekananda exalted Indian culture as a spiritual culture ...."[33] for him, Indian tradition is a spiritual tradition.[34] "Spirituality has been always in India"[35] and "The very air is full of the pulsations of spirituality."[36] Indian tradition had its beginnings in the spiritual

---

[20] R. K. Dasgupta, op.cit., 152, 315.

[21] Swami Vivekananda, *My India, The India Eternal* (Calcutta: Ramakrishna Mission Institute of Culture, 7th Reprint, 1998), 5; hereafter it will be denoted as *My India*.

[22] *CWSV*. 8: 92-93.

[23] *CWSV*. 4:324-325.

[24] *CWSV*. 3: 285; 4:160; *New Discoveries*. 4: 155-156.

[25] *CWSV*. 5:459.

[26] *CWSV*. 5: 444-445.

[27] *CWSV*. 8: 71.

[28] *CWSV*. 3: 165.

[29] *CWSV*. 9: 390.

[30] *CWSV*. 3:213.

[31] *CWSV*. 1:468.

[32] *CWSV*. 5: 308.

[33] R. K. Dasgupta, op.cit., 321.

[34] *CWSV*. 4: 475-476.

[35] *CWSV*. 3: 137.

[36] *CWSV*. 4: 313.

experiences of Vedic *ṛṣis*,[37] as Indians are "...the descendants of *ṛṣis* and sages who lived on roots and fruits in mountains and caves, meditating on the Supreme."[38] Therefore *ṛṣis* are the leaders of India, not political figures; as religion, not politics that leads Indian nation.[39] Further, for him, as a spiritual tradition, prayers, vigils and fasting have great place in India.[40] Moreover for Vivekananda, due to its spirituality, India is Christ – like in humility, love, gentleness, and affection towards all living beings.[41] Thus Vivekananda affirms that, spirituality is the foundation of Indian civilization and not materialism; as the Indian ideal is primacy of spirit over matter.[42] *Mokṣa* or freedom of the soul is the goal of India.[43] Therefore India did not give emphasis to materialistic enjoyment of the world, as this worldly life is impermanent and vanity.[44] Rather India is a 'land of renunciation'[45] and tried "...in lessening, in a great measure, the material needs of men."[46] Finally Vivekananda was able to see this spiritual, meditative, ascetic and renouncing tradition, in Sri Ramakrishna and has said: "Ramakrishna Paramahamsa …was the embodiment of all the past religious thoughts of India."[47] This view of Indian tradition as spiritual was in direct contrast to the materialistic and political civilization of the West.

Another peculiarity that Vivekananda considered as the foundation, backbone and bed-rock of Indian tradition was religion.[48] Therefore he stated: "India is the land of religion...."[49] "The Indian mind is first religious then anything else."[50] "In India, religious life forms the centre, the keynote of the whole music of national life. …"[51] Hence for him, religion is realization[52] and by religion he meant the eternal principles taught by the scriptures, not local customs and superstitions.[53] He saw religion as a creative force for integration

---

[37] R. K. Dasgupta, op.cit., 317.

[38] *CWSV*. 3: 139.

[39] *CWSV*. 3: 153, 175; 6: 161.

[40] *CWSV*. 9: 415.

[41] *CWSV*. 8: 206-207.

[42] *CWSV*. 8: 71-72.

[43] *CWSV*. 5: 458-459; 8: 70.

[44] *CWSV*. 3: 152.

[45] *CWSV*. 3: 137; 2: 272.

[46] *CWSV*. 6:462-463.

[47] *CWSV*. 6: 311.

[48] *CWSV*. 3: 148; 204; R. C. Majumdar, op.cit., 89.

[49] *CWSV*. 3: 165.

[50] *CWSV*. 3: 289.

[51] *CWSV*. 3: 220.

[52] *CWSV*. 3: 377.

[53] *The Life*. 2: 302.

and stability of India.[54] Hence, he defended against the missionary view that, the whole of India is 'pagan'.

Vivekananda further noted many characteristic features of Indian tradition. That Indian tradition, unlike the Western Christian tradition, is based, built and emphasises on principles, not on persons, as persons are only illustrations of principles.[55] It is transcendental and philosophical[56] and holds the divinity of man. Hence, he stated: "Our God is man!"[57] Further Indian tradition is calm and marked by silence and non-violence.[58] Another feature is its belief in *karma* and *saṃsāra* (metempsychosis).[59] He also said of other Indian features such as – tolerance, universal acceptance, hospitality, inclusiveness and equality of all religions.[60]

Again for Vivekananda, India is superior as a moral and religious nation,[61] the first and greater than other nations.[62] India is "...the motherland of philosophy, of spirituality, and of ethics, of sweetness, gentleness, and love."[63] India has attained the highest standards of humanity[64] and her religion and philosophy have reached their culminating points.[65] Thus, India got a highly developed metaphysics[66] as ideas of God, pre-existence, and immortality of soul first arose and fully developed in India than elsewhere.[67] Therefore the world is indebted to India; [68] that as a cultural force India has influenced all the cultures of the world.[69] Thus, he says: "There is not a system of religion or philosophy in the world that does not show the influence of India's speculation, even to the Catholic church."[70] For example, all religious thought in every part

---

[54] S. S. Mital, op.cit., 75.

[55] *CWSV*. 3: 182-184, 249, 280; 5: 207.

[56] *CWSV*. 3: 149, 353.

[57] *CWSV*. 9: 419.

[58] *CWSV*. 3: 274.

[59] *CWSV*. 6:103; 7:423.

[60] *CWSV*. 1: 3-4; 9: 429-430.

[61] *CWSV*. 5: 220; *The Life*. 1: 555.

[62] *CWSV*. 1: ix; 3: 147.

[63] *CWSV*. 3: 147.

[64] *CWSV*. 3: 105.

[65] *CWSV*. 3: 285.

[66] *CWSV*. 4: 144; 6: 390-391; 9: 193, 206.

[67] *CWSV*. 3: 154, 4: 263.

[68] Swami Nikhilananda, op.cit., 206.

[69] *CWSV*. 3: 105, 106; P. R. Bhuyan, *Swami Vivekananda Messiah of Resurgent India* (New Delhi: Atlantic Publishers and Distributors, 2003), 51.

[70] *CWSV*. 9: 504; *cf.* 3: 138.

of the world are derived from the *Vedas*.[71] Before Buddhism, Indian thought had reached China, Persia, Greece and other countries.[72] Hence for Vivekananda, Greek philosophy had its origins from India through Pythagoras,[73] as he traces the influence of Indian thought in Pythagoras, Socrates, Plato and Egyptian neo-Platonists.[74] He also traces connections between Asoka's missionaries and Christian origins.[75] Thus Christianity, for him, is "a collection of little bits of Indian thought,"[76] "a very patchy imitation"[77] and a "great offshoot"[78] of Indian tradition. Especially he found many similarities between Hinduism and Catholicism and compared the Holy Sacrament with the *prasādam* of the Hindu temples[79] and the confessional and the belief in saints in the Catholic Church are taken from Hindu religion.[80] These Indian influences on Western philosophy and Christianity is traced actually by Vivekananda, to give proof of the superior nature of Indian culture over the Western, hence to silence the colonizers and missionaries alike, against their suppositions.

Vivekananda thus contrasts Oriental with Occidental.[81] According to him Western civilization is too young, based on competition,[82] modern and yet to mature itself and achieve stability; whereas Indian tradition is ancient, mature and stable.[83] Therefore he was against Westernization of India and thereby uprooting of Indian tradition, which developed through centuries.[84] He says: "...imitation is not civilisation."[85] Further he continues: "In the first place, we cannot become Western; therefore imitating the Westerns is useless. Suppose you can imitate the Westerns, that moment you will die, you will have no more life in you."[86] So according to Vivekananda, India cannot become anything else; Indian tradition is most suitable for India and India can

[71] *CWSV*. 6: 105.

[72] *CWSV*. 3:275.

[73] *CWSV*. 2: 445; R. K. Dasgupta, op.cit., 175.

[74] *CWSV*. 3: 434.

[75] *CWSV*. 7: 347.

[76] *CWSV*. 3: 275.

[77] *CWSV*. 3: 275.

[78] *CWSV*. 7:287.

[79] Swami Nikhilananda, op.cit., 111.

[80] *CWSV*. 7:287.

[81] *CWSV*. 4: 12, 155.

[82] *CWSV*. 3: 433.

[83] V.K.R.V. Rao, *Swami Vivekananda The Prophet of Vedantic Socialism*, op.cit., 183; S. S. Mital, op.cit., 121.

[84] *CWSV*. 4: 406.

[85] *CWSV*. 3: 381.

[86] *CWSV*. 3: 172.

follow only India.[87] However, India by standing firmly in her own tradition must consciously accept and assimilate what is good, useful and novel from others, especially from the West says Vivekananda.[88]

Thus according to Vivekananda, Indian tradition got the capacity to assimilate new thoughts, to accept change without giving up her spiritual character.[89] He says: "My motto is to learn whatever good things I may come across anywhere."[90] Therefore according to him, "... each must assimilate the spirit of the others and yet preserve his individuality and grow according to his own law of growth."[91] He thus said; "Let us be as progressive as any nation that ever existed, and at the same time as faithful and conservative towards our traditions."[92]

Vivekananda, in contrast to dogmatic and exclusive Western Christian tradition, saw Indian tradition as an inclusive tradition, where pluralities and diversities co-exist harmoniously.[93] He says: "It is one of inclusion of every one, exclusion of none."[94] Thus "...each and all have a place..." in it.[95] For example, from the high spiritual flights of the *Advaita Vedānta* philosophy, to the low ideas of idolatry with its multifarious mythology, the agnosticism of the Buddhists, and the atheism of the Jains, have a place in Indian tradition.[96] In India, theists, atheists, monists, dualists, monotheists, materialists, etc. were allowed to exist together.[97] Moreover, India got the spirit of toleration and shows reverence and acceptance towards other religions.[98] Thus with its hospitable mind, India has sheltered the persecuted and the refugees of all religions and all nations of the earth.[99] As examples, he cites the cases of Jews, Zoroastrians and Christians.[100]

Along with inclusivism, Vivekananda also emphasised pluralism as another characteristic feature of Indian tradition. *Ekam Sat Viprāha Bahudhā Vadanti* – Truth is Absolute, Sages call it variously (*Ṛig-veda*. 1.164.46) was

[87] *CWSV*. 3: 220.

[88] *CWSV*. 3: 152, 381, 382; 9: 531, 541.

[89] *CWSV*. 1:157; 3: 176; *My India*, 5.

[90] *CWSV*. 6:234.

[91] *CWSV*. 1:24.

[92] *CWSV*. 3: 174.

[93] *CWSV*. 2:238.

[94] *CWSV*. 3: 132.

[95] *CWSV*. 1: xiii.

[96] *CWSV*. 1: 6.

[97] *CWSV*. 1:348.

[98] *CWSV*. 1:391.

[99] *CWSV*. 1: 3.

[100] *CWSV*. 1:391.

the core and foundation of Indian pluralistic tradition.[101] India got a wonderful catholicity to harmonize everything.[102] And Indian tradition looks charitably and kindly upon the different religious convictions.[103] Thus he says: "We have no quarrel with any religion in the world, whether it teaches men to worship Christ, Buddha, or Mohammed, or any other prophet."[104] Thus India is a land of religious harmony, where Hindus even built churches and mosques for Christians and Mohammedans.[105] Moreover, religious freedom is a great feature of India.[106] Therefore India does not know the words like 'exclusion'[107] 'persecution'[108] and 'intolerance'[109] says Vivekananda. One can sense that these characteristic features of India are in direct contrast to aggressive colonial civilization that came to India in the nineteenth century.

Thus, India, for Vivekananda is a conglomeration of various races, religions, cultures and languages.[110] It is "A mixed race in every sense of the word."[111] As a result, much cross fertilization has taken place in India and this has resulted in the evolution of a composite culture which upholds unity in diversity.[112] However, of these infinite varieties, he says, "The one common ground that we have is our sacred tradition, our religion. That is the only common ground, and upon that we shall have to build."[113]

This common ground for Vivekananda is *Advaita Vedānta*,[114] as it upholds, the "...Oneness of everything."[115] For him, *Advaita* is "the crest-jewel of all spiritual thought"[116] and harmonizes diversities into unity. He says: "The whole of this universe is one Unity. One Existence, physically, mentally,

---

[101] CWSV. 1: 3; 3: 186-187; 9: 259.

[102] *CWSV*. 8: 210.

[103] *CWSV*. 3: 187-188.

[104] *CWSV*. 3: 132.

[105] *CWSV*. 3: 186-187; 274.

[106] *CWSV*. 1: 425; 2: 115.

[107] *CWSV*. 9: 429-430.

[108] *CWSV*. 1:391, 425; 9: 436.

[109] *CWSV*. 9: 438.

[110] *CWSV*. 3: 286.

[111] *CWSV*. 4: 299, 296.

[112] K. P. Aleaz, *Harmony of Religions: The Relevance of Swami Vivekananda* (Calcutta: Punthi-Pustak, 1993), 224.

[113] *CWSV*. 3: 286.

[114] For Vivekananda, 'Hindu' means '*Vedāntist*'. He says: "What we really mean by the word Hindu is really the same as Vedantist." CWSV. 3: 396.

[115] *CWSV*. 2:153.

[116] *CWSV*. 3:432.

morally and spiritually."[117] In this *Advaitic* culture of India, not only 'human' but even the tiny creatures got a place in it and share in the unity and oneness of everything. Thus, Here, and here alone the human heart expanded till it included not only the human, but birds, beasts, and plants; from the highest gods to grains of sand, the highest and the lowest, all find a place in the heart of man, grown great, infinite. And here alone, the human soul studied the universe as one unbroken unity whose every pulse was his own pulse."[118] However, while emphasising this unity and oneness, Vivekananda affirms that unity is not uniformity, but the recognition of diversities as part of one spiritual unity[119] and the 'individuality' of each element is not destroyed.[120] Hence, this is a definite proclamation of the superiority of the *Advaitic* culture of India, which is totally against the superior-inferior approach, racism, colonial exploitation, denigration of other religions etc, which are the characteristic features of Western civilization founded on the Aristotelian epistemology.

Against the colonial missionaries' view that, they have only the 'mission' of Christianizing and civilizing other nations of the earth, Vivekananda said: "Each nation has a mission for the world."[121] India lives to this day, for it has a mission to fulfil in the spiritual ordering of the universe.[122] So he viewed India as the spiritual leader of the world – teaching religion and spirituality to the world nations.[123] Indian thought-philosophical and spiritual, must once more go over and conquer the world.[124] Because, Indian tradition got a therapeutic value and –"India's very atmosphere is soothing."[125] The world has to follow India, if it wants to live.[126]

Vivekananda did not accept the Christian missionary criticisms of Indian tradition. For him, Christian presentation of India to the West was totally negative and this misrepresentation by Christian missionaries was for money-making, which was used for the purpose of conversion.[127] Hence, he had to correct this negative picture of India.[128] He boldly asserted that India was far ahead of the western nations in spirituality and morality and that the

---

[117] *CWSV*. 2:249.

[118] *CWSV*. 4: 314.

[119] *New Discoveries*. 1:414-415.

[120] *CWSV*. 4: 310-311.

[121] *CWSV*. 8: 75.

[122] *CWSV*. 3: 169.

[123] *CWSV*. 5: 421; Dev Raj Bali, op.cit., 34; Swami Nikhilananda, op.cit., 206.

[124] *CWSV*. 3: 276.

[125] *CWSV*. 5: 210.

[126] *CWSV*. 3: 167.

[127] *CWSV*. 4: 414, 415.

[128] *CWSV*. 4: 201, 415.

western Christian missionaries were not required to preach and teach religion to India, rather they should learn from India.[129] He said, "let Jesus save Europe, than India."[130] "Missionary work is unwanted"[131] as "India does not want the Christianity of missionaries."[132] Vivekananda thus told the missionaries that, they could not convert India to Christianity;[133] so he requested them to work somewhere else.[134]

3.3. Mahatma Gandhi and Indian Tradition

In contrast to 'modern' Western civilization, Gandhi considered Indian tradition as 'ancient' and founded on the legacy and *tapasya* of *ṛṣis* and *munis*.[135] In modern times, he tried to revive, return and restore the ancient culture of India, against the onslaught of colonizers and Christian missionaries.[136] Hence Gandhi is highly indebted to Indian tradition[137] and he developed his ideas on the basis of it.[138] For example, Gandhi got inspiration from both āstika and *nāstika* traditions of India,[139] as *Vedas*, *Upaniṣads*, *Gītā*, Jainism and Buddhism form the basic sources of Gandhian thought.[140] Gandhi took *Vedas* as eternal and of divine origin; they are dateless.[141] Hence, Indian ideals became working principles in Gandhi[142] as he became a living example and personification of Indian tradition,[143] in fact, a genius of Indian civilization. So it is said: "Gandhi was India."[144]

---

[129] *CWSV*. 8: 206-207.

[130] *CWSV*. 5: 444-445.

[131] *CWSV*. 9: 468.

[132] *CWSV*. 8: 206-207; 9:441.

[133] *New Discoveries*. 1: 414-415.

[134] *CWSV*. 5: 444-445.

[135] *CWMG*. 14: 299.

[136] M. K. Gandhi, *Modern Vs. Ancient Civilization* (Mumbai: Bharatiya Vidya Bhavan, 1998), 21.

[137] Nirmal Minz, op.cit., 73.

[138] J. P. Naik, "Development and Gandhian Tradition in India," *The Review of Politics*, 45/ 3 (July, 1983): 353.

[139] S. K. Kim, op.cit., 253.

[140] Surendra Verma, *Metaphysical Foundation of Mahatma Gandhi's Thought* (Bombay: Orient Longman, 1970), 70-71.

[141] Gandhi, *Hindu Dharma*, op.cit., 22, 26.

[142] Rama Shanker Srivastava, op.cit., 159.

[143] Madhuri Wadhwa, *Gandhi between Tradition and Modernity* (New Delhi: Deep & Deep Publications, 1997), 11.

[144] E. Stanley Jones, op.cit., 32.

Gandhi loved India and was proud of her tradition, for he said: "Indian Civilization is unquestionably the best."[145] "Everything in India attracts me."[146] And "I cling to India like a child to its mother's breast."[147] These statements show the defence and superior place given to India by Gandhi, over against the denunciation of everything Indian, in the colonial period.

Gandhi, therefore had a deep and direct knowledge of India, which sprang from the grassroots level interaction with the Indian masses and villages.[148] He was thus firmly rooted in Indian tradition.[149] However, he was not a traditionalist,[150] as his regard for tradition was combined with a progressive outlook and dynamism;[151] for he re-interpreted the ancient values of India in a new way,[152] according to the needs of the times.[153] He, thus said: "I do claim to throw a new light on many an old truth."[154]

Gandhi perceived the continuity and survival of Indian tradition over against the 'threat' of its displacement by colonizers and missionaries. He observed that, while many of the mighty civilizations of the world disappeared, India is still 'living.'[155] He, thus asked: "Where is Rome and Greece?...Ancient India is still living."[156] He thus added: "I want India to recognize that She has a soul that cannot perish."[157] Therefore for Gandhi, India should realize that "her culture has a very important place in the universe" and "is likely to serve as an example for the whole world to copy."[158] India has a mission for all the world.[159] Even, he said of conquering the West by the East through truth and non-violence.[160]

---

[145] Gandhi, *Modern Vs. Ancient Civilization*, op.cit., 19.

[146] M. K. Gandhi, *India of My Dreams* (Ahmedabad: Navajivan Publishing House, 1959), 3.

[147] *Young India*, 06.04.1921.

[148] *CWMG*.13:524; 14:362, 513; 16:186; *Harijan*, 28.01.1939.

[149] Bindu Puri, *Gandhi and the Moral Life* (New Delhi: Mittal Publications, 2004), 20, 22.

[150] K. Aravindakshan, *Gandhiyude Jeevitha Darsanam* (Mal.) (Kozhikode: Mathrubhumi Books, 2008), 212.

[151] Madhuri Wadhwa, op.cit., 32.

[152] K. C. Chacko, op.cit., 3; Jaladhar Pal, op.cit., 192.

[153] J. P. Naik, op.cit., 360.

[154] R. K. Prabhu & U. R. Rao, *The Mind of Mahatma Gandhi* (London: Oxford University Press, 1946), 93.

[155] M. K. Gandhi, *Hind Swaraj or Indian Home Rule* (Ahmedabad: Navajivan Publishing House, 20th Reprint, 2008), 52; *CWMG*. 34:316.

[156] *Young India*, 24.11.1927.

[157] *Young India*, 11.08.1920.

[158] *CWMG*. 23:244.

[159] Gandhi, *India of My Dreams*, op.cit., 4.

[160] *CWMG*. 100: 473.

However, Gandhi argued that, although the Indian civilization was still living and fundamentally sound, it was inevitable that such an old civilization may over time develop 'defects' or 'excrescences.'[161] Thus he was a reformer of Indian tradition from social evils such as untouchability, child marriage, widowhood, *dévadāsīs*, etc.[162] He tried to reject all superstitions, inhuman, immoral and irrational elements in Indian tradition.[163] On the other hand, he was not a radical reformer for he said: "I am a reformer through and through. But my zeal never takes me to the rejection of any of the essential things ...."[164] So Gandhi distinguished between the essentials and non-essentials and accepted the essentials and rejected the non-essentials.[165] Being 'ancient' was not the criteria to accept anything by him.[166] For example, he did not accept the tradition of untouchability as an essential part of Indian tradition, but as an excrescence.[167] Untouchability is not founded on *Śāstras*[168] but originated out of ignorance and cruelty.[169] Therefore he called untouchability as 'a device of Satan,'[170] 'a grievous crime,'[171] and 'a grave sin.'[172]

Further, Gandhi understood Indian tradition as a spiritual tradition. He thus said: "India is...the place of spirituality. ...The basis of life is spiritual."[173] India gives emphasis to inner life than outward life.[174] "Her spiritual heritage is simple living and high thinking."[175] Its prime aim is God-realization.[176] Gandhi also saw Indian tradition as a moral one based on values, for he said: "The very essence of our civilization is that we give a paramount place to morality in all our affairs, public or private."[177] Moreover, for him, Indian tradition was

---

[161] Madhuri Wadhwa, op.cit., 36.

[162] *CWMG*. 34:536-537.

[163] *Young India*, 17.10.1929.

[164] *Young India*, 06.10.1921.

[165] K. S. Bharati, *Thoughts of Mahatma*, vol. 1, op.cit., 82.

[166] *CWMG*. 34:550-551.

[167] *CWMG*. 21: 250.

[168] *Harijan*, 11.02.1933.

[169] Gandhi, *Hindu Dharma*, op.cit., 58.

[170] *Young India*, 19.01.1921.

[171] *CWMG*. 46: 303.

[172] M. K. Gandhi, *Food for the Soul* (Mumbai: Bharatiya Vidya Bhavan, 1998), 40.

[173] *CWMG*. 96: 201.

[174] *CWMG*. 17: 57.

[175] *Young India*, 22.09.1921.

[176] P. K. Das, *Modern Vedanta Gandhi's Philosophy Compared with the Philosophies of Vivekananda, Raman Mahershi, Tagore, Aurobindo, Ramatirtha, Radhakrishnan and Deen Dayal Upadhyaya* (Meerut: Rahul Publishing House, 2004), 194.

[177] *Young India*, 23.01.1930.

a village tradition[178] as he found 'real India' in the villages,[179] and he said: "If the village perishes India will perish too."[180] These affirmations were against the 'ungodly' and 'materialistic' civilization of the West.

Against the 'violence' and 'bloodshed' by the 'brute force' of Westerners', Gandhi highlighted the supreme values of Indian tradition '*ahiṃsā*' and '*satya*'.[181] For him, the *ṛṣis* only discovered the law of non-violence[182] so they are the permanent and ancient aspects of India.[183] He thus said: "I have nothing new to teach the world. Truth and Non-violence are as old as the hills."[184] *Ahiṃsā* is thus central and deep-rooted in Indian tradition and it is the most valuable contribution of India for the progress of the world.[185] *Ahiṃsā* was not mere 'non-injury, but compassion and love of all living beings.[186] Moreover, Gandhi considered 'non-violence' superior to brute-force and atom bomb; it is based on soul-force and is the supreme force in the world.[187] He thus applied ancient and unbroken tradition of *ahiṃsā* in all aspects of his concrete life and found successful, especially in developing *Satyāgraha.*[188] He also observed that "...all that is permanent in ancient Hindu culture is also to be found in the teachings of Jesus...."[189] Thus Jesus Christ was a non-violent *Satyāgrahi* for Gandhi as Jesus used 'soul force.'[190] Hence, Gandhi believed in the superiority of 'soul force' over 'brute force' and used it in the form of *Satyāgraha* against the British colonialism and found successful through the independence of India.

In Gandhi's view, the Indian civilization was essentially 'synthetic' in nature. Over the centuries the Indian 'blended with one another with the utmost freedom' and made India a microcosm of the world.[191] Thus 'It is a mingling of the cultures represented by the different faiths and influenced by the geographic and other environment in which the cultures have met.' It was

---

178 *CWMG*. 41: 220.

179 *CWMG*. 100: 473.

180 *Harijan,* 29.08.1936.

181 *CWMG*. 100: 161, 162.

182 *Young India*, 11.08.1920.

183 *CWMG*. 35:327.

184 M. K. Gandhi, *On Myself* (Mumbai: Bharatiya Vidya Bhavan, 1998), 14.

185 *Young India*, 21.03.1929; *CWMG*. 40:57, 58.

186 *CWMG*. 23: 24; Bindu Puri, op.cit., 60.

187 Cited by Raghavan Iyer, ed., *The Essential Writings of Mahatma* Gandhi, op.cit., 209.

188 *CWMG*. 100: 317; S. K. Kim, op.cit., 192; R. K. Prabhu & U. R. Rao, *The Mind of Mahatma Gandhi*, op.cit., 168.

189 R. K. Prabhu & U. R. Rao, Ibid., 91.

190 C. F. Andrews, op.cit., 193.

191 *Harijan*, 09.05.1936.

not 'wholly Hindu, Muslim, or Christian' but a 'fusion' of all of them. Thanks to its history of tolerance and synthesis, a unique 'spirit' had grown up in India and become an integral part of its way of life. Indeed India had developed an unusual faculty, the 'faculty for assimilation' and an 'amazing tolerance of opposite ideas.'[192] "Indian culture is therefore Indian. It is neither Hindu, Islamic nor any other, wholly. It is a fusion of all and essentially Eastern."[193] Hence he was against the monolithic European view of Western culture and also against the missionaries' wish of making India 'wholly Christian'.

Further, India got a welcoming tradition for Gandhi. He says, "I do not want my house to be walled in on all sides and my windows to be stuffed. I want the cultures of all the lands to be blown about my house as freely as possible. But I refuse to be blown off my feet by any."[194] So he assimilated many good values and ideas wherever he found them, especially from the West, but never got Westernized by giving up his ancient traditions of India. Rather he retained in himself the basis of Eastern ethos at all times.[195] He said: "I should not imitate you but should assimilate you."[196] "Adaptability is not imitation. It means power of resistance and assimilation."[197]

Gandhi held the Indian tradition of equality of all religions, over against the 'only true religion' concept of the Christian West. He, therefore approached other religions with tolerance and respect.[198] In his view, different religions as enlightened world perspectives can coexist simultaneously in society; And that is nothing new, as it has its roots in ancient Indian traditions.[199] He thus declared, 'Diversity in Unity' is a wonderful law[200] and "India of the near future stands for perfect toleration of all religions."[201] He also affirmed, "We were never exclusive, we were inclusive."[202] For example, Gandhi tells that Christianity

---

[192] *Young India*, 11.08.1927.

[193] *Young India*, 30.04.1931.

[194] *CWMG*. 20:159.

[195] *Young India*, 02.09.1926; Gandhi, *Modern Vs. Ancient Civilization*, op.cit., 87.

[196] *CWMG*. 48:128.

[197] *Young India*, 07.10.1926. Gandhi was against imitation, but welcomed assimilation, as assimilation is not uprooting, but a 'selective' approach to accept the good in others in conformity with one's own ethos and culture.

[198] K. Aravindakshan, op.cit., 38.

[199] P. K. Das, op.cit., 374.

[200] *CWMG*. 85: 460.

[201] *Young India*, 22.09.1921.

[202] D. G. Tendulkar, *Mahatma Life of Mohandas Karamchand Gandhi*, vol. 2 (New Delhi: The Publications Division, Ministry of Information and Broadcasting, Government of India, 1988), 191. Hereafter it will be denoted as *Mahatma* with different volumes.

was tolerated and its good elements were imbibed by Indian tradition.[203] He even declared: "There is in Hinduism room enough for Jesus...."[204]

Thus Gandhi often contrasted East with West, and ancient with modern.[205] He was mostly negative to modern materialistic civilization of the West as reflected in his '*Hind Swaraj*'.[206] Gandhi did not accept the Westerner's inferior view of Asia.[207] Gandhi praised Indian tradition while blaming the Western civilization.[208] Western ideal of life, for Gandhi, is 'false.'[209] He thus said, European civilization is suited for the Europeans only but it will mean ruin for India, if we endeavour to copy it.[210] Therefore India should unlearn those things from the West, which are useless and unprofitable.[211]

Gandhi was against the blind imitation of the West and the act of forgetting the ancient Indian tradition.[212] He stated, India is not to copy Europe blindly.[213] He was, thus, against 'uprooting of tradition'[214] and said: "Any attempt to root out tradition, effects of heredity, climate and other surroundings is not only bound to fail but is sacrilege."[215] On the other hand, he stressed that the people of India should understand and follow Indian ideals and must consider India's ancient culture and civilization not as a relic of the past to be despised but as a precious heritage that had to be cherished.[216]

Gandhi, therefore denied the negative and prejudiced Christian criticisms of Indian religions and tradition. On the contrary, he saw a lot of good in Indian tradition[217] and admonished Christian missionaries to have a receptive and open mind towards the 'good' of Indian tradition.[218] He identified the message of non-violence in both Indian tradition and Christian tradition of Sermon on the Mount and he saw meeting points between the Indian tradition and the

---

[203] *CWMG*. 4:408; 64:424.

[204] *Harijan*, 30.01.1937.

[205] *CWMG*. 8: 244; 57:498.

[206] *CWMG*. 19:178.

[207] *Young India*, 21.03.1928.

[208] *CWMG*. 10:189.

[209] *CWMG*. 23:243-244.

[210] *CWMG*. 46: 55.

[211] *CWMG*. 16: 495.

[212] *CWMG*. 13: 521.

[213] *Young India*, 11.08.1920.

[214] *CWMG*. 34:550.

[215] *Young India*, 25.09.1925.

[216] *CWMG*. 41:62.

[217] *CWMG*. 27: 436.

[218] *CWMG*. 27: 437; 34:261.

Christian tradition.[219] He advised the Indian Christians not to take the Western Christianity for themselves, because Jesus of Asia has been misrepresented in the West; and they should follow the Asian Jesus, not the Christ of the Western Christianity.[220]

Gandhi also opposed conversions to Christianity, as it often meant denationalization and rejection of Indian culture.[221] For him, conversions destroy, the age-old social superstructure of India and result in the uprooting of tradition.[222] Moreover, Westernization came through Christian garb.[223] He, thus preferred inner transformation to outward conversion.[224] He, therefore, wanted the Christians to stop converting Indians, and to limit their activities to humanitarian service only.[225] The reason is that, "the great faiths held by people of India are adequate for her people. India stands in no need of conversion from one faith to another."[226] The *Swadeshi* and *Swaraj* concepts of Gandhi also affirmed the superiority of India in the colonial context.

3.4. Swami Vivekananda and *Advaita*

Vivekananda proclaimed: "I am the Advaitist."[227] He always took his stance in the *Advaita* tradition of *Vedānta*,[228] because his basic belief in the essential unity of everything, that is, in the completely monistic nature of reality, owed to the *Advaita Vedānta*.[229] He says that *Advaita* upholds "...Oneness of everything."[230]

To prove the supremacy of *Advaita*, Swami Vivekananda put forward, 'the ladder theory.' According to this, *Dvaita* and *Viśiṣṭādvaita* are the two lower stages of philosophic enquiry which find their fulfilment in the final

---

[219] *CWMG*. 48:421.

[220] *CWMG*. 89:112.

[221] P. S. Daniel, op.cit., 261; Robert Ellsberg, op.cit., 20.

[222] *Harijan*, 28.09.1935; *CWMG*. 34:550; 35:250.

[223] *CWMG*. 35:328.

[224] *CWMG*. 100: 222.

[225] *CWMG*. 100: 313.

[226] *CWMG*. 46:28.

[227] *CWSV*. 8: 525.

[228] *CWSV*.6:229; Nalini Devdas, *Svāmī Vivekānanda* (Bangalore: CISRS, 1968), 107.

[229] Basant Kumar Lal, op.cit., 2.

[230] *CWSV*. 2:153.

stage of *Advaita*.[231] Hence for Vivekananda, "It begins with dualism, goes through a qualified monism and ends in perfect monism."[232] He thus says:

> But this is my attempt, my mission in life, to show that the Vedantic schools are not contradictory, that they all necessitate each other, all fulfil each other, and one, as it were, is the stepping-stone to the other, until the goal, the Advaita, the Tat Tvam Asi, is reached.[233]

Because according to him, "monistic theory….is the most rational of all religious theories that we can conceive of. Every other theory, every other conception of God which is partial and little and personal is not rational."[234] Hence in *Advaita*, man realizes the Oneness and the solidarity of all beings and realizes that the diversity and variety are only an appearance of the Reality, the *Brahman*-Ātman, which is indivisible, distinctionless and impersonal.[235] Therefore, for Vivekananda, *Advaita* "is the last word of religion and thought,"[236] and monism (oneness) is higher than dualism (separateness).[237] However, since Western Christianity emphasised dualism, i.e., separateness among man, universe and God,[238] Vivekananda considered the Western Christianity at the lower stage of *Dvaita*.[239] Therefore he argues that, Indian tradition of *Advaita* (monism) is higher than the dualistic Christianity.

Another claim Vivekananda makes for the superiority of *Advaita* is that, it is qualified to be the 'Universal Religion'. He thus delineates the peculiarities of *Advaita* as the 'Universal Religion.' For example, *Advaita Vedānta* presented the idea of spiritual oneness of the whole universe, therefore, Vivekananda thought, it could easily become the religion of humanity.[240] *Advaita* can thus look to all mankind and behave as one's own soul.[241] Vivekananda thus says: "It

---

[231] Nalini Devdas, op.cit., 12. According to the *Dvaita* understanding of the *Vedānta*, the universe (*jagat*) and the plurality of souls (*jivas*) are different from, but totally dependent on, God who alone is totally independent and therefore pre-eminent. The *Viśiṣṭādvaita* system is based on the principle of unity comprehending internal differentiations. The universe and the plurality of souls are accepted as eternal and real distinctions within the Absolute. The *Advaita* teaching is that the Self within (the Ātman) is non-different from *Brahman*, the ultimate Substratum of the universe.

[232] *CWSV*. 2:252.

[233] *CWSV*. 3:324.

[234] *CWSV*. 2:337.

[235] P. S. Daniel, op.cit., 139.

[236] *CWSV*. 6:415.

[237] *CWSV*. 2: 415, 465.

[238] *CWSV*. 2:429, 415.

[239] *CWSV*. 5: 81-82. *cf.* 2: 241.

[240] *CWSV*. 6: 415.

[241] *CWSV*. 6: 415.

is not confined to any time and place, it is everywhere."[242] Another peculiarity of *Advaita Vedānta* is that, it is "the most ancient religion of the world,"[243] and is based on "impersonal principles."[244] That the God of *Advaita Vedānta* is principle, not a person.[245] On the other hand, Vivekananda believed that, "No religion built upon a person can be taken up as a type by all the races of mankind."[246] As Christianity is based on the person of Christ, it cannot become a 'universal religion', for Vivekananda.[247] Therefore, all people of the world can be brought together only through principles and not through persons. Here *Advaita Vedānta* offers ample scope for bringing together all people based on its impersonal principles."[248] He thus claimed that the *Advaitic* principles of *Vedānta* to be "the truest religion."[249] Hence for Vivekananda, *Advaita Vedānta* is the rationale of all religions.[250] Another difference he finds is that while *Advaita* is a universal religion, Christianity is not. The reason he gives is that, Christianity has one set of rules for all; so it is not capable to accommodate different kinds of people.[251] But *Advaita Vedānta* will be equally acceptable to all minds, as it is equally and harmoniously balanced in philosophic, emotional, mystical, and action domains of religion.[252] Hence he declares: "It is [*Advaita*] Vedanta, and [*Advaita*] Vedanta alone that can become the universal religion of man, and that, no other is fitted for the role."[253] As such, he considered *Advaita* as "the crest-jewel of all spiritual thought."[254] Therefore he has no doubt that, "Advaita will be the future religion of thinking humanity."[255] Here one can clearly see a counter-affirmation of *Advaita Vedānta* against the missionary claim that 'Christianity is the only true and universal religion'.

Moreover, contrary to the exclusive and dogmatic approach of the West, *Advaita* harmonises all other religions[256] and looks upon all religions

---

242 *CWSV*. 8: 137.

243 *CWSV*. 8: 122.

244 *CWSV*. 8: 122.

245 *CWSV*. 8: 133.

246 *CWSV*. 3:250.

247 *CWSV*. 3: 182-183; 249; 279-280; 5: 207; 6: 7.

248 *CWSV*. 3:184.

249 *CWSV*. 6: 470.

250 *CWSV*. 5: 212.

251 *CWSV*. 6: 120.

252 *CWSV*. 2:387-388.

253 *CWSV*. 3: 182.

254 *CWSV*. 3:432.

255 *CWSV*. 8: 348.

256 *CWSV*. 5: 279.

and sects with love."[257] He was, thus, convinced that mankind ought to be taught religions as varied expressions of the Oneness.[258] Hence, there were no distinctions between the so-called various religions for Vivekananda. He says: "I am a believer in all religions."[259] All religions are sacred[260] as God is in every religion.[261] It is God himself who became Christ and Krishna and Buddha and all these [great teachers].[262]

As an *Advaita Vedāntin*, Vivekananda gave prime importance for realisation. He accepts the *Advaita* teaching that the ultimate goal is the realisation of perfect non-duality.[263] He emphasised that *Brahman* cannot be attained by the arguments of the reasoning mind, but *Brahman* can be known only by direct realisation.[264] He says: "Realisation is real religion."[265] This superiority of experience or realisation in religion is thus, an argument against 'rational' form of Western Christianity. That it is not the 'reason' that is highest in religious experience, but realisation, which is supra-rational.

Again as an *Advaita Vedāntin*, for Vivekananda the one great lesson that man needs to learn is the essential unity of mankind and the oneness of the universe. He says: "Great theme of [*Advaita*] Vedanta, this Oneness of life, this Oneness of everything."[266] "...ours is the Gospel of oneness of all beings."[267] That, "The whole of this universe is one Unity. One Existence, physically, mentally, morally and spiritually."[268] That the spiritual, the material, the mental, and the world of energies are not separate; it is all one, but seen from different planes of vision.[269] Hence in this *Advaitic* culture of India, not only 'human' but even the tiny creatures got a place in it and share in the unity and oneness of everything. Hence, this *Advaitic* unity and oneness is higher than the dualistic thinking of the West that "Europe is superior and Asia is inferior", "Christianity is true and Hinduism is false", etc. Vivekananda also criticises such colonial separatism, oppression and hatred of India. He says, "Love

---

[257] *CWSV*. 6: 415.

[258] *CWSV*. 6: 416.

[259] *CWSV*. 9: 472.

[260] *CWSV*. 7:460.

[261] *CWSV*. 7:417.

[262] *CWSV*. 1: 414.

[263] Nalini Devdas, op.cit., 90.

[264] Ibid., 33.

[265] *CWSV*. 1: 232.

[266] *CWSV*. 2:153.

[267] *CWSV*. 8: 375.

[268] *CWSV*. 2:249.

[269] *CWSV*. 2: 31.

makes no distinction..."[270] *Advaitism* "looks upon and behaves to all mankind as one's own soul"[271] "As manifested beings, we appear to be separate, but our reality is one, and the less we think of ourselves as separate from that One, the better for us. The more we think of ourselves as separate from the Whole, the more miserable we become."[272] Because, for an *Advaitin* like Vivekananda, the idea of separateness was erroneous, that there was a unity which pervaded the whole universe – trees, shrubs, animals, men, *Devas*, even God Himself-all are, but the manifestation of the One.[273] Hence, Vivekananda tries to establish unity among things which appear to us to be different from one another.[274]

Therefore, as an *Advaitin*, Vivekananda condemned dualistic thinking, which was the basis of colonialism, that creates the 'sense of separateness' and divisions. He says: "To teach dualism was a tremendous mistake...."[275] "It is the delusion of separateness that is the root of misery."[276] For him, the perception of separateness is an error, and *Avidyā*, or nescience.[277] Hence he wanted to destroy the sense of separateness or false individuality,[278] which is based on *avidyā*.

Another feature of *Advaita,* according to Vivekananda, is love/non-violence, which is the result of the unity of all creation. He says: "Man is man's brother because all men are one. A man is not only my brother, say the Vedas, he is myself. Hurting any part of the universe, I only hurt myself. I am the universe."[279] Therefore in injuring his neighbour, the individual actually injures himself.[280] Thus, man must love others because, those others, are himself.[281] Thus Vivekananda repeatedly affirms the *Advaitic* realisation that, 'I' and 'Thou' are not two. 'I am' my 'Brother', I and my brother are not separable, but the non-dual Self.[282] Hence with his *Advaitic* belief in the unity of humanity, Vivekananda was greatly against colonialism and the racial separation of the whites, and he condemned such evils. On the other hand, with

---

[270] *CWSV*. 5: 78.

[271] *CWSV*. 6: 415.

[272] *CWSV*. 2: 334.

[273] *CWSV*. 5: 519-520.

[274] *CWSV*. 5: 519.

[275] *CWSV*. 2: 199.

[276] *CWSV*. 8: 101.

[277] *CWSV*. 5: 520.

[278] *CWSV*. 7: 58.

[279] *CWSV*. 8:101. *cf.* 3: 129-130.

[280] *CWSV*. 1: 384-385.

[281] *CWSV*. 7: 96; *cf.* 2: 414- 415.

[282] Swami Satprakashananda, *Vivekananda: His Contribution to the Present Age* (Kolkata: Advaita Ashrma, 2011), 195. *cf. CWSV*. 3: 189.

his *Advaitic* spirit of unity, Vivekananda stressed the need of the East and the West coming close to each other. Science of the West and the spirituality of the East must meet at a point where humanity stood as an indivisible entity. He thus visualised a new type of civilisation and culture for the good of humanity in which the differences and discrimination between the East and the West would be eliminated.[283] Hence, Vivekananda was proposing an alternative civilization for the world based on *Advaita*, which is totally different from the Aristotelian logical structure and colonial world-view.

3.5. Mahatma Gandhi and *Advaita*

Like Vivekananda, Mahatma Gandhi too explicitly declared that philosophically he belonged to the *Vedānta* school of *Advaita* and all his writings are based on this *Advaitic* vision of unity and oneness of everything. In a couple of statements he made it clear.[284] He said: "I am an *Advaitist*."[285] "I believe in the rock-bottom doctrine of *advaita*."[286] Hence he believed "...in the essential unity of man and for that matter of all that lives."[287] He thus asks: "I believe in the absolute oneness of God and therefore also of humanity. What though we have many bodies? We have but one soul. The rays of the sun are many through refraction. But they have the same source."[288] Hence the aim of life for Gandhi is to 'realize the oneness of life'[289] and find 'unity in all the variety that we see around us.'[290] All these *Advaitic* affirmations in the colonial context denote that Gandhi was against the ideological basis of classification, separation and division behind the colonial rule and the superior claims of Western Christianity.

Further, in his quest for *mokṣa*/realisation, Gandhi, by following the *Advaitic* method, emphasised the primacy of experience/*anubh*ūti (which can be mystical also) over and above against the use of reason/intellect by the West. For example, Gandhi says: "He [God] defies reason. But he is experienced."[291] "Reason is powerless to know Him. He is beyond the reach or grasp of

---

[283] Dev Raj Bali, op.cit., 40.

[284] T.M.P. Mahadevan, "The Advaita of Mahatma Gandhi," in *Facets of Mahatma Gandhi*, vol. 4 op.cit., 126.

[285] *Young India*, 21.01.1926.

[286] *Young India*, 29.09.1927.

[287] *Young India*, 04.12.1924.

[288] *Young India*, 25.09.1924.

[289] *CWMG*. 41: 291.

[290] R. K. Prabhu & U. R. Rao, *The Mind of Mahatma Gandhi*, op.cit., 89.

[291] Gandhi, *God is Truth*, op.cit., 12.

reason."[292] Therefore Gandhi says, "…I have realized through experience,"[293] as "My reason follows my heart."[294]

Gandhi also was against the Western view of God, as if God is somewhere above us. Against such views, he says: "God is present in all of us….though many we are all one."[295] He also said: "I recognize that God manifests Himself in innumerable forms in this universe, and every such manifestation commands my spontaneous reverence."[296] Because "...there is an underlying unity in the variety which we see in God's creation."[297]

Thus for Gandhi, human beings are an integral part of the nature.[298] He said: "We are the Universe. We are in it and it is in us. God also is within us."[299] Hence "The universe is not different from us, and we are not different from the universe."[300] Thus he emphasized the sacredness, kinship and "love of all life."[301] As a result he declared: "I want to realize brotherhood or identity not merely with the beings called human, but I want to realize identity with all life, even with such beings that crawl on earth....because we claim common descent from the same God, and that being so, all life in whatever form it appears must be essentially one."[302] Thus Gandhi held the equality of all creatures on earth and said: "In the eyes of God, the Creator of all, His creatures are all equal."[303] This *Advaitic* view of Gandhi is directly contradictory to the Aristotelian-colonial view of hierarchy of creatures and the centrality of man over nature.

Gandhi thus always stressed the oneness of God and the oneness of creation.[304] He believed that "all life is One"[305] that "All life in whatever form it appears must be essentially one."[306] As "... all life (not only human

[292] Ibid., 11.

[293] *CWMG*. 28: 447.

[294] *Harijan*, 06.04.1940.

[295] *CWMG*. 43:82.

[296] *CWMG*. 41: 293.

[297] *Harijan*, 26.05.1946.

[298] K. S. Radhakrishnan, *Gandhi- Sree Narayana Guru* (Kottayam: D. C. Books, 2013), 138.

[299] Gandhi, "Selected Letters," in *The Selected Works of Mahatma Gandhi*, vol. 4, edited by Shriman Narayan (Ahmedabad: Navajivan Publishing House, 2006), 290.

[300] Ibid., 315.

[301] *CWMG*. 61: 190, 191.

[302] *Young India*, 04.04.1929.

[303] *Harijan*, 22.12.1933.

[304] Boyd H. Wilson, "Ultimacy as Unifier in Gandhi," in *Religion in Modern India*, edited by Robert D. Baird (New Delhi: Manohar Publishers, 2001), 442.

[305] *Young India*, 14.04.1927.

[306] *Young India*, 04.04.1929.

beings, but all sentient beings) coming from the One Universal Source."[307] For example, "From the Imperishable Unmanifest down to the perishable atom everything in the universe is the Supreme and an expression of the Supreme."[308] Therefore there is the need for living in friendship and harmony with not only human beings but also with other living beings.[309] That's why Gandhi said: "To see the universal and all-pervading Spirit of Truth face-to-face one must be able to love the meanest of creation as oneself."[310] That means "...to realize God is to see Him in all that lives, i.e. to realize our oneness with all creation."[311] Hence, for Gandhi exploitation and oppression of any form of life is denial of God or oneself, as there is no distinction among God, oneself and the entire universe in this *Advaitic* vision. Therefore, Gandhi, as an *Advaitin* was against all kinds of divisions and distinctions. He thus asked: "How can there be room for distinctions of high and low where there is this all-embracing fundamental unity underlying the outward diversity?"[312] "All mankind in essence are alike."[313] "What though we have many bodies? We have but one soul."[314] Therefore "In spite of the differences of races and religions", Gandhi wanted everyone "...to tolerate and respect one another and consider all human beings as children of one God and, therefore, brothers and sisters of one another."[315] He said: "we have to find unity in diversity"[316] that, "There is a real and substantial unity in all the variety that we see around us."[317] Thus for Gandhi, the diversities in the world means neither inequality nor any kind of inferiority or superiority as thought by the colonizers.[318] He was thus able to overcome in his life and thought all these forms of inequalities, differences and distinctions between man and man as well as between man and nature, with his *Advaitic* vision of unity, equality

---

[307] *Harijan*, 26.12.1936.

[308] Gandhi, "The Voice of Truth," in *The Selected Works of Mahatma Gandhi*, vol. 5, op.cit., 92.

[309] Devis Kavungal, *The Philosophical Foundation of Mahatma Gandhi's Vision of Sarvodaya* (Bangalore: Dharmaram Publications, 2000), 215.

[310] *An Autobiography*, 463.

[311] *Harijan*, 02.04.1938.

[312] R. K. Prabhu & U. R. Rao, *The Mind of Mahatma Gandhi*, op.cit., 89.

[313] *Harijan*, 12.11.1938.

[314] *Young India*, 25.09.1924.

[315] *Harijan*, 01.12.1933.

[316] *Harijan*, 02.02.1934.

[317] R. K. Prabhu & U. R. Rao, *The Mind of Mahatma Gandhi*, op.cit., 89.

[318] *Harijan*, 12.12.1933.

and oneness of all forms of life. Gandhi, accordingly, fought the White men's superiority in South Africa and in India.[319]

Further he said, "On God's Earth, nobody is low and nobody is high. We are all His creatures...."[320] So he asserts his *Advaitic* belief in the equality of all men. He says: "I believe implicitly that all men are born equal. All ...have the same soul as any other."[321] Hence for Gandhi, there is no superiority or inferiority among men, but all are equal. This is the firm manifestation of Gandhi's *Advaitic* belief as he asserts it again and again that "All mankind in essence are alike. What is therefore possible for one, is possible for everybody."[322] Hence he directly condemns the 'White-men's Superiority' and 'Eurocentric' attitude which were based on Aristotelian epistemology and was the basis of colonial exploitation and missionary denunciation of India.

With his *Advaitic* belief, Gandhi too questioned the inferior view on the Eastern religions by the West. On the other hand, he emphasized the basic unity and equality lying behind all religions.[323] For him, all religions believe in the same one God and they come from the same source.[324] Hence, the final goal of all religions is to realize this essential oneness.[325] That's why he stated: "I consider myself a follower of Islam, Christianity, Zoroastrianism and every other religion .... All religions are equal and they are founded on the same faith."[326] Hence he was able to say: "I can pay equal homage to Jesus, Muhammed, Krishna, Buddha, Zoroaster and others that may be named."[327] Because there was no distinctions between religions or their gods, scriptures or abodes of gods for Gandhi. He says: "I have really not seen any fundamental distinction between Jesus and other teachers...."[328] "I have not been able to see any difference between the Sermon on the Mount and the Bhagavad Gita."[329] Gandhi has also made no distinctions between the abodes of God such as temples, mosques or churches.[330] Moreover Gandhi said: "Looking at all religions with an equal eye, we would not only not hesitate, but would think

---

[319] *Young India*, 29.09.1927.

[320] *Harijan*, 05.02.1934.

[321] *Young India*, 29.09.1927.

[322] *Harijan*, 12.11.1938.

[323] *CWMG*. 26: 396; *Harijan*, 22.09.1946.

[324] Gandhi, "The Voice of Truth," op.cit., 230.

[325] Ibid.

[326] *CWMG*. 87: 45.

[327] *CWMG*. 31:420.

[328] Gandhi, *The Message of Jesus Christ*, (Mumbai: Bharatiya Vidya Bhavan, 1998), 22; *CWMG*. 31:419.

[329] *Young India*, 22.12.1927.

[330] *Harijan*, 18.03.1933.

it our duty, to blend into our faith every acceptable feature of other faiths."[331] That means to assimilate all that is good anywhere else into one's own,[332] so that one will love all religions as one's own religion, which is thus a correction of 'love of one's own religion only' by the colonial missionaries.

Gandhian concept of *svarāj* (self-rule) is also based on his *Advaitic* logic. *Svarāj* was proclaimed in the context of British-raj. Hence, *svarāj* is superior to the colonial British-raj. As an *Advaitic* concept, it was not a mere political concept, but proclaims the inter-relatedness and oneness of different fields of life.[333] Thus the ideal of self-rule or *svarāj*, as Gandhi termed it, meant the Kingdom of God on earth[334] or *rāmarājya.*[335] This is in line with his concept of '*sarvodaya*', the 'welfare of all' or the upliftment of all.[336] The *Sarva-mukti* ideal of *Advaita* is also significant in this aspect.[337] In other words, *rāmarājya* was a moral and spiritual concept of society based on *Advaitic* philosophy. *Rāmarājya* is an egalitarian society founded on truth and non-violence.[338] Through the religious principles of truth and love Gandhi wanted to create a social order devoid of classes and castes[339] by changing the hearts of the people.[340] Hence, this is realised through spiritual life of soul-force[341]and self-control.[342] This *svarāj* is thus directly contrary to British-raj, which is amoral, colonial, exploitative, based on brute-force, self-indulgence and looked only for the 'welfare of Europe/Whites'.

3.6. Conclusion

The above discussions denote that, both Swami Vivekananda and Mahatma Gandhi are *Advaita Vedāntins*. Both of them explicitly stated that, they believe in *Advaita* philosophy and thereby in the oneness and unity of everything – of all creation. Nevertheless, their *Advaita* was modified to suit the needs of the modern times; hence they related their *Advaitic* beliefs in practical aspects

[331] Gandhi, *From Yervada Mandir*, op. cit., 23.

[332] Gandhi, *My Religion*, op.cit., 23.

[333] K. S. Radhakrishnan, *Gandhi- Sree Narayana Guru*, op.cit., 145.

[334] *Harijan*, 05.05.1946.

[335] Dev Raj Bali, op.cit., 125.

[336] Jacob Pulickan, ed., *Gandhiji Life and Philosophy* (Thiruvananthapuram: Centre for Gandhian Studies-University of Kerala, 1999), 7.

[337] Ibid., 31.

[338] Santhinikethanam Krishnan Nair, *Gandhijiyum Adhunika Darsanikarum* (Mal.) (Kottayam: D. C. Books, 1998), 96.

[339] Dev Raj Bali, op.cit., 119.

[340] Ibid., 129.

[341] *Young India*, 01-12-1927.

[342] *Harijan*, 28.04.1946.

of life, in socio-political fields of life. Hence their writings exemplify the *Advaitic* vision of non-duality, unity and love of all forms of life, and also inter-religious harmony in the context of British colonialism and Christian triumphalism, which questioned these fundamental values of Indian tradition and of *Advaita* philosophy of oneness and unity of all life. Therefore both were against divisions and distinctions in thought and practice; hence they opposed 'inferior' and 'superior' feelings and differences of colonialism. They thus stressed not only the oneness of humanity, but the entire universe as an integrated entity, having equal value for all forms of life. Thus *ahiṃsā* or non-violent love is the only attitude towards all beings and all religions for *Advaitins* like Vivekananda and Gandhi. They also stood for religious harmony and stressed equality of all religions. In all these aspects, one can see the re-assertion of the superiority of the ancient and pluralistic Indian tradition and all-loving *Advaita* philosophy, against the narrow, colonial and exploitative epistemology of the West, which had its basis in the epistemology of Aristotle.

Chapter 4

Vivekananda's and Gandhi's View of Christian Tradition, Religions and Christ from *Advaita Vedāntic* Perspective

4.1. Introduction

This chapter analyses the approach of Vivekananda and Gandhi towards Christian tradition, religions and Christ. Their own sayings and comments on these subjects are comprehensively analysed from their writings, in order to understand their approach. Nevertheless, it must be noted that, they have approached on these issues in the context of 19th century British rule and colonial Christianity, with its triumphalisitc attitude towards other religions and of their superiority complex and narrow interpretation of Christ. Vivekananda and Gandhi approached these issues from an *Advaita Vedāntic* perspective. Hence their treatment of Christian tradition, religions and Christ is significant, as their understanding on these issues arises from an *Advaitic* perspective, which is different from the colonial and missionary Christianity of those times.

4.2. Swami Vivekananda and Christian Tradition

Swami Vivekananda was familiar with Christianity through his visits and interaction in the West and had relations with both Catholics and Protestants. He had liberal and broad Christian friends in English, Episcopal and Presbyterian Churches.[1] He says: "...Christianity was divided into many

[1] *CWSV*.5:59-60; 221; 8: 368; *The Life*. 1:453; 2:549.

creeds."[2] Vivekananda understood Christianity as a missionary religion.[3] Thus he has responded to Western Christianity in the context of nineteenth century colonial India. The missionary attack of Hinduism, prompted him to look at Christian tradition critically from an Indian perspective, thus affirming Indian *Advaitic* superiority over the Western claims.

First of all, he believed that Christianity has been influenced by Indian thoughts.[4] For example, according to him Christ took his teachings from the *Vedas*[5] and Mother *Kāḷi* is metamorphosed into the Virgin Mary, the mother of Jesus Christ.[6] Thus he considered Christianity as "a collection of little bits of Indian thought,"[7] "a very patchy imitation,"[8] "a distant echo"[9] and a "great offshoot"[10] of India's great tradition. He found the way of Indian influence on Christianity through Buddhism[11] and traced the similarity between Buddha and Christ.[12] He thus uses the seniority of Buddha and Buddhism to trace its influence on Christianity through 'similarities;'[13] and argues that Christianity is an offspring of Buddhism and Buddhism is the foundation of Christianity.[14] According to him, King Asoka's Buddhist missionaries were present in Palestine area and Alexandria and founded many sects such as the Therapeutae, Essenes, Manichaeans, and the like and through them has exerted its influence in the formation of Christianity.[15] Hence he states: "Indian and Egyptian ideas met at Alexandria and went forth to the world, tinctured with Judaism and

---

[2] *CWSV*. 8: 233; 2: 483. *cf.* 7: 427-428. Vivekananda was familiar with different denominations of Western Christianity. Hence he spoke of Armenians (*CWSV*. 9: 486), Roman Catholics (*CWSV*. 5: 506; 8: 223), Greek Church (*CWSV*. 9: 486) Protestants (*CWSV*. 6: 63) English Church (*CWSV*. 8: 369) Presbyterians (*CWSV*. 6: 63) Methodists (*CWSV*. 8: 369) Unitarians (*CWSV*.6: 137) and Quakers (*CWSV*.4: 51-52).

[3] *CWSV*. 7:43. *cf.* 9: 24.

[4] *CWSV*. 9: 504.

[5] *CWSV*. 5:453-454.

[6] *CWSV*. 5: 445.

[7] *CWSV*. 3: 275.

[8] *CWSV*. 3: 275.

[9] *CWSV*. 9: 420.

[10] *CWSV*. 7:287; 6: 105.

[11] *CWSV*. 2:511; 3: 512.

[12] *CWSV*. 2:510.

[13] He found similarities between Hinduism, Buddhism and Catholicism in a number of points: sacraments, *saṇnyāsi* life, tonsure, incense, lights, belief in saints, confession, order, idol-worship, concept of marriage and mother worship (*Kāḷi* - Mary). *CWSV*. 3: 362; 5:180, 445; 7:287; 9: 377.

[14] *CWSV*. 2:510-511; 7:430; 9: 458.

[15] *CWSV*. 1: 390; 7: 347.

Hellenism, as Christianity."[16] Thus"...Christianity of the Roman Empire was a mixture of everything, something from Persia, from the Jews, from India, from Greece, everything."[17]

Besides, Vivekananda considered Europe as the inheritor of Greece[18] and therefore Greek and Roman culture deeply influenced Western Christianity.[19] Therefore, "Much in Christianity is the mere application of new names and meanings to old pagan beliefs and customs."[20] Moreover, it was the power of the sword used by kings like Constantine and Charlemagne forced the spread of Christianity into Europe.[21] Hence for him, the European mind is brutal and was attracted only by cruel actions, thus it praised crucifixion of Jesus on the cross.[22] Further, when Christianity flourished in Europe, it did not contribute for the growth of civilization,[23] rather it suppressed free thinking, progress and science; and Europe went through dark ages.[24] So in modern times, civilization, philosophy and science came up in Europe as a revolt against Christianity.[25]

As an *Advaitin*, Vivekananda did not admire the doctrinal beliefs of Orthodox Christianity.[26] Christian doctrines were not attractive to him, rather he said, it is "...horrible, barbarous, savage creed...."[27] Thus his *Advaita Vedāntic* mind, did not subscribe to many of the Christian doctrines, rather emphasised realisation as one's own direct religious experience.[28] He said: "... realisation is religion, not doctrine."[29] Further he stated: "The problem with Christianity is its idea that religion consists in doctrines."[30] He too observed that Christianity has one set of rules for all; so it is not capable to accommodate different kinds of people.[31] Therefore Church is good only for the children, not

---

[16] *CWSV*. 9: 377-378.

[17] *CWSV*. 9: 273.

[18] *CWSV*. 4: 401.

[19] *CWSV*. 3:217; *The Life*. 2:262.

[20] *CWSV*. 8:25.

[21] *CWSV*. 8: 212-213; 5: 508.

[22] *CWSV*. 8: 272.

[23] *CWSV*. 7: 283.

[24] *CWSV*. 4: 57.

[25] *CWSV*. 5: 532, 533.

[26] *CWSV*. 3: 489.

[27] *CWSV*. 3: 500-501.

[28] *CWSV*. 9: 279.

[29] *CWSV*. 9: 279.

[30] *CWSV*. 1: 468.

[31] *CWSV*. 6: 120.

for the grown up.[32] Thus he called Christianity as a 'kindergarten religion,'[33] and 'nursery'[34] as it leads nowhere.[35] Moreover, he understood church life in West as mere customary and mechanical with no in-depth spirituality.[36] And Christian worship in the Churches was a sort of pre-arranged and learned spiritual exercise, devoid of real experience.[37]

He thus used comparative method to show the superiority of Hinduism over Christianity,[38] and criticised almost all beliefs and practices of Christianity, such as, creation, prayer, heaven, judgment, hell, reward, God, Trinity, soul, sin, incarnation, salvation, baptism, Eucharist, atonement, etc. For example, he denied the Christian concept of creation, that God created everything out of nothing.[39] For him, something cannot be made out of nothing.[40] He viewed Christian prayer as 'begging' as it always asked for material blessings.[41] He further considered Christian concept of heaven as a low idea, as it conceived heaven as a material concept, and arises out of the desire for enjoyment.[42]

He also questioned the Christian Concept of Personal God. He says: "The Christian pictures God as a personal being seated somewhere above us."[43] On the contrary, as an *Advaita Vedāntin*, for Vivekananda, God is not somewhere above us, but is within us and emphasised Jesus' saying that "The Kingdom of Heaven is within you."[44] Therefore God as 'Father,'[45] 'Judge' [46] and 'King'[47] is not acceptable for him. As a result, he denied the Christian concept of God as 'judge' and doctrine of Last Judgment and the belief in heaven and hell;[48] hell as a terrifying place of torture has been completely questioned by him.[49]

---

[32] *CWSV*. 1: 325; 7:79.

[33] *CWSV*. 4:239.

[34] *New Discoveries*. 6: 289.

[35] *CWSV*. 4:239.

[36] *CWSV*. 5: 77, 202; *New Discoveries*. 1:197, 348.

[37] *CWSV*. 4: 56-57; 6: 81.

[38] *CWSV*. 9: 480. Vivekananda forces *Advaita Vedānta* into Christianity and sees *Advaitic* teachings in Bible. *CWSV*. 2: 194; 5:222.

[39] *CWSV*. 2:245-246.

[40] *CWSV*. 2: 426.

[41] *CWSV*. 2:245; 7:417; 8:202.

[42] *CWSV*. 6:25; 2: 158-159; 4:40; 7: 34, 84.

[43] *CWSV*. 3: 500.

[44] *CWSV*. 2: 148; 4:149.

[45] *CWSV*. 3: 504.

[46] *CWSV*. 8: 222.

[47] *CWSV*. 8:125.

[48] *CWSV*. 7: 420; 9: 518.

[49] *CWSV*. 4:345; 7: 435.

However, he appreciated the Christian Trinity. He says: "...the conception of the Trinity[50] was a great advance over the dualistic idea..."[51] He understood Trinity in terms of *Saccidanānda* - Father is *Sat* (existence), Son is *Cit* (knowledge) and Holy Ghost is Ānanda (bliss).[52]

Christian concept of 'soul', that only humans have soul and soul got a beginning at birth, etc. was denied by him.[53] He also differentiated the 'Love of Neighbour' in Christianity and in *Advaita Vedānta*.[54] He says: "...love every man as your own Self and not as your brother as in Christianity. Brotherhood should be superseded by universal Selfhood. Not universal brotherhood, but universal Selfhood is our motto."[55] Thus man must love others because those others are himself.[56] Further he totally attacked Christian doctrine of man as a sinner and the very sense of sin.[57] He said: "It is a sin to call a man so...."[58] Thus he was not able to tolerate the Christian view of man that man is a fallen sinner and if men do not accept Christ's atoning work, they will go to hell.[59] Salvation by Jesus' blood and death was totally unacceptable for him.[60] He said: "For the [Christians] the problem is how to escape the wrath of the terrible God. For the Indians it is how to become what they really are, to regain their lost selfhood."[61] Thus as an *Advaita Vedāntin*, he emphasised the divinity of man, for he said: "Our God is man!"[62] Hence for him, instead of atoning work, Jesus reveals the true nature of human beings which is divine.[63] Moreover, since man is not a sinner, no need of repentance also.[64] He too saw the so-called Christian baptism as simply ceremonies and formulas, without the 'living spirit of baptism.'[65]

---

[50] According to the Christians, God the Father, God the Son, and Holy Ghost are One in three and Three in One. *CWSV*. 9: 295.

[51] *CWSV*. 7:100.

[52] *CWSV*. 8:191.

[53] *CWSV*. 2: 258; 4: 188-189; 6:85.

[54] *CWSV*. 6: 107.

[55] *CWSV*. 6: 122.

[56] *CWSV*. 7: 96.

[57] *CWSV*. 2:237.

[58] *CWSV*. 1:11.

[59] *CWSV*. 8:132.

[60] *CWSV*. 8: 209; *New Discoveries*. 2:30.

[61] *CWSV*. 1: 468.

[62] *CWSV*. 9: 419.

[63] *CWSV*. 7: 4.

[64] *The Life*. 2: 518.

[65] *CWSV*. 8: 114-115.

He crucially criticised the ritual of Eucharist. For him, "The Eucharist is a survival of a very ancient custom of savage tribes."[66] The idea of eating and drinking flesh and blood in the Eucharist is compared by him with the savage custom of primitive tribes. Human sacrifice was also a cruel Jewish idea; so according to Vivekananda, Christ cannot be fit into these ideas. Hence he says: "...this cruel idea made Christianity depart from the teachings of Jesus himself and develop a spirit of persecution and bloodshed."[67]

He was fully aware of the Christian claim that Christ is only one and perfect incarnation of God and no other.[68] However, for Vivekananda there are many incarnations and Christ is one among them, for he said: "Let us, therefore, find God not only in Jesus of Nazareth but in all the great ones that have preceded him, in all that came after him, and all that are yet to come.... They are all manifestations of the same Infinite God…."[69] Vivekananda also vehemently opposed and criticised the exclusivist claims of being, 'only true', 'only way' etc. of Christians and superiority over other religions.[70] On the contrary, he opted for plurality of ways and methods in God-realisation.[71] He said: "Truth is nobody's property; no race, no individual can lay any exclusive claim to it."[72] Rather he holds that "one must embrace all the religions to become the perfect Christian."[73]

Vivekananda was able to see the deviation of Western Christianity, due to its incapability in understanding Christ's teachings. Because according to Vivekananda, Europeans were not able to understand the Asian originated Christianity and Christ, who was an Oriental,[74] because Jesus' Jewish background, ideas, imageries, and metaphors were unfamiliar and foreign to them.[75] Hence Christianity has been imperfectly understood in the West, and as understood hitherto is found to be insufficient.[76] Therefore, according to Vivekananda, the most profound and noble ideas of Christianity were never understood in Europe,[77] so the people get very little of the beautiful religion of

---

[66] *CWSV*. 7:71-72.

[67] *CWSV*. 7:71-72.

[68] *CWSV*. 4: 31; 9: 486.

[69] *CWSV*. 4: 152; *cf.*4: 120-121.

[70] *CWSV*. 1: 368; 6: 138.

[71] *CWSV*. 3: 131; 4: 125; 5: 447; 6: 16; 9: 486.

[72] *CWSV*. 2:358.

[73] *CWSV*. 3: 483.

[74] *CWSV*. 4: 142, 144.

[75] *CWSV*. 1: 321-322.

[76] *CWSV*. 3: 182.

[77] *CWSV*. 1: 321.

Jesus.[78] For example, Christ's saying, "I and my father are one", was repeated by European people for the last nineteen hundred years, without understanding it.[79] Thus European Christianity remained a dualistic religion.[80]

Further as an *Advaita Vedāntin*, Vivekananda found, "the whole essence of Christianity," in the first five verses of John as each verse is full of the profoundest philosophy.[81] He considered Jesus as an *Advaitin*, [82] a non-dualist[83] as "...the teachings of the Vedas...is identical with the teachings of Christ."[84] Hence "...there is very little difference between the pure religion of Christ and that of the [*Advaita*] Vedanta."[85] Because, "God became Christ to show man his true nature, that we too are God."[86] He thus found this 'idea of oneness' in Jesus' saying of 'I and my Father are one.'[87] But Christ also preached dualism to the masses, 'our Father which art in heaven' as they are not able to conceive of anything higher than a personal God, thus to give them something tangible to take hold of, to lead them up to the highest ideal.[88] Because "…through 'our Father in heaven' lies the way to 'I and my Father are One.'[89] However, the Western Christianity remained in the first stage of *Dvaita*,[90] without understanding the higher stage of 'I and my Father are one' on the one hand,[91] and by emphasising dualism - separateness among man, universe and God on the other.[92] Thus he says: "They [Europeans] make Christ the saviour of men. He is God and we are worms!"[93] Therefore Vivekananda places Western Christianity at the first stage and at the lowest state of religion, which for him is dualism,[94] since monism (oneness) is higher than dualism (separateness) for Vivekananda.[95]

---

[78] *CWSV*. 1: 321-322.

[79] *CWSV*. 8:141.

[80] *CWSV*. 5: 81-82. *cf.* 2: 241.

[81] *CWSV*. 7: 3.

[82] K. P. Aleaz, *Jesus in Neo-Vedanta*, op.cit., 55.

[83] *CWSV*. 2: 143.

[84] *CWSV*. 9: 447.

[85] *CWSV*. 2: 353.

[86] *CWSV*. 7: 4.

[87] *CWSV*. 2: 353, 143.

[88] *CWSV*. 2: 353, 143.

[89] *CWSV*. 2: 353.

[90] *CWSV*. 5: 81-82. *cf.* 2: 241.

[91] *CWSV*. 8:141.

[92] *CWSV*. 2:429, 415.

[93] *CWSV*. 8:141.

[94] *CWSV*. 2: 141; 8:190.

[95] *CWSV*. 2: 415, 465.

Further Vivekananda drew a very sharp line of distinction between Christianity and Christianity.[96] He said: "All this nonsense which people have built round Christ's name is not his teaching."[97] Christians give credit to the person of Jesus and ignore his teachings in practical life.[98] Thus "...the whole teaching of the Master is degenerated, and all the struggle and fight is for the personality of the Man."[99] Because the person of Christ became more important for Christianity, rather than his teaching;[100] on the contrary, the teaching of Jesus is important for Vivekananda, not his person.[101] And he found the essentials of Jesus' teachings in the Sermon on the Mount.[102] For him, Christ taught to lead a life of renunciation and love and service of fellow-men and not a life of worldly enjoyment.[103] However, "The Europeans never took the words of Jesus Christ seriously."[104] So the Western Christian countries became "thoroughly materialistic"[105] and "spirituality... is entirely absent" in these countries.[106] Hence he observed, the religion of Christ is the religion of renunciation, but the West has made it a religion of luxury, a "shop-keeping religion."[107] Thus "... a true Christian nowhere do we see."[108] "Not one in twenty millions is a real Christian."[109] Because "The Christian Church tries to fit Christ into it, it does not try to fit itself into Christ..."[110] Hence Vivekananda told to the Western Christians to go back to Christ, as one cannot serve God and Mammon at the same time.[111]

Nevertheless, principles are more important for Vivekananda, than persons. But Christianity is built upon the life of Jesus Christ.[112] Therefore

---

[96] *CWSV*. 4: 198.

[97] *CWSV*. 9: 121.

[98] *CWSV*. 4:150-151; 9: 519.

[99] *CWSV*. 4:150-151.

[100] Vivekananda says: "... the disciples make the saint the Principle, and then they forget the Principle in the person." *CWSV*. 7: 21.

[101] *CWSV*. 4: 150.

[102] *CWSV*. 2: 164; 4: 417; 8: 218.

[103] *CWSV*. 9: 121.

[104] *CWSV*. 5:453.

[105] *CWSV*. 6: 271.

[106] *CWSV*. 9: 456.

[107] *CWSV*. 8: 213; 4: 144-145, 149.

[108] *CWSV*. 8: 160.

[109] *CWSV*. 2:164.

[110] *CWSV*. 7: 30.

[111] *CWSV*. 8: 213; 4: 144-145, 149.

[112] *CWSV*. 3: 249; 279-280.

"Christianity cannot stand without Christ."[113] This dependence of Christianity on the historical Jesus as its founder is seen as a weakness of Christianity by Vivekananda and not appreciated by him. Because there is a great dispute as to whether there ever was born a man with the name of Jesus, as there is lack of data or historical records concerning the life of Jesus.[114] Moreover Vivekananda denied the historicity of Jesus as he said: "I am inclined to think Christ never existed."[115] Therefore he says, if the historicity of Christ is questioned, then the whole structure of Christianity founded and built on the person of Christ falls.[116] On the other hand, *Advaita Vedānta* is based on principles and persons are secondary in it.[117] Moreover only principles can bring together the universe together[118] and not persons,[119] as it is vain to gather all peoples of the world around a single personality.[120] Therefore *Advaita Vedānta* can only become 'Universal Religion' as it is based on principles, but Christianity cannot become a 'universal religion' as it is depended on a person.[121]

Vivekananda thus revered Christ and attacked Christianity in its homelands.[122] He said: "...you do not hear me praising your current Christianity or your ideals of civilization, or the peculiar forms of character and life that are developed by Western ethical standards."[123] So his criticisms of Western Christianity are that, "Christ's life of renunciation is totally ignored. His higher teaching about unity and divinity of man are misinterpreted; and sects are organized on the basis of superficial dogmas. Worse still, the missionaries identify themselves with colonialism."[124] Moreover, according to him, Christianity succeeded everywhere with the help of sword and the Christian nations have filled the world with bloodshed and tyranny.[125] Because when Christianity went into new lands, it extinguished aboriginal races by killing

---

[113] *CWSV*. 5: 207.

[114] *CWSV*. 7:370.

[115] *CWSV*. 9: 377-378.

[116] *CWSV*. 6: 7; 3:182-183, 249; 279-280.

[117] *CWSV*. 6: 7; 3:182-183.

[118] *CWSV*. 3:184

[119] *CWSV*. 3: 250.

[120] *CWSV*. 3: 184.

[121] *CWSV*. 3: 182-183; 249.

[122] *CWSV*. 5:40. Marie Louise Burke says: "...he has ever spoken with love and reverence of Jesus and His work. What he has done is to denounce the outward expression of so-called Christianity, the creeds, dogmas, superstitions and bigotry which degrade our faith on the one hand, and the dishonesty, cruelty, intolerance and utter selfishness which dominate our social and business life on the other." *New Discoveries*. 1: 350-351.

[123] *The Life*. 1:462.

[124] S. S. Mital, op.cit., 88.

[125] *CWSV*. 3: 474; 7: 43; 9: 455, 528.

their people and culture and occupying their lands.[126] Thus"...the prosperity of the Christian nation" depended "on the misfortune of non-Christian nations."[127] He thus challenged the Western Christians, "...where has your Christianity succeeded without the sword? Show me one place in the whole world."[128]

Vivekananda too says that the association between colonialism and Christian Missions resulted in the trampling of age-old Indian religions.[129] He says: "…with the Bible in one hand and the conqueror's sword in the other ... you are not like your Christ, whom we could honour and reverence."[130] Therefore "India requires help from Christ, but not from the antichrist; these men are not Christlike. They do not act like Christ..."[131] So he contrasted missionaries' criticism of Indian tradition, religion and culture and asked to Western missionary sending nations: "You train and educate and clothe and pay men to do what? To come over to my country to curse and abuse all my forefathers, my religion, and everything."[132] He could find the economic motif of missionaries behind these criticisms and dark picturing of India to the West.[133] He thus tried to correct this dark picture of India presented by the missionaries and raised the status of India in the West.[134]

Vivekananda also opposed missionaries' effort to convert India to Christianity by destroying Indian culture. He said: "...I do not believe in this idea of conversion."[135] And "...India can never be converted to Christianity...."[136] However, according to him, conversions happened not due to religious or spiritual needs, but due to force or sword and material attractions due to the poverty and hunger of the lower castes.[137] He thus observed: "... the way of converting is absolutely absurd."[138] And conversions are not to Christ's Christianity, but to Western Christian denominations.[139] Therefore, he urged Western Christian missionaries, to give bread and education to India,

---

[126] *CWSV*. 5: 531, 533; 8: 477.

[127] *CWSV*. 2:95.

[128] *CWSV*. 8: 212-213.

[129] *CWSV*. 9: 527.

[130] *CWSV*. 9: 527.

[131] *CWSV*. 8: 217.

[132] *CWSV*. 8: 211-212.

[133] *CWSV*. 4: 344-345.

[134] *CWSV*. 2: 481; 4: 414, 415.

[135] *CWSV*. 3: 483.

[136] *CWSV*. 7:460-461.

[137] *CWSV*. 2: 480; 7:246, 460-461; 9: 33, 432, 441.

[138] *CWSV*. 9: 33. *cf.* 9: 528-529.

[139] *CWSV*. 9: 33.

instead of preaching Christianity.[140] He also requested the West not to send missionaries to India, as missionary work is unwanted in India.[141] Moreover, he identified so many evils in the Western Christian culture,[142] which were coming to India as part of Christianization, so he wanted to stop the incoming of such a Western wave of civilization into India.[143] However, he welcomed Christ-like missionaries to India, for he said: "We want missionaries of Christ. Let such come to India by the hundreds and thousands. Bring Christ's life to us and let it permeate the very core of society. Let him be preached in every village and corner of India."[144]

4.3. Mahatma Gandhi and Christian Tradition

Gandhi's observations and criticisms of Christianity are original and well-known, and seem to be out of his sincerity. He had studied and reflected upon almost all aspects of Christianity and formed his views on them. He discussed about Bible, Sermon on the Mount, Jesus Christ, doctrines of 'Orthodox Christianity,'[145] Christian missions, etc. He thus said about himself as "...a humble and impartial student of religion with great leaning towards Christianity."[146] He even said: "... I have not read as many books on Hinduism as I have about Christianity."[147] Hence, through a genuine life involvement with Christians also he learned a good deal about Christianity. As situations arose and occasions demanded of him, he made serious attempts to look at Christianity as an enquirer would. Personal contacts with Christians, participation in congregational worship and other spiritual programmes, the study of the Bible, and Christian literature are the basic sources of Gandhi's understanding of Christianity.[148]

Gandhi had come to know Christianity from Gujarat, England and South Africa. He experienced Christianity through Western mediation: words,

---

[140] *CWSV*. 1: 20; 9: 433; *cf.* 9: 450; 452-456.

[141] *CWSV*. 9: 476, 480-481.

[142] *CWSV*. 2: 516, 517.

[143] *CWSV*. 3: 433.

[144] *CWSV*. 4: 198; 9: 454.

[145] By 'Orthodox Christianity' Gandhi meant the Western aggressive missionary churches. He did not mean either the Greek or Russian Orthodox or Syrian Orthodox churches. Gandhi believed that Orthodox Christianity sprang directly from the Roman imperialistic Christian faith and had remained so ever since. His reference here is to the expansion of Christianity by force in the West after Constantine, and also to the modern missionary movement which was accompanied by the economic and political imperialism of the West over the non-Western world. Nirmal Minz, op.cit., 43-44.

[146] *CWMG*. 13:220.

[147] *Harijan,* 18.07.1936.

[148] Nirmal Minz, op.cit., 38-39.

actions, and writings.[149] As his encounter was chiefly with Protestant tradition (Evangelical) of Western Christianity, he had practically no significant contact with the Catholic Church, the largest of all Christian bodies. He had none with the second largest group, the Orthodox churches, whether Greek, Russian, Syrian, or other. The Coptic Churches of Africa and the Mar Thoma Church of India also lay outside his experience.[150]

His childhood experience and earliest impressions of Christianity were negative and disturbing. In his autobiography, he says: "In those days Christian missionaries used to stand in a corner near the high school and hold forth, pouring abuse on Hindus and their gods."[151] And many Hindus converted to Christianity ate beef and drank liquor.[152] He thus said: "Only Christianity was at the time an exception. I developed a sort of dislike for it."[153]

All these denote Gandhi's refusal of the form of Christianity presented to him, which had close relation with Western culture and the British colonial power along with the missionaries' negative attitude to other religions with dogmatic superiority and methods of conversion. Thus "...he did not absorb Christianity in full for there were several aspects of Christianity which he did not approve. ..."[154]

In England, he read the Bible and was influenced by the Sermon on the Mount. However, "It was in South Africa ... where he lived from 1893 to 1915, that he enjoyed his first extensive contacts with Christians."[155] There he read extensive Christian literature, attended Christian meetings, even reached to the point of conversion to Christianity and was influenced by it.

He was highly influenced by many of the aspects of Christianity – non-violence, Kingdom of God, social service, charity and love, etc.[156] The Sermon on the Mount and the way of the Cross[157] were the meeting points between Gandhi and Christianity.[158] E. Stanley Jones even called him as 'a deeply Christianized Hindu, more Christianized than most Christians.'[159] Moreover, many of his Christian friends wanted him to be a Christian and called him

---

[149] Terrence J. Rynne, op.cit., 23.

[150] James D. Hunt, op.cit., 2-3.

[151] *An Autobiography*, 31.

[152] Ibid.

[153] Ibid.

[154] Madhuri Wadhwa, op.cit., 21-22.

[155] Robert Ellsberg, op.cit., xi.

[156] Terrence J. Rynne, op.cit., 23.

[157] "He found the symbol and centre of true Christianity in the cross." S. K. Kim, op.cit., 134.

[158] George Pattery, *Gandhi – The Believer an Indian Christian Perspective* (Delhi: ISPCK, 1996), 122.

[159] E. Stanley Jones, op.cit., 28.

a 'Christian' variously and in different contexts such as: "Sermon-on the-Mount Christian", 'Natural Christian", "Concealed Christian", 'Unbaptized Christian", etc. But Gandhi said, 'I am not a Christian.'[160] "Just because I respect...Christianity I do not become...a Christian."[161] Because Hinduism appealed to him more than Christianity so he declared over and again that he is a *Sanātani* Hindu.[162] Hence he said: "There was a time when I was wavering between Hinduism and Christianity. When I recovered my balance of mind, I felt that to me salvation was possible only through Hindu religion and my faith in Hinduism grew deeper and more enlightened."[163] He thus understood Christianity through Hinduism and believed that "the fullness of Christianity could only be found in its interpretation in the light and by the aid of Hinduism."[164] As a result, he defined, re-discovered and re-interpreted Christianity.

Christianity is for Gandhi two thousand years old[165] and is based on the person, life and teachings of Jesus Christ.[166] For Gandhi, Christianity began as a gentle and self-abnegating creed of Asia, but by fourth century with Constantine it became an imperial religion of the West.[167] Hence, it got misunderstood and negated the original teachings of Christ,[168] by becoming aggressive, proselytising and even sanctioned wars. So Gandhi's belief is that 'when Christianity had the backing of a Roman Emperor', it got distorted into an imperialistic faith' by incorporating a system alien to it, 'based on might.'[169] Therefore he considered India's contribution is to show this fallacy to the world.[170] However, he regarded Christianity as "a true religion, a noble religion and along with other religions it has contributed to raise the moral height of mankind."[171]

Gandhi was looking for the spirit of the Sermon on the Mount in modern Christianity[172] and found that the Sermon on the Mount is absent in the history

---

160 *CWMG*. 75:69.

161 *CWMG*. 69: 212.

162 *CWMG*. 31:351; *cf*. 89:193.

163 Mahatma Gandhi, *The Spirit of Hinduism*, op.cit., 73.

164 *CWMG*. 12: 176.

165 *CWMG*. 35: 106.

166 *CWMG*. 68: 30.

167 *CWMG*. 90: 283.

168 K. L. Seshagiri Rao, *Mahatma Gandhi and Comparative Religion* (Delhi: Motilal Banarsidass, 1978), 29.

169 *Harijan*, 30.05.1936.

170 Nirmal Minz, op.cit., 44.

171 *Harijan*, 06.03.1937.

172 K. L. Seshagiri Rao, op.cit., 5.

of Christianity. He realized the historical Christianity in Western countries as a negation of Christ and has distinguished between Christ and Christianity.[173] He was thus trying to recover the real Christianity of Christ. Hence it is said, "Gandhi had rediscovered and retaught the original creed of Christ."[174] Esme Wynne-Tyson is also of the opinion that "…original Christianity, as taught and practiced by the Early Church, was much more like the Gandhian way of life than what is thought of today as the Christian religion."[175]

In short, "The Sermon on the Mount" was for Gandhi "...the whole of Christianity..."[176] However, he said: "...much of what passes as Christianity is a negation of the Sermon on the Mount…."[177] While Christianity gave up the Sermon, Gandhi took it as the cardinal part of Christianity.[178] Hence, Gandhi demanded and reminded Christians to live according to the message of Jesus as recorded in the Sermon on the Mount.[179] He found such an ideal Christian in his friend C. F. Andrews. About whom he said: "I have not known a better man or a better Christian than C. F. Andrews."[180]

Thus Christianity for Gandhi is a way of life in the pattern of the Sermon on the Mount. He said: "...where there is boundless love and no idea of retaliation whatsoever, it is Christianity that lives."[181] Real Christianity hence for Gandhi is difficult to speak, define or propagate, but it is lived experience of boundless love in the heart. He says: "...it is something indefinable, not capable of being preached to men, not capable of being transmitted from mouth to mouth, but from heart to heart. But Christianity is not commonly understood in that way."[182]

Thus it has been said that Gandhi embraced Christ but rejected Christianity.[183] His criticisms of Christianity was mainly centred around two points, one its exclusivism and the other, giving up of its living faith in the

---

[173] *CWMG*. 35: 523.

[174] Esme Wynne-Tyson, "Gandhi's Rediscovery of Christianity," in *Facets of Mahatma Gandhi*, vol. 4, op.cit., 235.

[175] Ibid., 237.

[176] Cited by Gopinath Dhawan, *The Political Philosophy of Mahatma Gandhi* (Ahmedabad: Navajivan Publishing House, 1962), 25.

[177] *CWMG*. 35:248. The sum total of the activities of European nations is a denial of the teachings of the Sermon on the Mount. *CWMG*. 28: 335.

[178] *CWMG*. 48:421.

[179] *CWMG*. 40:58-59; 65:81; 90: 212.

[180] *CWMG*. 71:394.

[181] *CWMG*. 48:438.

[182] *CWMG*. 48:438.

[183] K. S. Bharati, *Thoughts of Mahatma*, vol. 2, op.cit., 32.

practicability of the Sermon on the Mount.[184] He says: "But I am placing before you my fundamental difficulties with regard to the appearance of Christianity in the world and the formulation of Christian beliefs."[185] For Gandhi, there is a contradiction in Christian tradition, between the law of love and its practical development through violence.[186] No other religion teaches as Christianity about active love, but more than any other religions, Christianity has been responsible for bloodshed and war.[187] Thus for Gandhi, the central teaching of Christ - "Love your enemy", is denied in Christianity. He regarded that Western Christianity had departed from the spirit and teachings of Christ and instead had used 'brute force' than 'soul force' for its growth.[188]

As Gandhi encountered the Western Christianity, he realised a huge gap between Christ's teachings and the Christianity practised in the West.[189] Thus he distinguished between Christ and the Christianity.[190] He said: "West ...although it professes Christianity, there is no Christianity or Christ in the West...."[191] He continues: "European Christianity is totally different from Christ's Christianity."[192] "Jesus was an Asiatic"[193] and "...Jesus lived every inch of him in Asia ...."[194] Gandhi says: "...Jesus ... came from the East." But "...Christianity became disfigured when it went to the West."[195] Thus for Gandhi, Christianity is essentially an Eastern religion, but somehow or other, it became synonymous with Western culture.[196] This so called Western

---

[184] Mathew Thomas, "Christian Missions in the Pluralistic Context of India – The Relevance of Gandhian Approach" (Ph. D Thesis, Mahatma Gandhi University, 2003).

[185] Gandhi, *The Spirit of Hinduism*, op.cit., 30.

[186] C. F. Andrews, op.cit., 196.

[187] *Young India*, 22.12.1927, 31.12.1931; *CWMG*. 36: 30; 68: 2.

[188] *CWMG*. 21: 70; 32: 588.

[189] He says: "When I began as a prayerful student to study Christian literature in South Africa in 1893, I asked myself again and again, "Is this Christianity?" And I could only say, "No, no. Certainly this that I see is not Christianity." And the deepest in me tells me that I was right; for it was unworthy of Jesus and untrue to the Sermon on the Mount." Gandhi, *The Spirit of Hinduism*, op.cit., 31.

[190] *CWMG*. 35:523.

[191] *CWMG*. 86:22.

[192] *Young India*, 26.01.1922; *CWMG*. 22: 246; *cf. Young India*, 24.11.1927.

[193] *CWMG*. 82:155.

[194] *CWMG*. 28:133.

[195] *CWMG*. 87: 192. So Gandhi asserted, "*...I rebel against orthodox Christianity*, as I am convinced that it has distorted the message of Jesus. He was an Asiatic whose message was delivered through many media, and when it had the backing of a Roman Emperor it became an imperialist faith as it remains to this day." *Harijan*, 30.05.1936.

[196] *CWMG*. 56: 235.

Christian culture was materialistic,[197] as it worshipped the body more than the spirit. It, for him, represented "powers of darkness" and "the spirit of Satan,"[198] and is the destructive show of 'Mammon's nine days' wonder.'[199] Therefore Western Christians "...do not know the true message of Jesus"[200] but misunderstood Jesus as a 'passive resister' and as 'weak.'[201] Therefore, for a proper understanding of Jesus' message "... light ... have to be thrown from the East."[202]

Moreover, Gandhi realised that Jesus is denied in the Western Churches.[203] He said: "...the Christianity of the West is a negation of Christ's central teaching"[204]– "love your enemy."[205] So Gandhi alleged: "Christian Europe is not all Christian."[206] But "... only nominally Christian. It is really worshipping Mammon."[207] They "...show little of that belief in actual practice."[208] Christ came into this world to preach and spread the gospel of love and peace, but what his followers have brought about is tyranny and misery. Christians who were taught the maxim of 'Love thy neighbour as thyself' are divided among themselves.[209] Gandhi also observed that Christendom has been responsible for the wars, which put to shame even those described in the Old Testament and other records, historical or semi-historical.[210] Therefore Gandhi concluded: "The *tapasya* of Jesus Christ, boundless though it was, was not sufficient for Europe's need. Europe has disapproved Christ. ...Many Christs will have to offer themselves as sacrifice at the terrible alter of Europe, and only then will realization dawn on that continent."[211]

Gandhi did not accept the superior and exclusive claim of missionary Christianity as the 'only' true religion. He asks: "How can I limit God's grace

---

197 *CWMG*. 25: 461.

198 *CWMG*. 100: 75.

199 *Young India*, 08.12.1927.

200 *CWMG*. 68: 273.

201 *Harijan*, 07.12.1947.

202 C. F. Andrews, op.cit., 122.

203 *CWMG*. 49: 367.

204 *CWMG*. 73:51. "I consider Western Christianity in its practical working a negation of Christ's Christianity. I cannot conceive Jesus, if he was living in the flesh in our midst, approving of modern Christian organization, public worship, or modern ministry." *Young India*, 27.09.1921.

205 *CWMG*. 68: 30.

206 *CWMG*. 35: 106.

207 *Young India*, 08.09.1920.

208 *Harijan*, 18.06.1936.

209 *CWMG*. 88: 472.

210 *Harijan*, 07.12.1947; *CWMG*. 90:129-130.

211 *CWMG*. 13: 524.

by my little mind and say this is the only way?"[212] He, thus radically questioned the exclusive claims of Christianity such as Bible is the only revelation, Christ as the only Son of God, Christians can only have salvation, and Christians as the only 'chosen' people of God, etc. He said: "I would ... dispute your claim that Christianity is the only true religion."[213] "Philosophically there was nothing extraordinary in Christian principles."[214] And thus "It was impossible for me to regard Christianity as a perfect religion or the greatest of all religions."[215] He also told Christians to stop looking at other religions as 'false'. "Our religion is in no way inferior to Christianity."[216] Moreover for Gandhi, "...to be a good Hindu also meant ... a good Christian."[217] Hence, his consideration is that "Christianity is as good and true as any other religion."[218] Thus Gandhi gave equal respect to all religions, including Christianity.[219] He did not deny that Christianity was a true religion. But he only denied the claim that Christianity was the only true religion.[220] All the prophets of all religions were equal to him, including Jesus.[221] Gandhi also "... saw the need for the reconciliation of Christianity with other religions."[222] He thus advised Christians to cultivate toleration, charity and humility, instead of arrogance and from the feeling of being custodians of truth.[223] He thus said: "My message to Christians would be to cultivate humility instead of arrogating to themselves the exclusive possession of absolute truth."[224] He thus advised to his Christian friends to give prayerful and sympathetic study of other scriptures of the world.[225]

Gandhi further questioned and denied the traditional dogmas and doctrines of orthodox/evangelical Christianity. He found it too narrow and exclusive,[226] because of its condemnation of a large section of humanity and it's demand

---

[212] *Harijan*, 18.07.1936.

[213] *CWMG*. 64:398.

[214] *An Autobiography*, 126.

[215] Ibid.

[216] *CWMG*. 88: 96.

[217] Robert Ellsberg, op.cit., 12.

[218] *Harijan*, 06.03.1937.

[219] *CWMG*. 68: 289.

[220] A. Pushparajan, *From Conversion to Fellowship The Hindu-Christian Encounter in the Gandhian Perspective* (Allahabad: St. Paul Press, 1990), 158.

[221] *CWMG*. 36: 305.

[222] K. L. Seshagiri Rao, op.cit., 31-32.

[223] *CWMG*. 48: 106; 63: 91; 62:388.

[224] *CWMG*. 41:392.

[225] *Young India*, 31.10.1929.

[226] *CWMG*. 34:262-263.

of them to believe as Christians do.[227] He therefore said: "I admire much in Christianity, I am unable to identify myself with Orthodox Christianity."[228] For example, he took 'Trinity' as figurative and not as literal.[229] He also told: "I do not consider the embracing of Christianity as in any way essential for salvation."[230] The text that "Jesus is the only begotten son of God" was not literally true and he could not "ascribe exclusive divinity to Jesus."[231] Hence, his conception of Jesus was as a 'great teacher' not beyond that.[232] Gandhi gave importance to behaviour than belief and told who is a true Christian? He said: "Do not flatter yourselves with the belief that a mere recital of that celebrated verse in St. John [that is 3:16] makes a man a Christian."[233] But "It is not he who says, 'Lord, Lord' but 'He that doeth the will of the Lord [Mathew. 7:21] that is a true Christian."[234] Thus Gandhi understood a true Christian as one who does the will of God, than professing or chanting certain articles of faith. Gandhi said: "...belief without doing is not believing."[235] Gandhi also proved that the message of Christ can be lived without being called as a Christian, or even without hearing the name of Christ or reading Bible.[236] He then went on to say: "...I came to the conclusion that there was no need for me to join your creed to be a believer in the beauty of the teachings of Jesus or to try to follow his example."[237]

Gandhi too was aware of the origins of Christianity in India and the St. Thomas tradition.[238] He has mentioned about the Portuguese Christianity in India.[239] But he encountered the Westernized missionary Christianity of 19th and 20th centuries, which was associated with British colonialism. He was critical of this alliance of Christianity with colonialism and considered it as a continuation of the old association between Christianity and the Roman Empire. For he says:

---

[227] *CWMG*. 61:47.

[228] Gandhi, *The Spirit of Hinduism*, op.cit., 22-23.

[229] *CWMG*. 25:85.

[230] *CWMG*. 35:376.

[231] *CWMG*. 100:333.

[232] *CWMG*. 30:241.

[233] *CWMG*. 27:437.

[234] *Harijan*, 11.05.1935.

[235] *Young India*, 04.09.1924.

[236] *CWMG*. 72:299; *Harijan*, 04.08.1940; *Young India*, 06.08.1925; *cf. Mahatma*. 2:190.

[237] Cited by Augustine Thottakara, *Spirituality of Dialogue: Indian Experiences* (Bangalore: Dharmaram Publications, 1994), 112.

[238] *CWMG*. 86: 211.

[239] *CWMG*. 4:407.

> Unfortunately, Christianity in India is inextricably mixed up for the last one hundred and fifty years with the British rule. It appears to us as synonymous with the materialistic civilization and imperialistic exploitation by the stronger white races of the weaker races of the world. Its contribution to India has been, therefore, largely of a negative character.[240]

He also said, "... when Christianity and Western Civilization came to be associated, the Hindus began to look upon that religion with disfavour."[241]

Nevertheless, Gandhi too acknowledged Christianity's positive impact on India, especially in reforming Hindu religion,[242] through its criticisms and thereby removing some of the defects of Hinduism[243] and generating new reform movements.[244] He thus said: "I think that some of the principles of Christianity are bound to leave their impress upon the future development of India."[245]

However, Gandhi admonished Indian Christians not to follow the Western Christianity.[246] Because he observed that "Jesus of Asia is misinterpreted in the West"[247] and what European missionaries have brought to India is Western civilization, not the life of Jesus.[248] Therefore he said: "I hope that the Christians of India will express in their lives Jesus the Crucified of the Bible, and not as interpreted in the West with her blood-stained fingers."[249] Gandhi was thus not against Indians following Jesus and the Sermon on the Mount, but he opposed Westernization of Indian Christians or the spread of Western Christianity in India; because often he found "...Christianity synonymous with denationalization and Europeanization."[250] He was particularly pained to see the new converts to Christianity adopting European dress and eating beef and drinking brandy and looking down everything Indian and criticising their ancestral religion.[251] Therefore he said, "Conversion must not mean

---

240 *Young India*, 21.03.1929.

241 *Indian Opinion*, 15.04.1905.

242 *CWMG*. 29:326.

243 *CWMG*. 4:407.

244 *CWMG*. 4:408.

245 *CWMG*. 15:304.

246 *CWMG*. 89:112.

247 *Harijan*, 07.09.1947.

248 Gandhi, *Modern Vs. Ancient Civilization*, op.cit., 84.

249 *Harijan*, 07.09.1947.

250 *CWMG*. 34:261.

251 *CWMG*. 28:91, 92; 61:46.

denationalization."[252] He doubted the motif behind 'proselytization' and opposed it strongly.[253] He said: "I have absolutely no faith in the proselytizing activity that is carried on today."[254] "I disbelieve in the conversion of one person by another."[255] Since it does not improve the moral standard of converts, but they just get Europeanized not even understanding the teachings of Jesus.[256] Moreover, Gandhi found that missionaries often using material attractions for converting poor *Harijans*. So he was "...not against conversion. But ... against the modern methods of it."[257] 'Conversion became a business.'[258] On the other hand, for Gandhi, "...conversion should be primarily based on a change of inner conviction."[259]

Besides, he considered that the sending of missionaries to India by the west was "part of imperialist exploitation."[260] Because missionaries send an 'adulterated Christianity,'[261] 'a Christianity of their belief,' and 'not the message of Jesus...."[262] Gandhi also observed that in missionary effort there is a lack of real humility, as it is based on the assumption that one's own belief is true, not only for oneself but for all the world.[263] Hence he said: "My quarrel with missionaries is that they think no religion other than Christianity is true."[264] This was against his *Advaitic* belief in the equality of all religions.

Gandhi was also unable to accept the prejudiced criticisms of Christian missionaries on India and its heritage.[265] Such criticisms of Indian religions and traditions by Christian missionaries were considered by him as "a negation of the spirit of Christ."[266] Therefore, he admonished the Christian missionaries to have a receptive mind towards India and its heritage.[267]

---

[252] *CWMG*. 28:92.

[253] *CWMG*. 61:46.

[254] *CWMG*. 27:204.

[255] *CWMG*. 40:60.

[256] *CWMG*. 29:326; *Young India*, 17.12.1925.

[257] *Young India*, 23.04.1931.

[258] *Young India*, 23.04.1931.

[259] *CWMG*. 33: 8.

[260] *CWMG*. 73: 29.

[261] *CWMG*. 73: 29.

[262] *Harijan*, 12.12.1936.

[263] *Young India*, 22.03.1928.

[264] *CWMG*. 68: 422.

[265] *CWMG*. 27: 436.

[266] *CWMG*. 68: 252.

[267] *CWMG*. 27: 437.

Gandhi was also a critic of missionary preaching, rather for him, 'to live the gospel is the most effective way.'[268] He thus told the English and American missionaries to refrain from 'telling' India about Christ and to live the life of the Sermon on the Mount.[269] According to him, they should confine their activities to the humanitarian service without the ulterior motive of converting India and her unsophisticated villagers to Christianity, and thereby destroying their time immemorial social superstructure.[270]

4.4. Swami Vivekananda and Religion

Basically Vivekananda was a man of religion.[271] He, however, understood religion from an *Advaitic* perspective, which was contrary to the Western colonial missionary treatment of non-Christian religions as 'pagan', heathen', etc. He, on the other hand, understood religion as experience, toleration of others, and service of man.[272] He considered religion as fundamental in the very soul of humanity.[273] It is "the highest plane of human thought and life"[274] as it is "the search after the highest ideal."[275] Religion is above and beyond reason, as it is supernatural.[276] It "transcends the senses"[277] and deals "with the truths of the metaphysical world"[278] as it is an "inquiry into the beyond."[279] According to Vivekananda, "...all the great religions of the world are very ancient ... and ... owes its origin to the country between the Ganga and the Euphrates."[280] He acknowledges three parts in every religion– *viz*., philosophy, mythology and rituals.[281] He stated that there are four types of religion – (1) the worker, (2) the emotional, (3) the mystical, and (4) the philosophical; and that a religion which gave scope to all these different types and characters that he found in the *Advaita Vedāntic* tradition of Hinduism would be perfect.[282] Further, Vivekananda considered religion as the bed-rock and main theme

[268] *CWMG*. 60:323.

[269] *Young India*, 20.10.1927.

[270] *Harijan*, 28.09.1935.

[271] N. Lekshmikutty, op.cit., 86.

[272] S. Radhakrishnan, *Our Heritage* (Delhi: Orient Paperbacks, 1976), 94.

[273] *CWSV*. 6: 46.

[274] *CWSV*. 2:375.

[275] *CWSV*. 2:463.

[276] *CWSV*. 7: 60.

[277] *CWSV*. 3: 175.

[278] *CWSV*. 6: 81.

[279] *CWSV*. 4: 208.

[280] *CWSV*. 2:361.

[281] *CWSV*. 1: 72; 2:377; 6: 6.

[282] *CWSV*. 9: 533.

of Indian civilization.[283] He thus said: "In India, religion is the one and the only occupation of life."[284] So religion is the life of India, the language of this country, and the symbol of all its movements.[285]

As an *Advaita Vedāntin*, Vivekananda said: "Religion is experience."[286] "Religion lies in being and becoming, in realisation."[287] Religion is "the relation between the soul and God,"[288] and is "the manifestation of the divinity already in man."[289] So, when it was discovered that "I and my Father are one,"[290] the last word was said of religion.[291] Vivekananda was also able to find the gist of all religions in Christ's words, that "Blessed are the pure in heart, for they shall see God."[292] Thus doctrines, dogmas, rituals, books, temples, forms, intellectual argumentation, etc. which were the central concerns in the Western concept of religion, particularly in Christianity, were not religion for Vivekananda, but only secondary details.[293]

Contrary to the missionary attitude, Vivekananda believed not only in religious toleration, but accepted all religions as true.[294] He, therefore declared: "I am a believer in all religions."[295] All religions are sacred as God is in every religion.[296] Therefore, Vivekananda considered all religions equal, as all religions are good and alike in their essentials and basic principles.[297] The differences are only in non-essentials.[298] He further said: "…if one religion is true, all others must be true."[299] And "What is not found in one religion is supplied by another."[300] Thus he very vividly expressed his attitude in the equality of all religions:

---

[283] R. C. Majumdar, op.cit., 89.

[284] *CWSV*. 3: 107.

[285] *CWSV*. 4: 462.

[286] *CWSV*. 8: 230.

[287] *CWSV*. 8: 229.

[288] *CWSV*. 4: 179.

[289] *CWSV*. 4: 358.

[290] *John*. 10: 30.

[291] *CWSV*. 4:216. For Vivekananda "Advaitism is the last word of religion ...." *CWSV*. 6:415.

[292] *CWSV*. 4: 26. *cf. Mathew* 5: 8.

[293] *CWSV*. 1: 257; 2: 43; 3: 175.

[294] *CWSV*. 1:3.

[295] *CWSV*. 9: 472.

[296] *CWSV*. 7:460, 417.

[297] *CWSV*. 5: 293; 8: 218; 9: 439.

[298] *CWSV*. 1: 318.

[299] *CWSV*. 1: 318.

[300] *CWSV*. 3: 483.

> I accept all religions that were in the past, and worship with them all; I worship God with every one of them, in whatever form they worship Him. I shall go to the mosque of the Mohammedan; I shall enter the Christian's church and kneel before the crucifix; I shall enter the Buddhistic temple, where I shall take refuge in Buddha and his Law. I shall go into the forest and sit down in meditation with the Hindu, who is trying to see the Light which enlightens the heart of every one.[301]

Along with this belief in the equality of all religions, Vivekananda by following his master Sri Ramakrishna and *Advaita Vedānta* philosophy stressed the unity and inter-religious harmony.[302] For example, in the Parliament of Religions, he stressed the common basis of various religions and appealed for universal tolerance and mutual respect.[303] He said: "upon the banner of every religion will soon be written, in spite of resistance: 'Help and should not fight', 'Assimilation and not Destruction', 'Harmony and Peace and not Dissension.'[304] So according to Vivekananda, religions must be inclusive, and should not look down with contempt upon one another, because their particular ideals of God are different.[305] Rather we must learn to love those who think exactly opposite to us and differ from us in opinion,[306] so that we may have no quarrel with any religion in the world, "whether it teaches men to worship Christ, Buddha or Mohammed, or any other prophet."[307] He thus stated: "... live in harmony with all."[308]

Hence, Vivekananda denounced religious exclusivism of the Christian missionaries, which asserts that "only this way" is true and only this way "leads to salvation, all others are wrong."[309] For example, he criticised Christians' claim that, 'there is no other true religion, there is no other revelation of God' other than Christianity.[310] He believed that such exclusivism was the root cause of religious hostility and intolerance.[311] That these names as Hindu, Christian,

---

[301] *CWSV*. 2:374.

[302] *CWSV*. 3: 201. R. K. Dasgupta, op.cit., 169; K. P. Aleaz, *Harmony of Religions*, op.cit., 224, 243; Augustine Thottakara, op.cit., 39.

[303] Augustine Thottakara, Ibid., 35.

[304] *CWSV*. 1: 24.

[305] *CWSV*. 2: 67.

[306] *CWSV*. 9: 487.

[307] *CWSV*. 3: 132.

[308] *CWSV*. 5: 83.

[309] *CWSV*. 8: 24, 210.

[310] *CWSV*. 6: 138.

[311] *CWSV*. 3: 359.

etc., stand as great bars to all brotherly feelings between man and man.[312] He thus asserted: "No civilisation can grow unless fanaticism, bloodshed, and brutality stop."[313] " We should, therefore, look charitably upon the religious convictions of others and positively be helpful to each other.[314] For example, Christians can learn from Hindus and Hindus from Christians;[315] so that a true Christian will become a true Hindu, and a true Hindu, a true Christian.[316] He also said about the need of Hindu-Muslim unity in India, that "Vedantic brain and Islamic body is the only hope."[317]

Vivekananda too affirmed the need of religious pluralism in the world as 'unity in variety' is the plan of the universe.[318] He said: "You can't make one religion for the whole world."[319] That must not be, because the same level of religious thought will lead to the death of religious thought; as variety was its life.[320] Hence if "there were not different religions, no religion would survive."[321] As "One cannot exist without the other...."[322]

Vivekananda was also against religious conversion. He said: "I do not believe in this idea of conversion."[323] As all religions being true, such conversions serve no good end.[324] So he pointed out: "The Christian is not to become a Hindu or a Buddhist, nor a Hindu or a Buddhist to become a Christian. But each must assimilate the spirit of the others and yet preserve his individuality and grow according to his own law of growth."[325] Thus "Each must follow his own religion."[326]

Finally he proposed the "Advaitic principles of Vedanta to be the truest religion,"[327] which can harmonise every possible religious system in the world[328]

---

[312] *New Discoveries*. 2:355.

[313] *CWSV*. 3: 187.

[314] *CWSV*. 3: 187-188.

[315] *CWSV*. 4: 190; 2: 502.

[316] *CWSV*. 5: 415.

[317] *CWSV*. 6: 416.

[318] *CWSV*. 9: 489.

[319] *CWSV*. 9: 486.

[320] *CWSV*. 9: 533; *cf.* 6: 65.

[321] *CWSV*. 8: 217.

[322] *CWSV*. 3: 234; 2: 253.

[323] *New Discoveries*. 1:203.

[324] *CWSV*. 9: 438.

[325] *CWSV*. 1: 24.

[326] *CWSV*. 8: 315.

[327] *CWSV*. 6: 470.

[328] *CWSV*. 9: 491; 5: 279.

and can become 'the universal religion' of man.[329] Because *Advaita* is "the crest-jewel of all spiritual thought"[330] and "the only position from which one can look upon all religions and sects with love."[331] Moreover *Advaita Vedānta* will be equally acceptable to all minds as it got an equal and harmonious balance in different types of religion such as philosophic, emotional, mystic and action.[332] Hence he predicted: "Advaita will be the future religion of thinking humanity."[333] This was against the Christian missionaries' wish of making the 'whole world or whole of India' into Christianity.

4.5. Mahatma Gandhi and Religion

Gandhi was a born *Vaiṣṇava* Hindu and practiced Hinduism all through his life. He was essentially a religious man,[334] as he declared that his whole life was governed by religion.[335] Hence, his understanding of religion arose as a religious person, particularly from an *Advaitic* perspective, with a broad understanding of all religions. He recognized religion as one of the fundamental aspects of human life and said: "Man without religion is man without roots. Therefore, religion is the basis on which all life structure has to be created, if life is to be real."[336] Religion is, thus "the permanent element in human nature"[337] and it is "a belief in ordered moral government of the universe."[338] Moreover, for Gandhi, religion and morality were synonymous terms,[339] and declared: "My religion begins and ends with truth and non-violence."[340]

For him, "Even as a tree has a single trunk but many branches and leaves, so there is one true and perfect religion, but it becomes many as it passes through the human medium."[341] For example, Islam, Christianity, Hinduism and Zoroastrianism are the main branches of the tree religion,[342] which transcends all these religions.[343] Thus, there are elements of truth as well as

---

[329] *CWSV*. 3: 182.

[330] *CWSV*. 3: 432.

[331] *CWSV*. 6: 415.

[332] *CWSV*. 2: 387-388; 9: 533.

[333] *CWSV*. 8: 348.

[334] Dev Raj Bali, op.cit., 117.

[335] *CWMG*. 100: 282.

[336] *CWMG*. 1:464.

[337] *Young India*, 12.05.1920.

[338] R. K. Prabhu & U. R. Rao, *The Mind of Mahatma Gandhi*, op.cit., 82.

[339] *Harijan*, 06.03.1937.

[340] *Young India*, 20.08.1925.

[341] Gandhi, *My Religion*, op.cit., 19.

[342] *CWMG*. 85: 31.

[343] *Young India*, 12.05.1920.

some errors in all religions;[344] therefore "...every religion is both perfect and imperfect."[345] However, he said: "... I do not regard any of the great religions of the world false."[346]

Unlike the missionaries, Gandhi had an inclusive attitude and believed in the equality of all religions. He said: "I consider myself a follower of Islam, Christianity, Zoroastrianism and every other religion .... All religions are equal and they are founded on the same faith."[347] Further he declared: "I believe in *sarvadharmasamanatva* having equal regard for all faiths and creeds,"[348] that "religions are different roads converging to the same point."[349] He, thus emphasized not mere tolerance, but "...equal respect of all religions."[350] Besides, he considered: "...a friendly study of the world's religions" as "a sacred duty."[351]

Gandhi was against truth claims especially by the Christian West that they are the 'only' true religion; because for him, "...there was no such thing as only one true religion, every other being false."[352] Hence he told the Christians that, "I would ... dispute the claim that Christianity is the only true religion. It is also a true religion, a noble religion, and along with other religions it has contributed to raise the moral height of mankind."[353] Hence "...Christianity is as good and true as any other religion."[354] So he suggested a respectful approach to others' religions. He said, "Ahimsa teaches us to entertain the same respect for the religious faiths of others as we accord to our own."[355] So he was able "...to understand another's point of view with an unprejudiced mind."[356] He thus said: "My approach to other religions...is never as a fault finding critic but as a devotee hoping to find the like beauties in the other religions and wishing to incorporate in my own the good I may find in them and miss in mine."[357]

---

[344] M. K. Gandhi, *The Way to Communal Harmony* (Ahmedabad: Navajivan Publishing House, 1994), 56.

[345] *CWMG*. 32:13.

[346] Gandhi, *The Way to Communal Harmony*, op.cit., 66.

[347] *CWMG*. 87: 45.

[348] Gandhi, *All Religions are True*, op.cit., 7.

[349] *CWMG*. 87: 29-30, 45.

[350] *Harijan*, 12.01.1947.

[351] *CWMG*. 31:350.

[352] *Harijan*, 06.03.1937.

[353] Gandhi, *All Religions are True*, op.cit., 46.

[354] *Harijan*, 06.03.1937.

[355] Gandhi, *My Religion*, op.cit., 19.

[356] *CWMG*. 69:212.

[357] *Harijan*, 12.08.1933.

Gandhi was against religious conflicts and therefore, he emphasised unity, harmony and commonalities between religions than differences.[358] For him, "Religions are not for separating men from one another, they are meant to bring them together."[359] He said: "Hindus, Mussalmans, Christians, Parsis, Jews, are convenient labels. But when I tear them down, I do not know which is which. We are all children of the same God."[360] "Then Hindu, Christian and Mussalman would be synonymous terms."[361] Thus he tried to harmonize all religions[362] by bringing better understanding among different religions [363] through his inclusive and broader approach based on *Advaita* philosophy. Thus in his view, there was no conflict among different religions.[364]

Nevertheless, like Vivekananda, Gandhi too, with his idea of equality and sufficiency of all faiths,[365] opposed the conversion from one faith to another. He said: "I disbelieve in the conversion of one person by another."[366] But he tried to make everyone a better follower of his own faith, [367] for he said: "...a Hindu should be better Hindu, a Muslim a better Muslim, and a Christian a better Christian."[368] Hence Gandhi emphasised pluralism as he said: "I do not expect the India of my dream to develop one religion, i.e., to be wholly Hindu or wholly Christian, or wholly Mussalman; but I want it to be wholly tolerant, with its many religions working side by side with one another."[369] "... as one indivisible nation, having common interest, then minorities will not feel themselves to be minorities."[370] Hence through his inclusive, equal and plural approach to all religions, he was able to bring about the kind of national integration he hoped for.[371] This was thus totally against the missionary wish of making all of India into 'Christian' by uprooting the traditional religions and cultures of India.

---

[358] *CWMG*. 23: 243; 26: 396; 69:212.

[359] Gandhi, *All Religions Are True*, op.cit., 228.

[360] *Harijan*, 18.04.1936.

[361] M. K. Gandhi, *In Search of the Supreme*, vol. 3 (Ahmedabad: Navajivan Publishing House, 1962), 55.

[362] *CWMG*. 100: 496.

[363] *CWMG*. 41:393.

[364] *CWMG*. 83:61.

[365] *CWMG*. 100: 222.

[366] *Mahatma*. 2: 343.

[367] Ibid.

[368] *Young India*, 29.05.1924.

[369] *Young India*, 22.12.1927.

[370] *CWMG*. 56: 384.

[371] S. J. Samartha, *The Hindu Response to the Unbound Christ* (Madras: CLS, 1974), 97.

4.6. Swami Vivekananda and Christ

Swami Vivekananda's knowledge of Christ and his teachings was considerable. In understanding Christ, he had special attachment to the Sermon on the Mount, and some of the mystical sayings of Jesus in John's Gospel.[372] Thomas A Kempis' *Imitation of Christ* was instrumental, in his getting closer to Christ.[373] He held the greatness of Christ[374] and was "a devotee of Christ." [375] For example, he said: "Had I lived in Palestine, in the days of Jesus of Nazareth, I would have washed His feet, not with my tears, but with my heart's blood!"[376] So according to him, Christ got an extra-ordinary personality[377] and he was attracted to the holiness and beauty of the character of Jesus Christ.[378] Hence, there is little doubt that the personality and ideals of Christ made a powerful impression on his mind.[379]

Vivekananda expressed multiple views on Christ at various contexts. In his lectures, he presented Christ powerfully with great reverence and eloquence.[380] For example, his lecture 'Christ, The Messenger,'[381] delivered at Los Angeles, California, 1900 is very famous. He viewed Christ as an ideal[382] who wielded immense spiritual power over humanity.[383] So, Christ, for him is an embodiment of spiritual values, knowledge of whose life would benefit any culture.[384] Thus he viewed Christ as an integral part of Indian tradition and placed Christ on par with Indian *ṛṣis*[385] and revered Jesus as "a true Guru."[386] Therefore he says: "I pity the Hindu who does not see the beauty in Jesus Christ's character."[387] So for Vivekananda, the Hindus cannot criticise Christ's beautiful life, character and Sermon on the Mount but only revere and welcome

---

[372] *cf. CWSV*. 2:143, 353.

[373] *CWSV*. 8:159; 9:292; V. R. Karandikar, op.cit., 125.

[374] *The Life*. 1:206.

[375] Ibid., 448-449.

[376] *CWSV*. 9: 423; Sister Nivedita, op.cit., 260.

[377] *CWSV*. 4: 121.

[378] *CWSV*. 4:222; 8:217; 9: 456.

[379] S. J. Samartha, op.cit., 49.

[380] *CWSV*. 9: 509.

[381] *CWSV*. 4: 138-153.

[382] *CWSV*. 4:145. *cf.* 8: 111.

[383] *CWSV*. 8: 181. *cf.* 6: 63.

[384] *New Discoveries*. 2:350.

[385] *CWSV*. 9: 527.

[386] *CWSV*. 8: 115.

[387] *CWSV*. 8: 219.

it.[388] Hence he said: "India requires help from Christ...."[389] "Bring Christ's life to us and let it permeate the very core of society. Let him be preached in every village and corner of India."[390]

Vivekananda expressed his opinion on almost all aspects of Jesus' life and ministry. For him, Christ denotes the rise of a 'new wave' from the fall of Jewish race and represents the best and greatest of the Jewish culture.[391] However, he considered it is unnecessary to claim a supernatural birth for Jesus,[392] that is the claim of his virgin birth.[393] He says Christ had long years of preparation for his public ministry;[394] and Christ with his message of love, being meek and lowly, lived, worked and suffered for others.[395] Christ associated with publicans and sinners and never put himself up over others.[396] Moreover, his voice - "Come unto Me all ye that labour and are heavy laden, and I will give you rest"[397] - makes people ethical and leads them to freedom.[398] Hence, according to Vivekananda, Jesus spoke with authority;[399] and he got fascination and attraction to many of Christ's extra-ordinary teachings in the Sermon on the Mount.[400] For example, Christ's words, "Resist not evil", that is, not to return anger for anger is a good policy and denotes true morality.[401] And we are safe in taking the teachings of the Sermon on the Mount as a guide.[402] Thus, a Christian is the one who feels and follows the Sermon on the Mount[403] and any man who truly realised the truth of the Sermon on the Mount would be perfect, and become a god immediately.[404] On the other hand, the miracles of Christ failed to impress Vivekananda. He says: "Miracles I do not know nor understand."[405] "I look upon miracles as the greatest stumbling-

---

388 *CWSV*. 8: 217; 9: 455.

389 *CWSV*. 8: 217.

390 *CWSV*. 4: 198.

391 *CWSV*. 4:140-142.

392 *CWSV*. 7:16-17.

393 *The Life*. 2 :523.

394 *CWSV*. 6: 114.

395 *CWSV*. 9: 527.

396 *CWSV*. 8: 18.

397 *Mathew*. 11:28.

398 *CWSV*. 2: 123, 126-127.

399 *CWSV*. 4:124.

400 *CWSV*. 6: 374; 7:15.

401 *CWSV*. 6: 136.

402 *CWSV*. 1: 328.

403 *CWSV*. 4:25-26.

404 *CWSV*. 2:164.

405 *CWSV*. 5:53.

blocks in the way of truth."[406] He thus preferred the spiritual power of Christ than miracles and says: "The great strength of Christ is not in His miracles or His healing... but the wonderful powers of the Spirit which makes man free, gives him control over the whole of nature, takes from him the badge of slavery, and shows God unto him."[407] Further Vivekananda views Jesus as a disembodied, unfettered and unbound spirit;[408] Christ "...was a soul! Nothing but a soul – just working a body for the good of humanity; and that was all his relation to the body."[409] Thus he denies the literal crucifixion of Christ, they could not kill Christ; and what was crucified was a semblance, a mirage of Christ and crucifixion was a mere *līlā* or play.[410] Moreover he says that "...to be great a man need no necessarily be murdered."[411] He also did not accept the resurrection of Christ in the literal sense.[412]

Further, as an *Advaitin*, Christ for Vivekananda is an eternal universal spiritual principle, uncreated and always existing.[413] Thus, his basic conviction that Christ is a principle, makes him to give little interest concerning the historic personality of Jesus Christ.[414] In fact, he doubted the very existence of historical Jesus,[415] as there is a great dispute as to whether there ever was a man born with the name, 'Jesus'.[416] Moreover there is lack of data on Jesus' historicity.[417] Thus he says: "I am inclined to think Christ never existed."[418] As a result he admired Christ, the spiritual principle, not the historical Jesus, for he says: "It does not matter at all, whether the New Testament was written within five hundred years of his birth, nor does it matter even, how much of that life is true. But there is something behind it, something we want to imitate…there must have been a nucleus, a tremendous power that came down, a marvellous manifestation of spiritual power – and of that we are speaking. It stands there."[419]

---

[406] *CWSV*. 1: 328.

[407] *CWSV*. 4: 32-33.

[408] *CWSV*. 4:145.

[409] *CWSV*. 4:145.

[410] *CWSV*. 1: 328; 8: 190, 262.

[411] *CWSV*. 2:114.

[412] *CWSV*. 9: 379.

[413] *CWSV*. 6: 8.

[414] *cf. CWSV*. 3: 182-184, 280, 412; 4:150-151.

[415] *CWSV*. 5: 348; 6: 346; 9: 354, 378.

[416] *CWSV*. 7:370.

[417] *CWSV*. 7:370.

[418] *CWSV*. 9: 377.

[419] *CWSV*. 4: 146.

Vivekananda was aware of the denominational versions of Christ, for he says: "All Christians believe in Christ; but think, how many different explanations they have of him. Each church sees him in a different light, from different standpoints....Each sect is bound to see him in its own way."[420] However, he did not subscribe to any of the versions of Christ by the different denominations of Christianity.[421] Rather, he ignored the traditional doctrines of Orthodox Christianity on the person and work of Christ and interpreted it in an *Advaita Vedāntic* perspective by emphasising direct experience of Christ. He says: "With us realisation is religion, not doctrine."[422] "If one feels like Christ, he will be a Christ... neither things written in books, nor intellectual convictions are the proofs for Christ or God; but realisation is the proof."[423] Therefore, he rejected the doctrine of atonement; and to him, the idea of salvation by the blood of Jesus was unacceptable and distortionable.[424] Further, he considered it as absurd to depend on the work of a single *avatāra* like Christ for the rescue of humankind,[425] for he says: "It is blasphemy to think that if Jesus had never been born, humanity would not have been saved."[426]

Further, Vivekananda separated Christ from Western colonial Christianity and considered Jesus as "the true son of the Orient"[427] and he calls Christ as "an Oriental of Orientals."[428] So according to him, the East can understand Christ better than the West.[429] Thus he looks at Christ as an Oriental and declares: "If I, as an Oriental, have to worship Jesus of Nazareth, there is only one way left to me, that is to worship him as God and nothing else."[430] Because 'Christ was God incarnate'[431] and represents God Himself in the form of man.[432]

Unlike the materialistic West, Vivekananda was deeply impressed by the spirit of renunciation in the life and work of Jesus Christ.[433] He said: "Christ

---

[420] *CWSV*. 4: 51-52.

[421] *cf. CWSV*. 4: 43, 51-52; 7:4.

[422] *CWSV*. 9: 279; 6: 98-99.

[423] *CWSV*. 2: 307-308.

[424] *CWSV*. 8: 209. *cf.* 7:71-72.

[425] Olav Hammer, ed., *Alternative Christs* (Cambridge: Cambridge University Press, 2009), 157.

[426] *CWSV*. 7: 78.

[427] *CWSV*. 4:144.

[428] *CWSV*. 4:142.

[429] *CWSV*. 1: 323; 4:142; 5: 453-454.

[430] *CWSV*. 4:147. *cf.* 8:190.

[431] *CWSV*. 1: 328.

[432] *CWSV*. 4:29.

[433] S. J. Samartha, op.cit., 50-51.

was a Sannyâsin, and his religion is essentially fit for Sannyasins only."[434] Jesus had "...no faith in this evanescent world and all its belongings."[435] Christ had nowhere to lay his head.[436] He taught to renounce this world and its enjoyments.[437] So the central message of Christ for Vivekananda is renunciation- "Give up."[438] To give up the material pleasures of the world.

Christ is also described by Vivekananda as an incarnation/manifestation, who reveals God, the Absolute. For him, God, the Absolute cannot be known directly, but through the manifestations/incarnations like Christ.[439] He says: "Christ, the special manifestation of the Absolute, is known and knowable. The absolute cannot be known: we cannot know the Father, only the Son."[440]

Thus Swami Vivekananda acknowledges Jesus Christ as an incarnation,[441] one of the most perfect manifestations of the eternal Self.[442] However he says it is a mistake to think that Christ is the only one incarnation,[443] as incarnations cannot be limited into one or two; but is unlimited.[444] He says: "Let us, therefore, find God not only in Jesus of Nazareth but in all the great ones that have preceded him, in all that came after him, and all that are yet to come. Our worship is unbounded and free. They are all manifestations of the same Infinite God…."[445] So Jesus is considered alongside with others and regarded as one among the many as 'it is the same God who became Christ, Krishna and Buddha.'[446] Thus there are many waves in the spiritual ocean and Jesus is one of such a wave.[447] Therefore he declares: "The divine ones of God are all my Masters. I learn of your Christ in learning of Krishna, of Buddha, in learning of Mohamet."[448] Because names do not make much difference, for an *Advaitin* like Vivekananda.[449] This acceptance of plurality of incarnations, is a denial of the missionary claims about Jesus as the 'only one incarnation'.

---

[434] *CWSV*. 6:109.

[435] *CWSV*. 4:144.

[436] *CWSV*. 8: 213.

[437] *CWSV*. 9: 121.

[438] *CWSV*. 2: 100; 4:149, 183-184; 6: 109.

[439] *CWSV*. 7:3; 8:190.

[440] *CWSV*. 7: 3. *cf. John*. 1:18; 6: 46.

[441] *CWSV*. 7:4.

[442] *CWSV*. 3: 9.

[443] *CWSV*. 4:150-151.

[444] *CWSV*. 4: 95; 9: 223.

[445] *CWSV*. 4:152.

[446] *CWSV*. 1: 414.

[447] *CWSV*. 6:134; 8:179, 180-181; 9: 271.

[448] *CWSV*. 9: 471.

[449] *CWSV*. 9: 121.

While discussing about incarnations, Vivekananda very often spoke about Christ along with Buddha and placed Christ next to Buddha.[450] Buddha and Christ are the two biggest "bubbles" the world has produced until now.[451] So Vivekananda sees many similarities between Buddha and Christ.[452] Moreover he says: "...the same soul who came as Buddha came afterwards as Christ."[453] And he traces back the very teachings of Christ to those of Buddha.[454]

Vivekananda thus in accordance with the Indian tradition admits the doctrine of pre-existence and reincarnation of souls and uses the Hindu theory of *karma* and *saṃsāra* in explaining the person of Jesus.[455] For him, Jesus believed in reincarnation of souls.[456] Moreover, Jesus Christ was a pre-existent soul, because Jesus says, "Before Abraham was, I am."[457] However, Jesus of Nazareth was a free spirit and he took the human form, not by the compulsion of his past actions, but just to do good to mankind.[458] So Christ was the result of his previous work; Jesus worked hard for ages in previous births as a preparation to become Christ.[459] He thus says, "Such a gigantic will as that of ...Jesus could not be obtained in one life," for his father was only a carpenter, hence Joseph the carpenter according to Vivekananda, cannot produce the gigantic personality of Jesus. Therefore he asks: "How do you explain the gulf between the carpenter and his son….It cannot be solved by the theory of heredity."[460] Hence for Vivekananda, the gigantic will of Jesus came through the accumulation of power through ages and ages, continually growing bigger and bigger, until it burst on society as Jesus.[461]

So Vivekananda explains Christ, the perfect man as the result of evolution. God, the cosmic intelligence gets involved in the process of evolution and in Christ this cycle of evolution becomes complete; hence Christ, the perfect man is the final product of this evolution.[462] It takes thousands of years and when intelligence is perfect, we get the Incarnation – the Christ.[463] And in this perfect

[450] *CWSV*. 7: 22, 77-78. *cf.* 7: 78; 8:28, 105.

[451] *CWSV*. 7:7.

[452] *CWSV*. 2: 510.

[453] *CWSV*. 9: 412. *cf.* 8:180.

[454] *CWSV*. 2: 510.

[455] *CWSV*. 2: 36; 5: 313.

[456] *CWSV*. 1: 319, 321, 491; 4: 264.

[457] *CWSV*. 1:321. *cf. John*. 8: 58.

[458] *CWSV*. 5: 285-286.

[459] *CWSV*. 4:230. *cf.* 4:139. 8: 136, 184.

[460] *CWSV*. 1: 30-31.

[461] *CWSV*. 1: 30-31.

[462] *CWSV*. 2: 209-210; 3:8-9.

[463] *CWSV*. 8: 136; 6: 128.

man, elements of philosophy, mysticism, emotion, and of work will be equally present in full.[464]

As an *Advaita Vedāntin*, Vivekananda used the *Advaitic* framework and understood Christ as the name of a certain state of realization.[465] Christ represents a stage, the highest stage of human glory demonstrating the science of "evolving a God out of the material man,"[466] the process of unfolding of the potentialities which are enfolded within.[467] Jesus had our nature and was a *bhakta* but he became Christ.[468] Jesus attained to that stage of Christhood by prayer.[469] He says: "Jesus of Nazareth goes into his transfiguration, and when he comes out, he has become Jesus the Christ."[470] Thus "When a man has reached that perfect state, he is of the same nature as the Personal God. "I and my Father are one." He knows that he is one with Brahman, the Absolute, and projects himself as the Personal God does."[471] Thus the words of Jesus were the fruit of realization[472] for Vivekananda and this realization of Christhood by Jesus is taken as a model by him for all to become the same.[473] Because Christ, The Messenger came to show the path,[474] "Christ would show us the way to become perfect. God became Christ to show man his true nature, that we too are God."[475] He thus says: "Jesus had our nature; he became the Christ; so can we, and so *must* we."[476] He continues: "Be not an imitation of Jesus, but be Jesus! You are quite as great as Jesus.... If we are not... we must struggle and be."[477] Because for Vivekananda, Christ's prayer was: "Father, just as I am one with you, so make them all one with me."[478] Thus we all are equal to Christ[479] "... as the divine Man, Christ and we are one."[480] Besides all these

---

[464] *CWSV*. 2:388.

[465] *CWSV*. 8:105.

[466] *CWSV*. 1:18.

[467] K. P. Aleaz, *Jesus in Neo-Vedanta*, op.cit., 206.

[468] *CWSV*. 1: 55; 7:29. *cf.* 1:185.

[469] *CWSV*. 1: 55, 303; 4:213.

[470] *CWSV*. 4:213.

[471] *CWSV*. 5: 266. *cf.* 8: 255.

[472] *CWSV*. 2:44.

[473] He says: The "...great ones, they manifest themselves in our souls, and they make us like unto them. Our whole nature changes, and we become like them." *CWSV*. 4:32.

[474] *CWSV*. 4:148.

[475] *CWSV*. 7: 4. *cf.* 4:145-146.

[476] *CWSV*. 7:29. *cf.* 1:185, 303; 4: 134; 8: 17-18.

[477] *CWSV*. 1: 483. *cf.* 2:307.

[478] *CWSV* 1: 381.

[479] *CWSV*. 7: 89. *cf.* 2: 307-308.

[480] *CWSV* 7: 4.

interpretations, one can understand that Vivekananda himself had this Christ-experience and identifies himself with Jesus, for he says: "I lived in Jesus of Nazareth...."[481] And "I was Jesus ...."[482] In this relation, it must be remembered that many in the West felt him as a Christ-like man,[483] "as if Christ himself... in their midst,"[484] and they approached him as if they were going to Christ.[485]

Above all, Vivekananda understood Christ from an *Advaita Vedāntic* framework[486] and attempted to construct a 'Hindu Christ.'[487] For example, the sayings of Jesus such as "The Kingdom of Heaven is within you" (Luke. 17:21), "Blessed are the poor in the heart, for they shall see God" (Mathew. 5:8) and "I and my Father are one." (John 10: 30) were interpreted by Vivekananda with the *Advaita Vedāntic* principle of realization and inwardness.[488] He thus considered Jesus as an *Advaitin*,[489] a non-dualist.[490] For him, Christ took his teachings from the *Vedas*,[491] and the teachings of the *Vedas* are identical with the teachings of Christ.[492] However according to Vivekananda, Christ taught three stages of religion,[493] depended on the level of his hearers;[494] but Christ was essentially an *Advaitin* and intended through all his teachings to lead his hearers to the last and highest stage of union -'I and my Father are One.'[495] Hence "...there is very little difference between the pure religion of Christ and that of the [*Advaita*] Vedanta."[496] Further as an *Advaitin*, everything was Christ

---

[481] *CWSV*. 2: 469.

[482] *CWSV*. 8: 505. *cf.* 7: 78.

[483] *New Discoveries*. 5:74, 159.

[484] *The Life*. 2:504.

[485] Tony Mathew, *Vivekananda Prasnothari* (Mal.) (Kottayam: Current Books, 2004), 29, 32.

[486] S. J. Samartha, op.cit., 52; K. P. Aleaz, *Harmony of Religions*, op.cit., 218-219.

[487] *CWSV*. 8: 219.

[488] *cf. CWSV*. 1: 324, 327; 2: 148; 4: 145-146, 149, 246; 8: 8.

[489] K. P. Aleaz, *Jesus in Neo-Vedanta*, op.cit., 55; P. S. Daniel, op.cit., 170; S. J. Samartha, op.cit., 55.

[490] *CWSV*. 2: 143.

[491] *CWSV*. 5: 453-454.

[492] *CWSV*. 9: 447.

[493] "To the masses who could not conceive of anything higher than a personal God, he said, 'pray to your Father in heaven'. To others who could grasp a higher idea, 'I am the vine, ye are the branches', but to his disciples whom he revealed himself more fully, he proclaimed the highest truth, 'I and my Father are one'." *CWSV*. 2:143.

[494] *CWSV*. 2: 142-143, 351; 4: 144; 8: 6.

[495] *CWSV*. 4:148.

[496] *CWSV*. 2: 353.

for Vivekananda[497] even the worm,[498] and the evils.[499] In all these interpretations of Christ by Vivekananda, it is clear that, he has totally rejected the Orthodox theological framework of Western Christianity and separated Christ from it and attempted to understand Christ as an Oriental and hence purely by using the concepts of Indian tradition and *Advaita Vedāntic* framework.

4.7. Mahatma Gandhi and Christ

Gandhi spoke of Christ authentically and as a national leader of India his observations on Christ became world-famous.[500] The moral and political application of non-violent strategies drew Gandhi to Christ.[501] The rich and radiant personality of Jesus cast a fascinating spell over Gandhi,[502] for he said; "My regard for the life of Jesus is indeed very great. His ethical teaching, his common sense, his sacrifice command my reverence."[503] Moreover he says: Jesus 'affects my life'[504] and 'occupies in my heart.'[505] Thus Jesus, for Gandhi was 'the greatest teacher'[506] and 'the highest example'[507] with 'considerable influence'[508] on his life. Gandhi aspired to be equal in love with Christ in his very life.[509] He was thus able to carry the spirit of Christ into the thoughts and feelings of Indian people.[510] To the Hindus, he said: "...your lives will be incomplete unless you reverently study the teaching of Jesus."[511] Because for Gandhi, Christ is 'the greatest source of spiritual strength that man has ever known'[512] and the world became rich from Jesus' life and it had great influence on generations.[513]

---

[497] *CWSV*. 7: 89.

[498] *CWSV*. 7: 7.

[499] *CWSV*. 2: 34.

[500] P. V. George, *The Unique Christ and the Mystic Gandhi* (Thiruvalla: The Malabar Christian Office, 1934), 15-16.

[501] Ignatius Jesudasan, *A Gandhian Theology of Liberation* (Anand: Gujarat Sahitya Prakash, 1987), 289.

[502] Gandhi, *The Message of Jesus Christ*, op.cit., Preface.

[503] *CWMG*. 25:85.

[504] *CWMG*. 62:334.

[505] Gandhi, *The Spirit of Hinduism*, op.cit., 29.

[506] *CWMG*. 75:69.

[507] *CWMG*. 75:69.

[508] Gandhi, *The Spirit of Hinduism*, op.cit., 29.

[509] *CWMG*. 19:179.

[510] Nirmal Minz, op.cit., 101.

[511] *CWMG*. 35:343.

[512] *CWMG*. 75:69.

[513] *Mahatma*. 1:196.

For Gandhi, "Jesus was an Asiatic"[514] as Jesus came from the East.[515] Christ's life was of self sacrifice and renunciation,[516] and he had attained self-realization.[517] He, thus distinguished Jesus' teachings from Western civilization and said: "Confuse not Jesus' teachings with what passes as modern civilization."[518] Further Gandhi separated Christ from the later developments of Christianity in the West;[519] because for him, Jesus preached "not a new religion, but a new life."[520] Moreover, Gandhi observed, if Jesus was living in the flesh, he would not approve many of the things done in the modern Western Christianity, as it negated Christ.[521] Hence, Gandhi liberated Christ from the hold of Orthodox Christianity and declared, Jesus belonged "not solely to Christianity, but to the entire world; to all races and people."[522] And Christ's influence is universal, as "The lives of all have, in some greater or lesser degree, been changed by His presence, His actions, and the words spoken by His divine voice."[523] Thus there was no need for Gandhi to join the Orthodox Christianity, "...to be a believer in the beauty of the teachings of Jesus or try to follow his example."[524] Rather for Gandhi 'to be a good Hindu also meant a good Christian,'[525] because he was confident that"…Jesus would own me as a true Christian."[526]

On the other hand, Gandhi was confused of different denominational versions of Christianity on Christ. He says: "... my difficulty is fundamental. Which Jesus am I to believe? Him of your conception or mine? You will say, 'Jesus of the Bible'. Then the question is: 'According to whose interpretation?' I solve the difficulty by going the way God takes me."[527] Thus he did not subscribe to anyone version as true and did not accept the traditional doctrines

---

[514] *Harijan*, 07.09.1947. *cf. CWMG*. 35:326, 328.

[515] *Harijan*, 20.04.1947.

[516] *CWMG*. 35:250.

[517] *CWMG*. 14: 133.

[518] *CWMG*. 35:250.

[519] S. J. Samartha, op.cit., 84-85.

[520] *CWMG*. 100: 341.

[521] *CWMG*. 21:169.

[522] *The Modern Review*, October, 1941, cited by Robert Ellsberg, op.cit., 28; *CWMG*. 75:70.

[523] *CWMG*. 75:70.

[524] *Harijan*, 14.10.1939.

[525] *Harijan*, 14.10.1939.

[526] *CWMG*. 86:22.

[527] *CWMG*. 61:181.

of Christianity concerning Christ.[528] Because for Gandhi, Christ-like life was more important than belief in certain doctrines, for he said: "It is not he who says "Lord, Lord" that is a Christian, but "He that doeth the will of the Lord" that is a true Christian."[529]

Gandhi thus did not take the 'Immaculate Conception' (virgin birth) of Jesus literally.[530] Gandhi also did not believe in the so-called miracles of Jesus, as they were against 'natural laws.'[531] He said: "I do not need either the prophecies or the miracles to establish Jesus's greatness as a teacher."[532] The second coming of Christ was not taken that seriously by Gandhi.[533] He interpreted the Cross and Resurrection in symbolic and metaphorical language.[534] He thus said:

> God did not bear the Cross only 1,900 years ago, but He bears it today, and He dies and is resurrected from day to day. It would be poor comfort to the world if it had to depend upon a historical God who died 2,000 years ago. Do not then preach the God of history, but show Him as He lives today through you.[535]

Gandhi did not approve the Christian belief in the theory about the atoning death of Christ.[536] He says: "My reason was not ready to believe literally that Jesus by his death and by his blood redeemed the sins of the world."[537] "I do not believe in the doctrine of appropriation of another's merit. His sacrifice is a type and an example for us. Every one of us has to be "crucified" for salvation."[538] Hence Gandhi could only accept Jesus' death on the cross as an example of love, but not as a substitute for the sins of the world as there was nothing like "a mysterious or miraculous virtue in it."[539]

---

[528] *CWMG*. 34:10; Balwant A. M. Paradkar, "Hindu Interpretation of Christ from Vivekananda to Radhakrishnan," *The Indian Journal of Theology* 18/1 (January-March, 1969): 71. For example, he did not accept Virgin birth, prophecies, miracles, resurrection, second coming, Jesus as the only way of salvation, Jesus is God, Jesus as the only begotten Son of God, etc.

[529] *CWMG*. 61:47; *Harijan*, 25.05.1935.

[530] Gandhi, *The Spirit of Hinduism*, op.cit., 35.

[531] *CWMG*. 65:82; Gandhi, *The Message of Jesus Christ,* op.cit., 73.

[532] *Harijan*, 17.04.1937. *cf. CWMG*. 52: 56; 62: 333.

[533] *CWMG*. 14: 139.

[534] Nirmal Minz, op.cit., 40; Ravi Tiwari, *Reflections and Studies in Religion* (Delhi: ISPCK, 2008), 122.

[535] *CWMG*. 34:261.

[536] S. J. Samartha, op.cit., 95.

[537] *An Autobiography*, 126.

[538] *CWMG*. 25:85.

[539] *An Autobiography*, 126.

Further he said: "I do not accept the orthodox teaching that Jesus was or is God incarnate in the accepted sense or that he was or is the only son of God."[540] So Gandhi did not take the text in John 3: 16, that "Jesus is the only begotten son of God" as literally true.[541] Thus he did not regard Jesus as the only begotten son of God,[542] because God cannot be the exclusive father of Jesus,[543] as metaphorically we are all begotten sons of God.[544] Moreover "If God could have sons, all of us were His sons."[545] So the epithet 'only begotten son' in its material interpretation was quite unacceptable[546] for him as it was against his reason to believe that God can marry and beget children.[547] Hence the word 'son' for Gandhi is figurative, not literal;[548] the adjective 'begotten' implied spiritual birth for Gandhi[549] and not a physical event.[550] However, Gandhi recognised Jesus as the Son of God, in the sense that, Jesus was near to God; and he expressed, as no other could, the spirit and will of God in his own life.[551]

Nevertheless, Gandhi was not able to give the 'higher place' for Jesus as Christians gave.[552] He explicitly said: "I consider Christ as one of the great teachers of the world. Beyond that I have not gone…."[553]

> I consider him as an incarnation in the Hindu sense of the term. I do not believe him to be the World Saviour in the sense which orthodox Christianity understands the expression, but he was a saviour in the same sense as Buddha, Zoroaster, Mohammed, and many other teachers were. In other words, I do not believe in the exclusive divinity of Jesus.[554]

---

540 *CWMG*. 25:85.

541 *Harijan*, 06.03.1937.

542 *CWMG*. 65:82.

543 *Harijan*, 06.03.1937.

544 *CWMG*. 65:82.

545 *An Autobiography*, 126.

546 *CWMG*. 65:82.

547 *CWMG*. 64:398.

548 *CWMG*. 64:398.

549 *CWMG*. 62:334.

550 Nirmal Minz, op.cit., 43.

551 *CWMG*. 75:69.

552 Gandhi, *The Message of Jesus Christ*, op.cit., 41-42.

553 *CWMG*. 40:315.

554 *CWMG*. 15:304-305.

Hence Gandhi paid equal homage to Jesus along with other prophets and incarnations[555] as they were all equally 'divine' for him.[556] He says:

> In spite of most devout attention to every word ascribed to Jesus in the New Testament, and in spite of my having read in a humble spirit all about Jesus, I have really not seen any fundamental distinction between Jesus and other teachers I can understand and appreciate.[557]

Because as an *Advaitin*, Gandhi saw no distinctions between Christ and other incarnations, as "the names Rama and Krishna signify the same as Jesus,"[558] for Gandhi.

Moreover Gandhi saw Jesus as a human being, who became Divine by perfecting himself. He says: "I regard Jesus as a human being...."[559] "The gentle figure of Christ, so patient, so kind, so loving, so full of forgiveness that he taught his followers not to retaliate when abused or struck, but to turn the other cheek – I thought it was a beautiful example of the perfect man."[560] But not "the most perfect man ever born."[561] Because for Gandhi, "God alone is absolutely perfect" and Jesus came near to perfection as possible for a human being, however, Jesus is not perfect as God.[562] On the other hand, Gandhi considered Jesus as an example of the flowering of the spark of divinity within man.[563] Thus "... we can all become...as Jesus was."[564] Because as Jesus is a son of God,[565] "...every one of us is a son of God and capable of doing what Jesus did, if we but endeavour to express the Divine in us."[566]

Unlike in the West, the historicity of Jesus Christ had no special significance to Gandhi. On this point he wrote: "…I have never been interested

---

[555] *CWMG*. 31:420.

[556] M. K. Gandhi, *What Jesus Means to Me* (Ahmedabad: Navajivan Publishing House, 2009), 8. Gandhi does not deny divine self-disclosure in the person and self-understanding of Jesus. What he denies is the exclusive unicity or exclusive uniqueness of that self-disclosure in Jesus. Jesus is also a self-disclosure of God, not the only self-disclosure. Ignatius Jesudasan, *A Gandhian Theology of Liberation*, op.cit., 291.

[557] Gandhi, *The Message of Jesus Christ*, op.cit., 22.

[558] Ibid., 21.

[559] *CWMG*. 34:10.

[560] Gandhi, *The Message of Jesus Christ*, op.cit., 23.

[561] *An Autobiography*, 126.

[562] *CWMG*. 65:82.

[563] *CWMG*. 75:70.

[564] *CWMG*. 29: 454.

[565] *CWMG*. 72:297-298.

[566] *Harijan*, 04.08.1940.

in a historical Jesus."[567] "I do not know the Jesus of history."[568] However, he considered Jesus as a historical person,[569] but said, we do not know the whole life of Jesus,[570] as there are less data on him,[571] apart from what is given in the four Gospels of the New Testament.[572] However, Jesus for Gandhi was truer than history[573] and even if the person Jesus never lived, still the Sermon on the Mount was true for him.[574] Further, Gandhi preferred 'Christ of imagination'[575] than 'Jesus of history'[576] and experienced Christ as 'divine presence.' He says: "If you mean the historic Jesus, then I do not feel his presence. But if you mean a spirit guiding me, a presence nearer to me than hands and feet, than the very breath in me, then I do feel such a presence."[577] Thus Gandhi understood 'Christ' as a common name, not limited to any single historical person, so any teacher who has attained to complete purity and sinlessness can be called as Christ; he also considered Truth, the only infallible teacher and guide, as Christ.[578] Therefore Christ is an adjective signifying one of the names of God, as God has one thousand names to denote Him.[579]

Finally the two things most impressed Gandhi in relation to Christ as a teacher, was the Sermon on the Mount and Jesus' example of suffering death on the cross.[580] For him, "The message of Jesus ... is contained in his Sermon on the Mount unadulterated and taken as a whole."[581] And it is that Sermon which has endeared Jesus to him.[582] Further Gandhi could see *ahiṃsā*; the permanent aspect of ancient Indian tradition present in the teachings of Jesus as seen in the Sermon.[583] So for Gandhi, Christ represented the principle of non-

---

[567] *Young India*, 31.12.1931.

[568] *CWMG*. 36:40.

[569] *CWMG*. 58:402.

[570] *CWMG*. 64: 224-225.

[571] *CWMG*. 64:398-399.

[572] *CWMG*. 40:315.

[573] *Mahatma*. 7: 233.

[574] *Young India*, 31.12.1931.

[575] Gandhi, *All Religions Are True*, op.cit., 65.

[576] *CWMG*. 57:406.

[577] Cited by S. K. George, *Gandhi's Challenge to Christianity* (Ahmedabad: Navajivan Publishing House, 1947), 8. *cf. Young India*, 06.08.1925.

[578] *CWMG*. 31:420; 57:327.

[579] *Young India*, 06.08.1925.

[580] In an article entitled, *The Jesus I love*, he wrote that what impressed him most in Jesus Christ's life and teaching was 'the almost new law that He gave' and the stress on non-retaliation which Christ exemplified in his own life and death. *Young India*, 31.12.1931.

[581] *CWMG*. 100: 152-153.

[582] *CWMG*. 48:438.

[583] *CWMG*. 9:243; R. K. Prabhu & U. R. Rao, *The Mind of Mahatma Gandhi*, op.cit., 91.

violence,[584] which is the purest form of soul force.[585] Christ was strong with his soul-force of non-violence;[586] he stood for non-co-operation with corrupt authorities and struggled against the evils of his times such as hypocrisy, pride and lying and sought to banish corruption from temple and society.[587] Christ uncompromisingly challenged the might of the Sadducees, Pharisees and the Roman Empire.[588] So Gandhi detects no passivity, no weakness about Jesus; rather he finds Jesus as the bravest individual[589] and "the most active resister" in history.[590] Thus Gandhi calls Jesus Christ as a "Heroic satyagrahi,"[591] "a prince among politicians."[592] This anti-colonial nature of Jesus inspired Gandhi to fight against British raj through *satyāgraha*.

Further for Gandhi, Jesus was truly non-violent. He overcame evil with good, hatred by love. Jesus preferred gentleness,[593] forgiveness and love and not vengeance and hatred;[594] he did not support the use of sword.[595] Gandhi says:

> He who when being killed bears no anger against his murderer and even asks God to forgive him is truly non-violent. History relates this of Jesus Christ. With his dying breath on the cross, he is reported to have said: "Father, forgive them for they know not what they do.[596]

Nevertheless, Gandhi saw Jesus' death on Calvary as a victory over the might of a whole Empire,[597] that by his death his teaching spread far and wide[598] and his influence became greater after his death.[599] He asks: "What did it matter if the body was dissolved in the process, so long as by Christ's act of

---

[584] *Young India*, 31.12.1931.

[585] *CWMG*. 9:243.

[586] *Mahatma*. 8:280.

[587] *CWMG*. 19:179; 23: 105; 54: 50.

[588] *CWMG*. 23:104, 105; 18: 115, 126.

[589] *CWMG*. 90:129-130.

[590] *CWMG*. 84: 372.

[591] *CWMG*. 18: 126.

[592] *CWMG*. 18: 196.

[593] *CWMG*. 17:408.

[594] *CWMG*. 16: 313.

[595] *Harijan*, 14.04.1946.

[596] *Harijan*, 28.04.1946. *cf. Luke*. 23: 34.

[597] *CWMG*. 17:408; 20: 284.

[598] *CWMG*. 66: 432.

[599] *CWMG*. 77: 325.

non-resistance, the forces of good were released in society?[600] Hence, Christ gained life by losing it.[601]

Hence Jesus' suffering and death on the Cross had a lasting impact on Gandhi.[602] He says: "I saw in the Vatican art collection a statue of Christ on the Cross which simply captured me and kept me spell-bound."[603] Gandhi was thus influenced by Christ in his definition of the concept of non-violence for he says,

> ...the example of Jesus' suffering is a factor in the composition of my undying faith in non-violence which rules all my actions, worldly and temporal.... Jesus lived and died in vain if he did not teach us to regulate the whole of life by the eternal Law of Love.[604]

And "...if I raise resistances of a non-violent character I simply and humbly follow in the footsteps of the great teachers" like Christ.[605] Thus Gandhi gave so much importance for the cross-experience of Christ. In the hard days of freedom struggle, Jesus was a fountain of strength and inspiration to Gandhi,[606] as Jesus and his teachings became an important source of his philosophy of *satyāgraha*.[607]

Hence Gandhi brought a deeper meaning to the suffering figure of Christ on the cross and gave a 'universal meaning' to the cross and did not accept the narrow interpretation of the cross by Orthodox Christianity.[608] For him, cross is not an event of past history, but happening in the day today lives of individuals and nations.[609] He says: "Christ is daily manifested through suffering."[610] "... Living Christ means a living Cross, without it life is a living death."[611] Thus Jesus' was a *yajña* on the cross, i.e., laying down his life for true welfare.[612] That "The love that Jesus taught and practised was not a mere personal virtue, but that it was essentially a social and collective virtue."[613]

---

[600] *CWMG*. 89:63-64.

[601] *CWMG*. 89:63-64.

[602] Daniel Mangalath, op.cit., 30.

[603] *CWMG*. 63: 416.

[604] *Harijan*, 17.01.1939.

[605] *CWMG*. 17:408.

[606] Jaladhar Pal, op.cit., 32.

[607] Gopinath Dhawan, op.cit., 24.

[608] M. K. Gandhi, *My Dear Child* (Ahmedabad: Navajivan Publishing House, 1956), 86.

[609] *CWMG*. 34:261; 100: 231.

[610] *Harijan*, 30.03.1934.

[611] *Young India*, 31.12.1931.

[612] *CWMG*. 17: 493.

[613] *CWMG*. 68: 307.

4.8. Conclusion

The approaches of Vivekananda and Gandhi towards the Christian tradition, religions and Christ show, the Indian understanding on these issues, particularly from an *Advaita Vedāntic* perspective. Both experienced Christianity in the context of 19th century colonial India; hence the Christian civilization which came to India from the West[614] was colonial and was viewed by them as a foreign religion, alien to the soil of India. Moreover the deepest conflicts between Hinduism and Christianity were manifested in the fact that the former was *swadeshi* and the latter a *pardeshi* religion for the Hindu.[615] Vivekananda and Gandhi, thus denounced the false Western form of Christianity which they encountered with. However, it is to be noted that, even in such a colonial context, they loved and admired Christ, by separating Christ, from what they considered the Christianity. For example, Vivekananda had deep respect for Christ, but he was critical to the missionary activities and its negative impact in India.[616] Gandhi particularly noted that this form of Christianity came to India in 'a tainted form.'[617] He thus said, the missionaries "present a Christianity of their belief but not the message of Jesus,"[618] as they negated the Sermon on the Mount.[619] Gandhi too did not identify himself with the 'Orthodox Christianity'[620] as it negated 'Christ's Christianity.'[621] Gandhi thus separated Christ from Christianity, as Christ himself would not approve much of what passes as Christianity.[622] Moreover, they distinguished the true Christianity from Western cultural forms and said Indian Christianity must dissociate itself from the Western civilization, which is based on violence and materialism.[623] So the Indian understanding of Christianity suggested for a 'correction' in Western Christianity.

In relation to religions, Gandhi wilfully questioned the accepted western interpretations of the Bible based on colonial hermeneutics.[624] He, rather suggested for the re-interpretation and re-reading of the Bible by the missionaries. He especially advocated re-formulation of Christian faith in relation to other faiths. Both Gandhi and Vivekananda thus did not accept

[614] M. M. Thomas, op.cit., 243.

[615] Nirmal Minz, op.cit., 170.

[616] Sisir Kumar Das, op.cit., 140.

[617] *Harijan*, 06.03.1937.

[618] *Harijan*, 12.12.1936.

[619] *Young India*, 08.12.1927.

[620] *Young India*, 06.08.1925.

[621] *Young India*, 22.09.1921.

[622] *Young India*, 22.09.1921.

[623] M. M. Thomas, op.cit., 211.

[624] *Young India*, 11.08.1927.

the colonial missionary view that, other religions are 'false', 'non-valid' and represent 'darkness'. They especially challenged the missionary critique of Hinduism and Indian tradition. Thus they affirmed the pluralistic and inclusive tradition of *Advaita Vedānta*, which according to them, was superior but affirmed the equality of all religions. This negated the exclusive, narrow and negative views of the missionary Christianity on other religions.

Further, in their understanding of Christ, they separated Christ from the so called Christianity. Their understanding of Christ, in many respects, was different from the so called doctrines and dogmas of Western Christianity. Because in Indian minds, "...there was a conflict between the respect for Christ and antipathy to Christian missionary action."[625] One of the main causes of this hatred of Christianity and the resultant dissociation of Christ from Christianity was the wide gap between the precepts and practice of Christianity. Vivekananda and Gandhi realised that racial discrimination, the superior attitude of the White race towards the Asiatic and the African people, social, economic, and political injustices perpetuated by Christian Whites - all these did not go with the teachings of Christ.[626] For example, Gandhi made a sharp distinction between Jesus' teaching and what was followed in modern Western civilization.[627] His *swadeshi* principle also forced him to reject the formal foreign religion and to accept Hinduism as his and his countrymen's faith.[628] Hence, Gandhi and Vivekananda stood firmly within their own Indian religious and philosophical heritage and their understanding and interpretation of Christianity and Christ was from within the Indian *Advaitic* tradition. Nevertheless, Gandhi drew inspiration for his understanding of Christianity and Christ from Tolstoy and others, who held a vision of reality similar to that of the Hindus.

Vivekananda and Gandhi were sceptical of Western Christianity's presentation of Christ and were selective in their understanding of Christ, because the Western missionaries, as the primary transmitters of Christianity, left behind a Western image of Jesus. Vivekananda and Gandhi, therefore, sought an Indian understanding of Jesus by employing new interpretative resources, cultural symbols, and thought patterns from India, in order to domesticate Jesus in India and to reclaim the 'Asiatic Christ'. Hence, they separated Christ from Western Christianity and understood/experienced Christ as an Asian/ Indian from an *Advaitic* (metaphysical and ethical) perspective. They, thus re-interpreted Christ in line with Indian tradition. For example, Gandhi expressed

---

[625] Sisir Kumar Das, op.cit., 40.

[626] Nirmal Minz, op.cit., 166.

[627] Ibid., 41.

[628] Ibid., 80.

the view that the message of Jesus of Nazareth was little understood in the West, and it was time that light upon it has to be thrown from the East.[629]

They, thus had soon noticed that there was ample room for Christ in Hinduism, in its philosophic-religious structure.[630] This Indian response to Christ was to interpret Christ in an entirely new way.[631] It may be that the *Advaita Vedānta* provides a better method for the study of the message of Christ than Western philosophical frameworks.[632] For example, Vivekananda made a sharp distinction between the Asiatic and European approaches to life and emphasized on the Oriental feature of the Christ figure. This orientalization of Christ attains deeper dimensions in the *Advaita Vedāntic* attempt to make out of Christ a mystic of the *Sanātana Dharma*, a true *Advaitic Yōgi*. By this Christ is not only just oriental, but also properly Indian, or more precisely, "Hindu". Vivekananda, thus sees Christ as an *Advaitin* who realised his essential oneness with God. Christ is, thus, an example for the realisation of man's essential divinity.[633]

Gandhi, too, is prepared to consider Jesus Christ as one of the many teachers and prophets of mankind, and even as one of the many names and incarnations of God, but without giving credit to his exclusive divinity, his atoning deed or his mediation between God and mankind as understood by Orthodox Christianity.[634] According to Gandhi, these teachings of Christianity concerning Jesus Christ contradicted the law of reason, natural law, and the rules of logic; and therefore, he rejected the Orthodox Christian doctrines.[635] On the other hand, Christ is the 'Prince of *Satyāgrahis*' in Gandhi's view.[636] *Satyāgraha* led Jesus Christ to the cross which is the supreme manifestation of *ahiṃsā*.[637] So, in these attempts of Indian interpretation of Christ, Vivekananda and Gandhi were able to trace out and recover some aspects of Jesus not seen in the Western traditional history of Christianity. They held, in fact, that Western culture was not quite congenial to Christianity, and that Christianity had lost

---

[629] Ibid., 168.

[630] *Harijan*, 30.01.1937.

[631] Carl Keller, "The Vedanta Philosophy and The Message of Christ," *The International Review of Missions* 42/168 (October, 1953): 383.

[632] Ibid., 384.

[633] Mathew Vekathanam, *Indian Christology Perspectives and Challenges* (Bangalore: Asian Trading Corporation, 2004), 277.

[634] M. M. Thomas, op.cit., 204.

[635] Nirmal Minz, op.cit., 67.

[636] Ibid., 199.

[637] Ibid., 191-192.

some of its cardinal points while moving through the Western world. These lost values, they argued, must be regained through Indian tradition.[638]

As the Western Christianity was dogmatic; it gave importance to some intellectual belief in certain doctrines and dogmas, while Indian understanding is to realize/experience Christ as a living reality/presence. While Christian missionaries wanted to safeguard the Christian dogmas on the historicity of Jesus' life, death and resurrection; for the Hindu leaders, on the other hand, these dogmas and doctrines about Incarnation, the natures of Christ etc. were not so important, but what was important for them was the set of moral precepts to be practised by everyone that they discovered in the teachings of Christ, especially in the Sermon on the Mount.[639] For example, while the colonial Christianity ignored the 'Sermon on the Mount', it was Gandhi who unearthed it. Hence, Vivekananda and Gandhi wanted to experience Christ directly (*anubhava*), first-hand and not through the Western mediation of doctrinal/ denominational/dogmatic aspects. The Western theological and ecclesiastical traditions and cultural baggage accompanying the missionary enterprise in India were rejected by them. They wanted to free themselves from all these Western religious and cultural bondages and enter into a direct experience of the original nucleus of Christianity.[640] That was their Christ-experience. Thus, theirs was not the historic Christ, but the experiential Christ. Instead of doctrines and dogmas, Vivekananda and Gandhi made Christ-experience, the central norm of their thinking, which was in accordance with the Indian tradition of *Advaita Vedānta* and its emphasis on 'realization'.

---

[638] Ibid., 114.

[639] Thomas Mampra, "Encounter Between Hinduism and Christianity," *Journal of Dharma* 1/3 (January, 1976): 258.

[640] Nirmal Minz, op.cit., 114.

Chapter 5

Christ – Experience of Vivekananda and Gandhi as Metaphysical and Ethical

5.1. Introduction

Vivekananda and Gandhi realized that the Western Christendom, barring certain individuals was nominal, Christ-less and was devoid of Christ-experience. The church life was mechanical and their understanding of Christ meant customary belief in certain doctrines/dogmas, which were formulated in its historical evolution in relation to Aristotelian epistemology. This doctrinal approach to Christ was more of rational and intellectual, than experiential. Their epistemological tools also centred on the 'historical figure' of Jesus, rather than an active and living relation with Christ. Hence the Western Christians emphasised on the 'belief' in the person of Christ as saviour and in his atoning death on the cross, than following the moral precepts of Jesus, in their lives. The participation in certain sacraments, which became mere rituals, was also given prominence in Western churches. Furthermore, the conflicting denominational versions and the resultant debates on the person and work of Christ, also camouflaged the Western understanding of Christ. It is in this context that, we have to analyse the Indian *Advaitic* approach to Christ by Vivekananda and Gandhi and their emphasis on Christ-experience (*Kristanubhava*).

5.2. Differences between Western Christian Epistemology and Indian *Advaitic* Epistemology

Against the Western missionary presentation of a Western dogmatic Christ, both Vivekananda and Gandhi, as *Advaita Vedāntins* interpreted and understood Christ from an *Advaitic* perspective. They did not subscribe to any versions or doctrines on the person and work of Christ by the different denominations of Christianity. On the other hand, in line with the Indian tradition, they emphasised on the direct experience of Christ. For example, Vivekananda said: "With us realisation is religion, not doctrine."[1]

Hence, there are serious differences between Western Christian Epistemology and Indian *Advaitic* Epistemology in relation to Christ-experience. With the Aristotelian epistemology, which approves binaries such as body and mind, saints and sinners, God and Satan, etc. as its basic framework, the Western Christian thinking gave too much emphasis on the faculty of senses and reason, in developing and explicating the doctrines and dogmas on Christ. This Western approach tried to be "rational" and "objective" in obtaining the knowledge of Christ, and lost the "experiential" dimension, as the church life in the West denotes. They gave too much emphasis on the historicity of Christ, His atoning death on the cross and on the dualistic thinking which saw God as above in heavens and is holy; whereas man is viewed as a sinner, below on earth. Thus the Westerners made Christ as the 'Saviour' and men as 'sinners'. 'Belief' in these doctrines, was considered as essential for one's salvation, than on practising the precepts of Jesus or entering into a 'living relationship' with Christ.

In contrast to this colonial church epistemology, Vivekananda and Gandhi proposed a totally different epistemology based on *Advaita* in relation to their Christ-experience. This shows the inseparable inter-link between metaphysics and epistemology in *Advaita* methodology. For example, they recognised senses and reason as apt epistemological tools in knowing the physical realities, but in knowing the metaphysical principles or spiritual realities like Christ, they stressed the incapacity and limitations of senses and reason and suggested inspiration/intuition[2] as the apt tool, which is capable to reach and realise the metaphysical truths.[3] Hence, unlike the colonial epistemology, they gave less importance to the world of senses and reason in their epistemology in relation to spiritual truths; rather they stressed the limitations of these tools. For example, Vivekananda says, "Jnana is never sense-knowledge."[4] He too remarked about the limitation of senses and reason in knowing the religious/ spiritual truths.[5] He says: "The truths of religion, as God and Soul, cannot be perceived by the external senses. I cannot see God with my eyes, nor can I touch Him with my hands, and we also know that neither can we reason

[1] *CWSV*. 9: 279; 6: 98-99.

[2] *CWSV*. 2: 389-390; Gandhi, *God is Truth*, op.cit., 17, 19, 36, 61; *Young India*, 21.03.1929; *CWMG*. 64:398.

[3] *CWSV*. 1: 150, 181; 2: 449; 7: 60; 8: 20-21; *CWMG*. 64:398.

[4] *CWSV*. 8: 21-22.

[5] *CWSV*. 1: 150; 8: 20.

beyond the senses. Reason leaves us at a point quite indecisive ...."[6] So we need to go beyond senses and reason, for realising the metaphysical principle and spiritual truths of religion.[7]

Like Vivekananda, for Gandhi also, the spiritual truth was not to be realised by dialectical skill or conceptual cognition but by spiritual experience.[8] He states: "He [God] defies reason. But he is experienced."[9] "Reason is powerless to know Him. He is beyond the reach or grasp of reason."[10] He further continues, "There are subjects where Reason cannot take us far, and we have to accept things by faith. Faith, then, does not contradict Reason but transcends it. Faith is a kind of sixth sense which works in cases which are without the purview of Reason."[11] For Gandhi, this faith is experience.[12] He says: "Faith can be turned into knowledge by experience...."[13] Hence he says: "...I have realized through experience."[14] Gandhi, further states that this Faith, which he calls as 'intuition' is capable to know God because it is free from the limitations of senses and reason.[15]

Thus along with this emphasis on the limitation of Western epistemological tools, Vivekananda and Gandhi suggested intuition/inspiration which is called 'direct religious experience' as the only epistemological tool to know/realise the Metaphysical Reality. Hence the Indian understanding of Christ-experience, by following the *Advaitic* method, emphasised the primacy and centrality of direct experience/*anubhava*. For example, Vivekananda says: "Religion is, after all, realisation...intuitive experience. What we experience in the depths of our souls is realisation."[16] Gandhi, too, talks about this religious experience, that "Religious truth comes to us mysteriously."[17]

Hence, contrary to West, reason is not ultimate in India, but only a part of our cognitive process and subsidiary to intuition. That's why Gandhi told,

---

[6] *CWSV*. 1: 232.

[7] *CWSV* 2: 449.

[8] Prakash Chandra, *Modern Indian Political Thought* (New Delhi: Vikas Publishing House, 2000), 136.

[9] Gandhi, *God is Truth*, op.cit., 12.

[10] Ibid., 11.

[11] *CWMG*. 64:398.

[12] K. S. Radhakrishnan, *Gandhijiyude Ramarajyadarsanam* (Mal.) (Kottayam: Sahithya Pravarthaka Co-operative Society, 2012), 136, 175.

[13] *Harijan*, 18.06.1938.

[14] *CWMG*. 28: 447.

[15] Gandhi, *God is Truth*, op.cit., 19.

[16] *CWSV*. 3:54.

[17] *CWMG*. 48:126.

"My reason follows my heart."[18] So religious truth is not a matter of rational argument and proof, but has to be experienced through intuitive realization. In the words of Vivekananda, "...realisation is religion, not doctrine."[19] Further he has stated that, "The problem with Christianity is its idea that religion consists in doctrines."[20] But on the other hand, the Indian emphasis on experience/ *anubhava* is not what results from an intellectual process – but is the fruit of an inner experience,[21] which is called 'realisation'. In Gandhi's words, this "Realization is the final fruit of constant effort."[22] Hence in *Advaitic* epistemology, supreme knowledge (*brahmajñāna)* is gained not by the mediation of reason but by its transcendence.[23] Spiritual reality is experienced not through rational argument, but by direct experience (*anubhava*).

This *anubhava* is experiential knowledge (experience itself as knowledge) and it is *anubhava* that leads one to *sākṣātkāra* or realization.[24] This experience ... is a kind of consciousness, an awareness to which man finds himself raised beyond the reach of his faculties, hearing, seeing, feeling or even thinking.[25] Therefore, it is a superconscious, super-sensuous and supra-rational experience. In this experience, there is no distinction between the subject and the object, since knowledge, knower, and the known are merged into one.[26] Hence it is this *Advaita Vedāntic* non-dual experience, which is the goal of one's very existence. [27] This *anubhava* is of great importance in the Indian tradition as it is recognized as a *Pramāṇa* (criterion or source of valid knowledge).

In this *anubhava*, the Western dualistic concept of Jesus as saviour and men as sinners, is challenged by the *Advaitic* metaphysics and epistemology. For example, Vivekananda had no sympathy towards the Christian concept of sin.[28] For him, it is sin, to call a man 'sinner', rather for him, man is God. So, in this *Advaitic* non-dual state of realisation, one is identical with the non-dual reality of the universe; hence knowledge, knower, and the known are merged

---

[18] *Harijan*, 06.04.1940.

[19] *CWSV*. 9: 279.

[20] *CWSV*. 1: 468.

[21] Mathew Vekathanam, op.cit., 597.

[22] Gandhi, *God is Truth*, op.cit., 49-50.

[23] Anantanand Rambachan, *The Limits of Scripture Vivekananda's Reinterpretation of the Vedas*, op.cit., 134.

[24] Mathew Vekathanam, op.cit., 156.

[25] Cited by Bradley Malkovsky, "Advaita Vedanta and Christian Faith," *Journal of Ecumenical Studies* 36/3-4 (Summer-Fall, 1999): 420.

[26] *CWSV*. 4:515.

[27] Mathew Vekathanam, op.cit., 575.

[28] Sunand Sumithra, *Christian Theologies from an Indian Perspective* (Bangalore: Theological Book Trust, 1995), 228.

into one.[29] Thus, the distinction between God (as 'holy' and 'above') and man (as 'sinner' and 'below') is denied and bridged in *Advaita* metaphysics. Thus, as the *Advaita* epistemology stresses the fundamental divine character of each man, and Jesus Christ can only be an example, not ransom or saviour (in the Christian sense) in Indian *Advaita Vedāntic* context.[30]

5.3. Metaphysical Dimension of Christ-Experience

Metaphysically, Christ is understood as a 'spiritual/meta-physical reality' in Indian context, than a 'historical person'. While Western epistemology is focused around the 'physical/historical Jesus' as a person, in India, the focus is not on the historical Jesus as a 'person', but on Christ, the impersonal, eternal, meta-physical, and spiritual principle. Therefore, the Indian insistence is on the 'Christ-principle' than on 'Christ as a person of history'. This is because, the modern manner of 'historical thinking' did not occupy an important place in Hindu epistemology, as it treated history as transience or change and was thus, equated with *māyā*/illusion. Therefore, historical details were not given much significance in *Advaitic* epistemology, as historical truth was important only as an exemplification of universally valid spiritual truths.[31] So, the historical Jesus is only an example or model of God-realisation. Jesus is not 'the only one' who exemplified this spiritual principle of realisation, but there are many *avatārs* and God-men who had realised God. Hence there is no 'exclusive divinity' for Christ (as in the Western sense) in India, as Jesus is only a historical manifestation of the Christ-principle in time and space. Nevertheless, tremendous respect is given to the 'Christ-ideal' in India. Thus, in Indian understanding, the importance of Christ lies not in his historicity, but in the fact that, he realised God, and became an example and model of God-realisation for others to realise the same. Therefore the Indian emphasis is on the 'Christ-principle' than on the 'person of Christ'.

As a result of this *Advaitic* epistemology, Vivekananda's and Gandhi's Christ is not a person, but a transpersonal reality. So, Vivekananda and Gandhi are interested in Christ, only as a universal, spiritual meta-physical principle and not in the particular historical Jesus as a person. For them, the historical earthly physical Jesus cannot be experienced / seen today, as he is limited by time and space in the first century Palestine, which comes under the domain of *māyā*. But Christ, the universal spiritual principle is not limited to geography or Christianity, but it is universal, unbound and timeless; so the 'Christ-principle' can be experienced at any time by anyone.

---

29 *CWSV*. 4:515.

30 Mathew Vekathanam, op.cit., 476.

31 Bhikhu Parekh, op.cit., 252.

Hence, as an *Advaita Vedāntin*, for Vivekananda Christ is an eternal universal spiritual principle, uncreated and always existing.[32] Thus his basic conviction that, 'Christ is a principle', makes him to give little interest to the historic personality of Jesus Christ.[33] So he admired Christ, the spiritual principle; not the historical Jesus.[34] In fact, Vivekananda views Jesus as a disembodied, unfettered and unbound spirit;[35] Christ "...was a soul! Nothing but a soul – just working a body for the good of humanity; and that was all his relation to the body."[36] Thus he denies the literal crucifixion of Christ, and says that they could not kill Christ; and what was crucified was a semblance, a mirage of Christ and hence crucifixion was a mere *lila* / play for Vivekananda.[37]

The historicity of Jesus Christ had no special significance to Gandhi also. On this point he wrote: "…I have never been interested in a historical Jesus."[38] "I do not know the Jesus of history."[39] Gandhi does not want a historical God, but a living God, as he said:

> God did not bear the Cross only 1,900 years ago, but He bears it today, and He dies and is resurrected from day to day. It would be poor comfort to the world if it had to depend upon a historical God who died 2,000 years ago. Do not then preach the God of history, but show Him as He lives today through you.[40]

So Gandhi preferred 'Christ of imagination'[41] than 'Jesus of history'[42] and experienced Christ as 'divine presence.'[43] Because as an *Advaitin*, Gandhi denies any person as reality; person is limited, but Truth as reality is impersonal and unlimited. So Gandhi could not accept the historically limited person of Jesus as the highest/ultimate reality. Hence, for Gandhi too, Christ is an 'impersonal principle' than a 'person'. For he says: "If Jesus represents not a person, but the principle of non-violence, India has accepted its protecting power."[44]

---

[32] *CWSV*. 6: 8.

[33] *cf. CWSV*. 3: 280, 182-184, 412; 4:150-151.

[34] *CWSV*. 4: 146.

[35] *CWSV*. 4:145.

[36] *CWSV*. 4:145.

[37] *CWSV*. 1: 328; 8: 190, 262.

[38] *Young India*, 31.12.1931.

[39] *CWMG*. 36:40.

[40] *CWMG*. 34:261.

[41] Gandhi, *All Religions Are True*, 65.

[42] *CWMG*. 57:406.

[43] Cited by S. K. George, *Gandhi's Challenge to Christianity*, op.cit., 8. *cf. Young India*, 06.08.1925.

[44] *Young India*, 31.12.1931.

Thus, the Indian *Advaita Vedāntic* approach to Christ put more stress on supra-historical dimensions of Christ-experience.[45] While colonial epistemology tries to establish the historicity of Christ, *Advaita* tries ...to liberate Christology from the shifting sands of historicity.[46] Because in India, 'the Christ of history' must become 'the Christ of experience'. In this *Advaitic* approach any question regarding the historicity of Jesus is irrelevant. History belongs only to the realm of empirical reality. Jesus as one among many manifestations of the divinity in the repeating cyclic historical process, He cannot lay claim to any so called historical uniqueness.[47] Therefore, the *Advaita Vedāntic* Christ as the universal principle, the meta-historical Christ-principle serves...to 'liberate' Christ, from the Western colonial epistemology. Hence, once Christ is freed from his historical limitations it becomes easy to present him as an omnipresent principle.[48] This spiritual principle is called the 'Christ-ideal', 'Christ-Principle' or 'Christhood'.

Since this 'spiritual/metaphysical principle' of Christ is insisted on in India, Vivekananda and Gandhi suggested the need of transcending the senses and reason to realise this 'spiritual principle', which is 'beyond' the reach of senses and reason. Hence, with the change of perception from the Western understanding of Christ, the epistemological tools are also changed in India. So, the apt epistemological tool to realise the metaphysical reality of Christ-principle is 'intuition/inspiration', which can be termed as *anubhava*/ realization, the direct religious experience. For Vivekananda and Gandhi, realising this metaphysical principle of non-duality is the goal of religious life. And Christ is one of the examples or models of realising this spiritual principle.

Another peculiarity of the metaphysical dimension of Christ-experience in Indian *Advaita Vedāntic* context is that, it emphasises metaphysical equality of everyone with Christ. While the Western Christian epistemology with its dualistic thinking tried to keep the distinctiveness and uniqueness of Jesus, in *Advaitic* epistemological thinking, there is no metaphysical distance between Christ and other human beings, rather there is a fundamental equality. However, the importance of Christ is that, he realised God, and became a model of God-realisation for others to realise the same, but he is not the only one. So as a model/example of God-realisation, Christ is not the end, but only a means for God-realisation for Vivekananda and Gandhi. And the end is not different for

---

[45] Mathew Vekathanam, op.cit., 341.

[46] Ibid., 452.

[47] Ibid., 352.

[48] Ibid., 269.

the man, so whatever that was proper to Jesus, is applicable to each individual self also. [49]

Metaphysically speaking, Vivekananda, as an *Advaita Vedāntin* presents an *Advaitic* Christology. Vivekananda sees Christ as an *Advaitin*, as Christ's central idea is metaphysical oneness -'I and my Father are One.'[50] However, this self-realisation of his true identity was revealed by Christ to his disciples only in progressive stages, starting pedagogically from the ordinary God-experience of the masses and reaching the climax in the small group of his disciples.[51] So Vivekananda sees no difference between the religion of Christ and *Advaita Vedānta*,[52] but sees in Christ an example for the realisation of man's essential divinity. [53]

Therefore, unlike the dogma of the Church, Vivekananda understood Christ as the name of a certain state of realization.[54] Christ represents a stage, the highest stage of human glory demonstrating the science of "evolving a God out of the material man,"[55] the process of unfolding of the potentialities which are enfolded within.[56] Jesus had our nature and was a *bhakta* (devotee) but he became Christ.[57] Jesus attained that stage of Christhood by prayer.[58] He says: "Jesus of Nazareth goes into his transfiguration, and when he comes out, he has become Jesus, the Christ."[59] Thus, "When a man has reached that perfect state, he is of the same nature as the Personal God. "I and my Father are one." He knows that he is one with Brahman, the Absolute, and projects himself as the Personal God does."[60] Thus, for Vivekananda, the words of Jesus were the fruit of realization[61] and this realization of Christhood by Jesus, is taken as a model by him for all to become the same.[62] Because Christ, The Messenger came to show the path,[63] "Christ would show us the way to become perfect.

---

[49] Ibid., 489.

[50] *CWSV*. 4:148.

[51] Mathew Vekathanam, op.cit., 278.

[52] *CWSV*. 2: 353.

[53] Mathew Vekathanam, op.cit., 277.

[54] *CWSV*. 8:105.

[55] *CWSV*. 1:18.

[56] K. P. Aleaz, *Jesus in Neo-Vedanta*, op.cit., 206.

[57] *CWSV*. 1: 55; 7:29. *cf.* 1:185.

[58] *CWSV*. 1: 55, 303; 4:213.

[59] *CWSV*. 4:213.

[60] *CWSV*. 5: 266. *cf.* 8: 255.

[61] *CWSV*. 2:44.

[62] He says: The "...great ones, they manifest themselves in our souls, and they make us like unto them. Our whole nature changes, and we become like them." *CWSV*. 4:32.

[63] *CWSV*. 4:148.

God became Christ to show man his true nature, that we too are God."[64] He thus says: "Jesus had our nature; he became the Christ; so can we, and so *must* we."[65] He continues: "Be not an imitation of Jesus, but be Jesus! You are quite as great as Jesus.... If we are not... we must struggle and be."[66] Because for Vivekananda, Christ's prayer was: "Father, just as I am one with you, so make them all one with me."[67] Thus we all are equal to Christ;[68] "... as the divine Man, Christ and we are one."[69] Besides all these interpretations, one can understand that Vivekananda himself had this Christ-experience and identifies himself with Jesus, for he says: "I lived in Jesus of Nazareth...."[70] And "I was Jesus ...."[71] Therefore, he finds metaphysical equality between himself and Christ. Metaphysically speaking, Christ and we are essentially one and the same (identical), says Vivekananda.[72] Hence, he goes on to say that his soul is the soul of Jesus and identifies himself with Jesus.[73] In this relation, it must be remembered that many in the West felt him as a Christ-like man,[74] "as if Christ himself...in their midst,"[75] and they approached him as if they were going to Christ.[76]

Metaphysically, Gandhi also, did not accept the Christian dogmatic claims on Christ. For example, Gandhi had problem with the Christian claim of 'Jesus as the only begotten Son of God' i.e., limiting 'sonship' to Christ alone. He says: "I do not believe in the exclusive divinity of Jesus."[77] "Thus, to believe that Jesus is the only begotten son of God is to me against Reason."[78] On the other hand, as an *Advaitin*, Gandhi sees the essential identity between us, Jesus and God. Hence he does not allow any metaphysical distance between Jesus and us,[79] as there is nothing special in Jesus. He rather says: "If God could have sons, all of us were His sons. If Jesus was like God, or God Himself,

---

[64] *CWSV*. 7: 4. *cf.* 4:145-146.

[65] *CWSV*. 7:29. *cf.* 1:185, 303; 4: 134; 8: 17-18.

[66] *CWSV*. 1: 483. *cf.* 2:307.

[67] *CWSV* 1: 381.

[68] *CWSV*. 7: 89. *cf.* 2: 307-308.

[69] *CWSV* 7: 4.

[70] *CWSV*. 2: 469.

[71] *CWSV*. 8: 505. *cf.* 7: 78.

[72] *CWSV*. 1: 341; 2: 469.

[73] *CWSV*. 1: 483; 7: 89.

[74] *New Discoveries*. 5:74, 159.

[75] *The Life*. 2:504.

[76] Tony Mathew, op.cit., 29, 32.

[77] *CWMG*. 15:304-305.

[78] *Harijan*, 06.03.1937.

[79] Ignatius Jesudasan, *A Gandhian Theology of Liberation*, op.cit., 220.

then all men were like God and could be God Himself."[80] Therefore, Gandhi affirmed the metaphysical oneness and equality between Christ and us, which was contrary to the Western belief.[81] Because we are capable of becoming another Christ,[82] as Gandhi considered Jesus as an example of the flowering of the spark of divinity within man.[83] Thus, "...we can all become...as Jesus was."[84] Because as Jesus is a son of God,[85] "...every one of us is a son of God and capable of doing what Jesus did, if we but endeavour to express the Divine in us."[86] So Christ is only a model and example of God-realisation for Gandhi.

This shows that the Christian claim of Jesus' uniqueness is a great problem for the *Advaita Vedāntic* mind.[87] There is no 'exclusive divinity' for Jesus in India, because the Indian tradition considers everybody as the son of the living God.[88] Therefore, the divine sonship of Christ is at the same time the divine sonship of every man.[89] Just as Jesus is God or the Son of God, in the *Advaitic* sense, every human being is by right the Son of God and each one has the capacity to realize in one's own life what Jesus attained in his *Advaitic* consciousness.[90] So unlike the dogmas of the Western Christianity, according to *Advaitic* understanding, the possibility of manifesting a 'Christhood' is open to every human being and is not to be considered as restricted to Jesus of Nazareth only.[91] The concrete historical figure called 'Jesus of Nazareth' is only an example; but the 'Christ-hood' is a universal principle; one of the embodiments of this 'universal Christ' is Jesus.[92] So Jesus is the one who shows us the way to become perfect by our efforts; Jesus Christ shows us our true human nature that we too are God.[93] Therefore in the *Advaitic* context, Christ is seen as the embodiment and realisation of the highest possibilities of human existence.[94] Hence, Jesus of Nazareth is recognized as a representative

---

[80] M. K. Gandhi, *Christian Missions, their Place in India* (Ahmedabad: Navajivan Publishing House, 1940), 13.

[81] *Harijan*, 04.08.1940.

[82] *CWMG*. 29: 454.

[83] *CWMG*. 75:70.

[84] *CWMG*. 29: 454.

[85] *CWMG*. 72:297-298.

[86] *Harijan*, 04.08.1940.

[87] Mathew Vekathanam, op.cit., 299.

[88] Ibid., 314.

[89] Ibid., 297.

[90] Ibid., 490.

[91] Ibid., 271.

[92] Ibid., 291.

[93] Ibid., 490.

[94] Ibid., 924.

figure for the rest of mankind, that Christ as a man realized all the divine potentialities that are already in man and thus he becomes a model for others.[95] Thus, according to *Advaita Vedānta*, as Christ realised God, we can also realise God and become another Christ; thus there can be many Christs, and its aim is to make every man Christ.[96] So Vivekananda and Gandhi affirmed metaphysical equality with Christ.

5.4. Ethical Dimension of Christ-Experience

Vivekananda's and Gandhi's ethical dimension of Christ-experience is also developed in contrast to the colonial ethics of Christendom. As colonial ethics is self-centred and based on dualistic thinking, it possesses the policy of hatred and exploitation against 'others'. The *Advaita* ethics is based on love, unity and oneness of all life, hence it emphasises love of all life and based on self-denial for the sake of the one and all.

Hence for Vivekananda, colonialism is 'other-negating' and exploitative. It is immoral and selfish. But *Advaita* ethics is 'other-regarding,[97] loving and recognizing the other as one's own self.[98] Therefore *Advaita* is ethically good. He thus said: "Advaita is the basis of ethics."[99] He, therefore, derived his ethics from *Advaita Vedāntic* oneness and unity, and stressed the denial of 'little self' and selfishness in his ethics. For him, a life of renunciation is the basis of an ethical life. He was, therefore, able to find this *Advaita Vedāntic* ethics in Christ, as Christ lived for others and suffered himself in love for others. So, the ideal of Christ is against colonial, immoral and exploitative practices of Western Christianity.

Vivekananda was, thus, deeply impressed by the spirit of renunciation in the life and work of Jesus Christ.[100] He said: "Christ was a Sannyâsin, and his religion is essentially fit for Sannyasins only."[101] Jesus had "...no faith in this evanescent world and all its belongings."[102] Christ had nowhere to lay his head.[103] He taught to renounce this world and its enjoyments.[104] So the central message of Christ for Vivekananda is renunciation- to "Give up."[105]

---

[95] Ibid., 508.

[96] Ibid., 580.

[97] *CWSV*. 1:110; 2: 353; 6: 5; 7: 58.

[98] *CWSV*.8: 101; 9: 500-501.

[99] *CWSV*. 5: 257.

[100] S. J. Samartha, op.cit., 50-51.

[101] *CWSV*. 6:109.

[102] *CWSV*. 4:144.

[103] *CWSV*. 8: 213.

[104] *CWSV*. 9: 121.

[105] *CWSV*. 2: 100; 4:149, 183-184; 6: 109.

Hence, for Vivekananda, Christ is ethical, as he is egoless and unselfish. Christ transcended his 'little self' when Christ realised, 'I and My Father are one.'[106] Thus Christ was a renouncer[107] for Vivekananda, who destroyed his 'self' and individuality and realised oneness with the greater Self, which is the basis of *Advaita* ethics.[108] But Christianity's emphasis on the historical personality of Christ and his individuality, cannot be the basis of ethics according to Vivekananda.[109] The principle of oneness and unity of everything constitutes ethics for Vivekananda, rather than emphasis on the 'individuality' of any historical figure. As a result, unlike the Western Christian doctrines, there is an added emphasis on the ethical dimension of Christ-experience in Vivekananda, which he finds in the life of self-denial, renunciation and love for others.

In contrast to the colonial policy of self-indulgence and increase of material pleasures at others' cost; like Vivekananda, Gandhi also very emphatically stressed an ethically disciplined life of self-restraint, limitation of wants and vows in his ethics.[110] For him, a truly moral life consisted in leading a truthful and non-violent life. As a result, Gandhi gave greater importance to the ethical aspect of Christ-experience in his life and thought. First of all, he considered Christ as a great ethical teacher. He explicitly said: "I consider Christ as one of the great teachers of the world."[111] And Christ's 'ethical teaching' commanded Gandhi's reverence.[112]

He saw the essential moral teachings of Christ in the Sermon on the Mount,[113] which has endeared Jesus to him.[114] What attracted Gandhi most in the Sermon was, the principle of non-resistance to evil as exemplified by Jesus, in which he could see *ahiṃsā*; the permanent aspect of ancient Indian tradition.[115] So for Gandhi, Jesus was the representation of the principle of non-violence, which is a door towards the infinite possibilities of universal love.[116] Hence, when the colonial Christianity negated the ethical teachings of Christ in the Sermon on the Mount, Gandhi practised the ethics of Christ in the Sermon. Therefore, there is a great emphasis on this ethical dimension

---

[106] *CWSV*. 4:148.

[107] *CWSV*. 2: 100; 4:149, 183-184; 6: 109.

[108] *cf. CWSV*. 2: 63, 173; 7: 58.

[109] *CWSV*. 2: 353; 3: 189, 250-251.

[110] *cf. CWMG*. 41: 274.

[111] *CWMG*. 40:315.

[112] *CWMG*. 25:85.

[113] *CWMG*. 100: 152-153.

[114] *CWMG*. 48:438.

[115] *CWMG*. 9:243; R. K. Prabhu & U. R. Rao, *The Mind of Mahatma Gandhi*, op.cit., 91.

[116] Mathew Vekathanam, op.cit., 483.

of Christ-experience in Gandhi, which is often over-looked by the traditional Christian teachings.

Another ethical aspect of Christ-experience in Gandhi is centred around the self-sacrificing and suffering death of Jesus on the Cross. Unlike the West, for Gandhi, cross was not mere atonement, but an image of non-violence.[117] So the challenge of the Cross is to suffer for the sake of love for others.[118] Hence, Gandhi brought a deeper meaning to the suffering figure of Christ on the cross and gave a 'universal meaning' to the cross and did not accept the narrow interpretation of the cross by Orthodox Christianity.[119] For him, cross is not an event of past history, but happening in the day today lives of individuals and nations.[120] He says: "Christ is daily manifested through suffering."[121] "... Living Christ means a living Cross, without it life is a living death."[122] Thus Jesus' was a *yajña* on the cross, i.e., laying down his life for true welfare,[123] and that "The love that Jesus taught and practised was not a mere personal virtue, but that it was essentially a social and collective virtue."[124]

Further, this ethical dimension of the suffering love of Christ on the cross, for Gandhi, represented the principle of non-violence,[125] which is the purest form of soul force.[126] Hence Christ was a *Satyāgrahi* for Gandhi, who was strong with his soul-force of non-violence.[127] Christ non-co-operated with the corrupt authorities and struggled against the evils of his times such as hypocrisy, pride and lying, and sought to banish corruption from temple and society.[128] Christ, thus uncompromisingly challenged the might of the Sadducees, Pharisees and the Roman Empire.[129] So Gandhi, unlike the West, perceives no passivity, no weakness about Jesus; rather he finds Jesus as the bravest individual[130] and "the most active resister" in history.[131] Thus Gandhi

---

[117] *CWMG*. 25:85.

[118] Mathew Vekathanam, op.cit., 529.

[119] M. K. Gandhi, *My Dear Child*, op.cit., 86.

[120] *CWMG*. 34:261; 100: 231.

[121] *Harijan*, 30.03.1934.

[122] *Young India*, 31.12.1931.

[123] *CWMG*. 17: 493.

[124] *CWMG*. 68: 307.

[125] *Young India*, 31.12.1931.

[126] *CWMG*. 9:243

[127] *Mahatma*. 8:280.

[128] *CWMG*. 19:179; 23: 105; 54: 50.

[129] *CWMG*. 23:104, 105; 18: 115, 126.

[130] *CWMG*. 90:129-130.

[131] *CWMG*. 84: 372.

calls Jesus Christ as a "Heroic satyagrahi,"[132] "a prince among politicians."[133] Therefore, for Gandhi, Christ as a *Satyāgrahi*, was also against colonialism. So in the hard days of freedom struggle, Jesus was a fountain of strength and inspiration for Gandhi,[134] as Jesus and his teachings became an important source of his philosophy of *satyāgraha.*[135] Hence, Gandhi, like Jesus, chose to meet evil courageously and non-violently.[136] In this relation, Gandhi was especially influenced by Christ in his definition of the concept of non-violence, for he says, "...the example of Jesus' suffering is a factor in the composition of my undying faith in non-violence which rules all my actions, worldly and temporal.... Jesus lived and died in vain if he did not teach us to regulate the whole of life by the eternal Law of Love."[137] And "…if I raise resistances of a non-violent character I simply and humbly follow in the footsteps of the great teachers" like Christ.[138] Thus, the cross-experience of Christ was full of ethical vigour for Gandhi to fight against the immoral practices of the Western colonial Christianity, which he met in the 19th century. However, he fought this moral battle in Christ's way of non-violent love.

Thus, when the colonial Christianity negated the ethical aspect of Christ-experience, Vivekananda and Gandhi emphatically emphasised it in their *Advaitic* dimension of Christ-experience. Hence, they understood Christ as a great teacher and as an example of the one who had realised God through his ethical life of renunciation and non-violent love. As *Advaita Vedāntins*, both shunned violence and affirmed non-violent love in their ethics, as understood from the Sermon on the Mount. They stressed on the unity of all life and considered injury to the 'other' as injury to oneself as the 'other' is not different from oneself. Thus for them, Christ-experience requires an egoless life and ethical discipline. Non-violent love (*ahiṃsā*) as manifested in the cross is the means to realise this oneness and true welfare of all beings.

5.5. Conclusion

As the Western Christianity was dogmatic; it gave importance to some set of intellectual beliefs in certain doctrines and dogmas, while Indian understanding is to realize/experience Christ as a living reality/presence. While Christian missionaries wanted to safeguard the Christian dogmas on the historicity of Jesus' life, death and resurrection; for the Hindu leaders like Vivekananda and

[132] *CWMG*. 18: 126.

[133] *CWMG*. 18: 196.

[134] Jaladhar Pal, op.cit., 32.

[135] Gopinath Dhawan, op.cit., 24.

[136] K. L. Seshagiri Rao, op.cit., 30.

[137] *Harijan*, 17.01.1939.

[138] *CWMG*. 17:408.

Gandhi, these dogmas and doctrines about Incarnation, the natures of Christ, etc. were not so important, but what was important for them was the set of moral precepts that they discovered in the teachings of Christ, especially in the Sermon on the Mount.[139] For example, while the colonial Christianity ignored the 'Sermon on the Mount', it was Gandhi who unearthed it. Hence Vivekananda and Gandhi wanted to experience Christ directly, first-hand and not through the Western mediation of doctrinal/denominational/dogmatic aspects. The Western theological and ecclesiastical traditions and cultural baggage accompanying the missionary enterprise in India were rejected by them. They wanted to be free themselves from all these Western religious and cultural bondages and enter into a direct experience of the original nucleus of Christianity.[140] That was their Christ-experience. Thus theirs was not the historic Christ, but experiential Christ. Instead of the doctrines and dogmas, Vivekananda and Gandhi made Christ-experience the central norm of their thinking, which was in accordance with the Indian tradition of *Advaita Vedānta* and its emphasis on 'realization'.

Therefore Both Vivekananda and Gandhi as *Advaita Vedāntins* completely rejected Christ of the colonial Christianity and interpreted and understood Him from an *Advaitic* perspective. As a result, their Christ-experience lies outside the Western Christian dogmatic approach. This Indian response to Christ was to interpret Christ in an entirely new way.[141] It may be that the *Advaita Vedānta* provides a better method for the study of the message of Christ than Western philosophical frameworks.[142] Hence ethically also, Christ's *ahiṃs*ā is practised better in India than in the Christian West. This may be due to the principle of non-violence and love for the enemies is a very part of the age-old tradition of India.[143]

The peculiarity of Indian emphasis is that, it sees Christ as representing the spiritual/metaphysical principle and its inseparable relation with epistemology. Therefore, the Indian *Advaitic* epistemology exalts direct intuitive experience (*anubh*ūti), above senses and reason in relation to Christ-experience. This can be seen as a reaction against the colonial Christian epistemology, which exalts 'reason' above everything. Hence reason is not the absolute criterion in India, but *anubhava*, so that reason only prepares oneself for the higher state of realisation; so Indian approach gives a higher place for experiential knowledge over the Western emphasis on rational knowledge. While in Vivekananda, this

---

[139] Thomas Mampra, op.cit., 258.

[140] Nirmal Minz, op.cit., 114.

[141] Carl Keller, op.cit., 383.

[142] Ibid., 384.

[143] Mathew Vekathanam, op.cit., 488.

experience is purely mystical;[144] in Gandhi, this takes the form of experiments and the practical and gradual realisation of the Absolute Truth through relative truths.[145]

Thus the Indian approach to Christ-experience was centred on its metaphysical and ethical dimensions. Metaphysically, Vivekananda and Gandhi, as *Advaita Vedāntins* consider Christ's importance in his showing the way to the realization of man's innate divinity, and, they see in Christ, a great ethical teacher of humanity. In both cases the role of Christ is not considered as that of a Saviour in the Christian sense.[146] *Advaita Vedānta,* thus ignores the basic distinction between the person of Jesus Christ and other human individuals in the course of history.[147] Therefore, Christ is a mystic *Yogi*, an example, a model and a *Satyāgrahi*, who through the path of non-violent love realised God/Truth. So, Christ is only an example for the realisation of man's essential divinity.[148] Ethically speaking, Sermon on the Mount is greatly relevant in India, than the so-called doctrines and dogmas of Western Christendom. The Hindu understanding of the Cross of Christ is also not in line with the Western atonement/redemption theories, but as the supreme example of dedication to moral principles and self-purification.[149] Hence, the Christology of Vivekananda and Gandhi is purely in *Advaita Vedāntic* categories, which emphasises the metaphysical and ethical dimensions of Christ-experience.[150]

---

[144] *CWSV*. 6:81.

[145] *An Autobiography*, xiii; *CWMG*. 61:81, *Harijan*, 25.05.1935; Gandhi, *God is Truth*, op.cit., 49-50.

[146] Mathew Vekathanam, op.cit., 476.

[147] Ibid., 508.

[148] Ibid., 277.

[149] Ibid., 525.

[150] Ibid., 612.

Chapter 6

Critical Analysis and Observations

6.1. Introduction

The sporadic encounters between Christians and *Advaitins* took place in the late nineteenth century. However, it was not characterized by a real openness by either side to learn from the other. Both parties tended to feel themselves superior to the other in their attempts to convert or to repel the attempts of the other to triumph in debate. The relationship between Hindu intellectuals on the one hand, especially important figures of the Hindu Renaissance such as Vivekananda and Gandhi, and Christian missionaries of the colonial period on the other, was markedly polemical and apologetic in nature. Hence there remains much misunderstanding as to what Christianity and *Advaita Vedānta* really teach.[1] Christianity's association with colonialism and its Western structures and thought patterns also contributed to this issue.

The missionary criticisms and denunciations of Hinduism and Indian tradition and also the colonial effort to displace the Indian religion and culture did hurt them deeply. This caused, in 19th century, a reactionary response from Hindus against the colonial tide of Western Christianity. Vivekananda and Gandhi were actually products of this reaction. Hence to counter-act and to defend Indian tradition and Hinduism, they used the same colonial/missionary comparative method, which did not understand 'the other' as they were. Their aim was to project the superiority of Indian tradition and Hinduism through *Advaita Vedānta*. In this process, they adopted the language of Christ to fight against colonial Christianity.[2] As, the colonizers and missionaries denunciated Indian tradition, Vivekananda and Gandhi also used the same denunciative

[1] Bradley Malkovsky, op.cit., 403-404.

[2] Sisir Kumar Das, op.cit., 61.

methods. They were in fact using comparative method in the philosophy of religions, in order to prove the superiority of Indian tradition and *Advaita,* and thereby to enunciate the inferiority of the Christian West. Hence, Vivekananda and Gandhi committed the same mistake of missionaries in understanding the other (methodological error), because theirs were mostly reactions against the colonial invasion of facts to make objective analysis.

6.2. Issues of Comparative Approach

Thus there are various issues arising in Hindu-Christian relations, from the use of this comparative method by Vivekananda and Gandhi, to prove the 'superiority' of their Hindu religious tradition over the Christian tradition. It is generally considered today that, the comparative approach as an immature [biased] view, that religions be compared in order to decide which is the best. This is a tendency to argue in favour of one's own religious truth, over against the truth of other religions, which is certainly an unhealthy tendency in today's pluralistic context. Hence, Vivekananda and Gandhi were using the norms and premises of Hindu religious tradition, consciously or unconsciously, in considering Christian tradition,[3] which originated in an entirely different context and was totally different from the *Advaitic* view of reality. Hence the two religious contexts, concepts and traditions are not the same, but different. They have to be seen as self-valid, incomparable, and equal and therefore no need to justify before any other as true or false. Because in today's context, 'superior-inferior' approach is unhealthy and undemocratic, as no person genuinely committed to his/her religion, will be satisfied with an inferior position assigned to his/her faith, by the adherents of another religion.[4] The aim of studies of religion is not to establish the superiority of one over the other, but to know and be known to each other. It should be a dialogical process of sharing and exchange rather than a monological form of confrontation and exclusivism.

6.3. Comparative Approach of Vivekananda – A Critical Analysis

Hence for example, to the missionaries' superior thesis that 'Christianity is the only true religion', Vivekananda responded in an equally competitive manner with an anti-thesis that '*Advaita* is the only universal religion' and is superior to Christianity.[5] Hence he compares *Advaita* in relation to Christianity in order to prove that, *Advaita* is superior and Christianity is a lower religion. He, thus

---

[3] Anantanand Rambachan, *The Limits of Scripture Vivekananda's Reinterpretation of the Vedas*, op.cit., 4.

[4] P. S. Daniel, op.cit., 263.

[5] *CWSV*. 3: 182-183; 249.

interprets Christianity in terms of *Advaita*.[6] He goes on to use *Advaita* as a criterion to understand Jesus Christ and the New Testament. He says: "Even Christians cannot understand their New Testament, without understanding the [*Advaita*] Vedanta. The [*Advaita*] Vedanta is the rationale of all religions. Without the [*Advaita*] Vedanta every religion is superstition; with it everything becomes religion."[7] Further, he propounded the ladder theory in religions, in which a hierarchical scheme is enunciated, in order to place *Advaita* at the top of the hierarchy and Christianity at the lowest step of the ladder/bottom of his scheme in order to prove the superiority of *Advaita*. He, thus considered Christianity as the dualistic *Vedānta* [*Dvaita*] adapted to the people of Europe. When he holds such positions of comparative approach, the following issues arise from a critical and analytical point of view.

6.3.1. Self-contradiction

Abraham Stephen observes that, in any reading of Vivekananda, he was a man of contradictions. He used the same words with different emphases to different audiences, in his unprepared lectures around the world, in his personal letters, in his more considered statements and writings.[8] For example, he talks about 'equality of religions' and at the same time holds the 'superiority of *Advaita Vedānta* form of Hinduism'? Therefore one can say that, Vivekananda is contradicting himself between two divergent and equally opposing philosophical positions between 'equality of all religions' and 'superiority of *Advaita Vedānta*'. However, both positions cannot be held together, because either all religions should be 'equal' or *Advaita* should be 'superior' over all others. If all religions are equal, then no single religion *viz., Advaitic* Hinduism can never become superior. If one religion is superior, then there is no equality among all religions, but all religions will be subjected under the 'one superior religion', which for Vivekananda is *Advaita Vedānta*. Therefore, according to Vivekananda, other religions are mere "steps" or "stages" on the way to the goal of *Advaita*,[9] hence not equal with *Advaita*. However, the important question is: If all paths are legitimate ways to reach God and have "the same saving power", why undermine dualism and qualified non-dualism for *Advaita*?[10] Hence some sort of differentiation, inequality, dominance and rank are institutionalized in his neo-*Vedāntic* structure....[11]

---

[6] M. M. Thomas, op.cit., 148.

[7] *CWSV*. 5: 212.

[8] Abraham Stephen, op.cit., xvii.

[9] Ibid., 286-287.

[10] Ibid., 262.

[11] Ibid., 286-287.

and Vivekananda never resolved this contradiction in his writings.[12] Thus Vivekananda, who condemned the patronizing attitude of those who claimed that theirs is a superior religion fulfilling all other religions, himself upholds the same attitude in elevating *Advaita* as the fulfilment of all other religions, and "thinking himself in a high position"...[13] Thus he contradicts himself.

6.3.2. Reductionism

Another criticism is that Vivekananda's understanding of Christ from an *Advaita Vedāntic* perspective was reductive. He did not do justice to the New Testament portrayal of Christ. He interpreted the New Testament narratives in a selective way, in order to suit Christ into his *Advaitic* mould. He thus exalted the ethical teachings, mystical aspects and principle of Christ, at the cost/negation of Christ's miracles, virgin birth, crucifixion, etc. He, just tries to explain them away as not vital to the understanding of Christ.[14] For example, he exalted 'Christ-principle', which for him, is meta-historical, at the cost of the historical Christ.[15] Therefore, there are defects in the understanding of Christ by Vivekananda, despite the importance given to 'Christ-experience.'[16]

6.3.3. Offending the 'Other'

Anantanand Rambachan notes that "...there are many aspects of Vivekananda's approach to the Christian tradition which are not conducive to meaningful dialogue."[17] Because many of the views of Vivekananda on Christ are contradictory to what Christians believe concerning Christ, hence his views can offend Christians. For example, his placing of Christ next to Buddha,[18] is unacceptable to Christians. Because by placing Christ next to Buddha, Vivekananda denies originality to the life and thoughts of Christ, as he says: "...the same soul who came as Buddha came afterwards as Christ."[19] And he also traces back the very teachings of Christ to those of Buddha.[20] This will definitely unacceptable to Christians, as these views are contrary to the conception of Jesus by Christian believers. According to Vivekananda's view, Christ is just a re-incarnation of Buddha and Christ is also indebted to Buddha

[12] Ibid., 296.

[13] P. S. Daniel, op.cit., 144.

[14] M. M. Thomas, op.cit., 137.

[15] Mathew Vekathanam, op.cit., 560.

[16] Ibid., 302.

[17] Anantanand Rambachan, "Interpreting Another Tradition: Vivekananda on Christ and Christianity," *Anima* 20/2 (September, 1994): 133.

[18] *CWSV*. 7: 22, 77-78. *cf.* 7: 78; 8:28, 105.

[19] *CWSV*. 9: 412. *cf.* 8:180.

[20] *CWSV*. 2: 510.

for his teachings, thus Vivekananda totally denies any originality to Jesus' personality and teachings, but duplicates it with that of Buddha.

6.3.4. Selective of the 'Other'

Another criticism concerning the comparative method of Vivekananda is in relation to his selective approach to Christian sacred scriptures. He takes what agrees with his vision of religion and ignores everything else. For example, Vivekananda has a great deal to say about the teachings of Christ about men's relation to God, but he has almost nothing to say regarding the Cross and Resurrection of Jesus.[21] Thus Anantanand Rambachan observes that,

> Vivekananda was extremely selective in his use of Christian scriptures. He emphasized those passages in which he could detect affinity with his Non-dualistic outlook, overlooking the long established and influential traditions of interpretation within the Church.[22]

But an objective approach to any religions requires that it is taken in its entirety.[23] Therefore the argument against Christianity by Vivekananda is incomplete and selective.

6.3.5. Avoidance of the Community of Faith and Placing of the Individual Views above the Community

Coming from a decentralized and individualistic spirituality, Vivekaṇanda, in fact, showed no concern for the role of the Church in Christian religion, as an exegetical community.[24] Rather he placed high authority on 'direct experience' hence negates the role of religious community as well as scriptures in religious experience. However, such an over-emphasis on *anubhūti* apart from the scriptural tradition and the believing community can become 'a matter of individual fancy'[25] and 'extreme subjectivism'.

6.3.6. Neglecting the Serious Differences between Religions

Another critic about Vivekananda's comparative approach is that, he has not taken seriously the radical differences between Hinduism and Christianity as these are two religious traditions originated and developed in different

[21] M. M. Thomas, op.cit., 127.

[22] Anantanand Rambachan, "Interpreting Another Tradition: Vivekananda on Christ and Christianity," op.cit., 133.

[23] Mathew Vekathanam, op.cit., 478.

[24] Anantanand Rambachan, "Interpreting Another Tradition: Vivekananda on Christ and Christianity," op.cit., 133.

[25] Mathew Vekathanam, op.cit., 616.

contexts with differing conceptions of reality. On the other hand, very often in his writings, he slips into making general assertions.[26] For example, he saw very little difference between what he understood to be the religion of Christ and the teachings of *Advaita Vedānta*.[27] However, if we take the differences seriously, we must be attentive to ways in which religious traditions define themselves, and should not superimpose our own philosophical and theological constructions on 'other' traditions.[28]

6.3.7. Quoting the Text by Ignoring its 'Original' Context

Another criticism is that, in his writings, Vivekananda mishandles the Christian Scriptures by taking the texts of the Bible out of context and interpreting them in a philosophical framework alien to the Bible.[29] Thus he forces his *Advaitic* assumptions into Bible.[30] For example, he applies *Advaitic* metaphysics of oneness to the New Testament passage of 'I and thy Father are same'[31] –in explaining Jesus' non-dual experience, but this passage can have a different meaning in its original context, so Vivekananda does not do justice to the original passage in his interpretation. Hence, his estimate of Christianity is based on his reading of the biblical passages out of context and interpreting them in ways alien to the contextual limitations of biblical religion.[32]

6.3.8. Against Historical Facts

Another fallacy of Vivekananda is that, while constructing his 'ladder theory' (in order to prove the superiority of *Advaita* and thereby to place Christianity at a lower level), he ignores the historical development of *Viśiṣṭādvaita* and *Dvaita*. He reverses the historical order and puts *Advaita* as the culmination and the third and final stage of spiritual growth and realisation, which comes after the first two stages of *Dvaita* and *Viśiṣṭādvaita*. But one can historically (historical development of ideas) see that, the *Advaita* School of *Śaṅkara* was developed first (c. 8th century), and after then only *Viśiṣṭādvaita* of *Rāmānuja* (c. 11th century) and *Dvaita* of *Madhvā* (c. 12th century) came into being. Even it is historically proved that, *Viśiṣṭādvaita* and *Dvaita* Schools of *Vedānta* philosophy developed after the development of the *Advaita* School

---

[26] Anantanand Rambachan, *The Limits of Scripture Vivekananda's Reinterpretation of the Vedas*, op.cit., 108.

[27] Anantanand Rambachan, "Interpreting Another Tradition: Vivekananda on Christ and Christianity," op.cit., 132.

[28] Ibid., 133.

[29] M. M. Thomas, op.cit., 147-148.

[30] *CWSV*. 5:222.

[31] *CWSV*. 1: 321; 2: 142 ff; 4: 142, 144,

[32] M. M. Thomas, op.cit., 133.

of philosophy, as a result of dissatisfaction with the *Advaita* School.[33] But Vivekananda ignores this historical fact and just do the reverse, in order to construct his ladder theory, which is creative and interesting but, historically ungrounded and contrary to it. Moreover, it is yet to prove that all people who belong to *Dvaita* and *Viśiṣṭādvaita* stage will discard their respective philosophical positions and move to the *Advaita* position as Vivekananda thinks. Further Vivekananda himself places *Advaita* (*jñāna mārga*) in the hard position of the third stage of spiritual development, and admits that only a few can follow it.[34]

6.4. Comparative Approach of Gandhi – A Critical Analysis

Gandhi emphatically denied that he was a Christian and affirmed repeatedly that he was a *Sanātani* Hindu. In the midst of colonial Christianity and its denunciation of everything Indian and Hindu, he was, thus compelled to act from the Hindu point of view for the preservation of Hindu culture and religion. Therefore, critically speaking, there is a clear-cut Hindu bias in Gandhi. For example, he used comparative method in his study of religions[35] and affirmed the superiority of East over the West.[36] So his understanding and interpretation of Christianity was from within the Hindu world view. He drew upon Tolstoy and others like, esoteric Christians and Quakers, who held a vision of reality similar to that of the Hindus and closer to *Advaita Vedānta*. He, thus believed that "the fullness of Christianity could only be found in its interpretation in the light and by the aid of Hinduism."[37] This approach of Gandhi towards Christianity, which got many similarities with that of Vivekananda, got many critical points and defects, when analysed in an objective way in today's world.

6.4.1. Avoidance of the Community of Faith and Placing the Individual Views above the Community

Gandhi followed his own interpretation, rather than any accepted or official interpretation of the Orthodox religious communities. Hence he says: "...my own interpretation of the Bible..."[38] So the Christ he admired was not the New Testament Christ or the Christ of the major Christian orthodox interpretations, but, the Christ of his own imagination. He, thus reinterpreted Christianity for his own purposes, and did not give any respect for the accepted views of

[33] S. Radhakrishnan. *Indian Philosophy,* vol. 2. (London: George Allen & Unwin Ltd, 1966), 716.

[34] *CWSV*. 2:252.

[35] *An Autobiography*, 146-149.

[36] Ibid., 148.

[37] *CWMG*. 12: 176.

[38] *Young India*, 02.09.1926.

the Christian community concerning the person and work of Christ. Hence for him, what he says only is true about Christianity, rather than what the Christians say it is?[39] Thus he makes himself an authority over Christianity. So there is no 'bracketing of his views' by Gandhi in approaching the 'other', rather it seems that he persuades his views on the other. The 'other' should act as what he says or accordingly. This is also a kind of colonial attitude – that is, the colonialism of the colonized, probably as a reaction against the superior attitude of Christian missionaries in the colonial period. Separating 'Christ' from Christianity also may not be acceptable to Christians, as Christ is the very core and integral part of Christianity and, without Him, it has no existence. So, there are many individual assertions in Gandhi in avoidance of a faith community, which may not be healthy in a pluralistic context, as the views of a community on its beliefs got its due place and importance.

6.4.2. Selective Approach

A much criticised weak point in Gandhi, in approaching a religion in general is that, he claims he is not bound to accept everything that is written as parts of a religious text. He claims that, he is bound to accept only whatever gets approval of his moral conscience and logical certainty. He practised Hinduism in accordance with this principle and he claimed that his practise of Hinduism gave him a pluralist space for the other religions. But the institutionalized versions of prophetic religions as a whole never allow pluralism in their religious practise.

However, Gandhi enjoyed 'tremendous freedom' in reading any text, as he did not accept anything wholly. At this point, he is totally different from a traditionally faithful reader of a religious text. A reader, who has faith in it, accepts the text in toto, that too, in letter and spirit. But Gandhi is not like a committed faithful reader of any religion, but he accepts only the things that keep conformity with logical reasoning and moral principles.

6.4.3. Avoidance of the Background of the Scriptural Text

Gandhi's method of reading religious material on the whole was random; he selected passages that appealed to him personally; and he then gave an interpretation which was not conditioned by dreary questions of background, history, context, language, or any other of the considerations which, for example, are usually considered by the biblical scholars.[40] So, his was not a customary approach towards the passages he quoted from scriptures of other faiths. But it is often subjective and inspirational and such interpretations of

[39] P. S. Daniel, op.cit., 222.

[40] Peter D. Bishop, "Ahimsa and Satyagraha the interaction of Hindu and Christian religious ideas, and their contribution to a political campaign,"*The Indian Journal of Theology* 27/2 (April-June, 1978): 55.

scriptural passages can be creative, but at the same time it may do injustice to the background and to the original meaning of the scriptural texts by the customary practitioners. Naturally, this approach of Gandhi towards the religious texts in general, invites criticism from the so called faithful and customary practitioners of religious texts.

6.4.4. Reductionism

Another criticism is that, Gandhi's views on Christ and His teachings became reductive, in relation to Christian faith concerning Christ. For example, he identified the essence of Christianity and Christ's Gospel with the Sermon on the Mount.[41] But actually, Christianity is more than that; Jesus' entire teachings are not limited to the Sermon alone, but more than that. So Gandhi reduces the person and teachings of Christ as portrayed in the New Testament, for the purpose of his selective interpretation and understanding of Christ. However, this might have done to correct the colonial Christianity, which gave over-emphasis to the rituals of New Testament and subsequently avoided the ethical aspect of the Sermon on the Mount.

6.4.5. Offending the 'Other'

Like Vivekananda, Gandhi's interpretations of Christian beliefs also are, at many points, not acceptable to Christians and they offend many, even today. Nevertheless, he was offended by the missionary preaching and his response to Christianity was also reactionary; hence it seems that he was not concerned about his reading and interpretation of the scriptures and the beliefs of other religions, even if, sometimes they offended, the followers of those religions. However, is it not a breach of his principle *ahiṃsā*?

6.5. Towards Mutual Understanding and Mutual Correction

In today's independent and secular India, it is a necessity to avoid the combative and competitive manners of encounter between Hinduism and Christianity characteristic of the bygone days of colonialism. The confrontational relations between Hinduism and Christianity, should be revised in the new context of secular-independent democracy, i.e., from confrontation to co-operation. We have to understand that, when two traditions interact and encounter, there will be both pros and cons. But much of the tension and rivalry are due to the misunderstanding of the principles of other religions.[42] Even if, the views of each other were biased towards each other, it is the mutual responsibility, to understand and correct it today and co-exist in an amicable and peaceable way in the multi-religious and multi-cultural context of India. Hence the past mistakes

---

[41] Mathew Vekathanam, op.cit., 479.

[42] P. S. Daniel, op.cit., 265.

should not affect the Hindu-Christian relations today; rather we should build better understanding for a better existence. Although, the Hindu reaction of the 19th century was caused by the criticisms of a colonial Christianity, however, it must be understood today that, all Christians in India do not support the colonial subjugation of India by the Western powers any longer, even while they hold the traditional beliefs of Christianity. In the Hindu reactionary response also, which is reflected in the views of Vivekananda and Gandhi, there are many points, which cannot be agreeable to the religious feelings of the Christian minority today. But we have to consider their arguments against Christianity as a 'reaction' only, against the Western Christian missionary criticism of the Hindu religion in a particular context rather than as having any particular epistemological value in itself. [43] Therefore, the former prejudices of Christian-Hindu relations reflecting the attitude of a superior to an inferior, of truth to falsehood, and of light to darkness have no place in the new world cultural context.[44] On the other hand, the attitude toward the traditions of Christianity and Indian religion and culture should be a balanced one. They have to be re-interpreted amicably in the light of the new cultural context of a secular democratic India.[45] Unlike the past, in the Hindu-Christian relations, today, the focus should be one of assimilation with mutual respect, rather than of substitution. Hence, after almost a century after Vivekananda and Gandhi, we need to see the areas of philosophical disputes between Hinduism and Christianity as not contradictory, but as natural differences between them, as they had grown, developed and existed by their own. These differences cannot be eliminated, as they constitute their basic identities and existence. Hence, we have to go beyond the comparative-superior approach towards the 'other' and be able to realise and accept the differences of the 'other' in a spirit of love, harmony, respect and co-existence of the two different, but equal religious traditions.

There should be correction from both sides. First of all, the condemnation of Hinduism by the missionaries as evil, as the very work of the devil[46] and their superior colonial attitude that 'their Christianity is the only true religion' should be revised, because such a doctrine of the monopoly of Truth has no place in India,[47] nor any philosophical basis for such claims. [48] Rather Christian missions should happen in a quite new way in the new context of post-colonial

[43] Abraham Stephen, op.cit., 188.

[44] Nirmal Minz, op.cit., 121.

[45] Ibid., 120.

[46] I. Jesudasan, "Gandhian Perspectives on Missiology," op.cit., 69.

[47] Santhosh Thomas, op.cit., 313.

[48] Thomas Mampra, op.cit., 265.

and secular democratic relations.[49] All this involves a critical look at and re-conception of the past missionary aims and their assumptions.[50] As Gandhi told, the missionaries "...have to alter their attitude...they tell people that there is no salvation for them except through the Bible and through Christianity. It is customary to decry other religions and to offer their own as the only one that can bring deliverance, that attitude should be radically changed."[51] Hence along with giving up of this "arrogant thesis,"[52] Christianity should be ready to acknowledge its wrong association with inhuman and exploitative colonialism. So that Christians can function in today's India, with conviction, but without fanaticism, with belief and action, but without arrogance or self-centredness or pride.[53] As C. F. Andrews argued, Christianity in India should be a helper and fulfiller, a peacemaker and a friend.[54] Indian Christianity should give up its 'Western grab' and should adopt its idioms and patterns of life in accordance with Indian tradition.

At the same time, the *Advaitic* conceptions of Christianity also need correction in today's context.[55] Because the problem of Vivekananda and Gandhi was that, they used consciously or unconsciously the same methodology of colonial missionaries in a reactionary mood i.e., the comparative approach in evaluating 'the other' (Christians) with prejudice and superiority of Hinduism and Indian tradition of *Advaita*. This has to be corrected in the post-colonial era, as every tradition has to be understood in its own terms, rather than evaluated by the concepts of a different tradition. Vivekananda's neo-*Vedāntic* scheme of hierarchy of religions, in which *Advaitic* Hinduism is placed at the top, should be critically evaluated and revised, as we live in a world of secularism. Again, the *Advaitic* devaluation of Christian concept of history, personhood, doctrines, etc. should be re-conceived and critically evaluated. Moreover the offending elements in *Advaitic* understanding of Christ and placing of individual views of Vivekananda and Gandhi over that of the Christian community has to be re-checked and re-thought in the context of minority-majority issues.

---

[49] Santhosh Thomas, op.cit., 293.

[50] I. Jesudasan, "Gandhian Perspectives on Missiology," op.cit., 71.

[51] *Young India*, 14.07.1927.

[52] Santhosh Thomas, op.cit., 312.

[53] Ibid., 312-313.

[54] B. R. Nanda, op.cit., 234.

[55] Mathew Vekathanam, op.cit., 801.

6.6. Dialogical Process for a Harmonious Multi-religious Context of India

The following observations are made based on this study, for a better perception, understanding and harmonious co-existence of Hindus and Christians through dialogical process in the context of multi-religious India.

i. Past prejudices and conceptions which caused misunderstandings, such as Hinduism is full of darkness and Christianity is a colonial religion, etc. should be revised and avoided today. We need to avoid past mistakes and work toward a better future, lest wrong assumptions of the past should affect the future Hindu-Christian relations. Hence, extreme and negative aspects should be totally rejected. For example, the use of strong self-assertive aggressive language should be avoided, as it will paralyse the real communication between religious communities. Therefore, inter-religious fellowship and co-operation are sincerely and emphatically advocated.[56]

ii. Further, in Hindu–Christian encounter, mutual offending elements should be avoided, which include forceful conversion, hostile criticisms, reductive view of the other, exclusive assertions or imposition of one's views over others, etc. In this context, thinkers like Vivekananda and Gandhi must make a note to give attention to the totality of the Christian experience, scriptural, personal, communal and institutional.[57]

iii. Another suggestion is to avoid the language of blame. As basically it is a cultural and religious interaction, it is necessary to avoid dichotomizing statements (as West versus East, or East versus West) to do away with the inter-religious tension, to see the overlapping cultural elements and some hope for a more peaceful future. As overlapping of cultures and religions in the past had not always been just, rather they had tended to be unjust, especially colonialism; but now that does not mean that, it is the only way they can be. There are ways in which we can come to understand one another better and improve the present relations.[58] So there are rooms for re-interpreting the old and promoting good, as no culture/religion is absolutely negative or wholly pure.[59]

---

[56] Santhosh Thomas, op.cit., 286.

[57] Anantanand Rambachan, "Interpreting Another Tradition: Vivekananda on Christ and Christianity," op.cit., 133.

[58] Eric Bain-Selbo, "Understanding the Other: The Challenge of Post-Colonial Theory to the Comparative Study of Religion," *Religious Studies and Theology* 18/1 (June, 1999): 92.

[59] M. Stephen, op.cit., 113.

iv. Then no religion needs to be seen as superior or inferior to any other religion, as all are mutually complementary.[60] As Gandhi says, we cannot approach a religion from a position or attitude of superiority.[61] On the other hand, the relation should be of the relations of equals, hence the irrelevant comparative method should be discarded and every religious tradition must be understood in itself rather than primarily relative to other traditions.[62] Thus, Hinduism should be understood as Hinduism, and Christianity as Christianity. Thus, they are unique and incomparable and must be understood in their own terms and in their historical context and setting. Disregarding the 'other', cannot be approved. There should be 'bracketing' in approaching the other and there should not be reductionisms. The other has to be understood as the 'other', and not according to a different criterion. Hence we need to enable the other to exist in its otherness, which is the true spirit of democracy. Further, one must know that one's understanding of another religion is right only if the followers of that religion can agree with it. [63]

v. Hence, the challenge of the philosophical encounter of *Advaita Vedānta* and Christianity is that, neither a pure metaphysical approach of the Hindu philosopher, nor a pure historical and personalistic emphasis of the Western Christian tradition is of much help,[64] so both the metaphysical and subjective (experiential) aspects of the Christ-Experience are to be stressed without losing sight of its historical dimensions (objective dimension of the Christ-experience).[65] The certainty and reliability of today's Christ-experience is essentially based on what happened in the past, in the history of Jesus of Nazareth, as the Christ.[66] So, both intellectual and intuitive kinds of knowledge are justified and balanced.

vi. Another aspect is that, since *Advaita* overemphasises the divinity of man and thus ignores the sinful nature of man, and Christianity over-emphasises the fallen and sinning nature of man and forgets the divinity of man, we have to find a 'mean' between these extreme positions, as man is not fully divine as there is evil and crime by men

---

[60] P. S. Daniel, op.cit., 58.

[61] *Young India*, 23.04.1931.

[62] Eric Bain-Selbo, op.cit., 86.

[63] P. S. Daniel, op.cit., 265.

[64] Nirmal Minz, op.cit., 133.

[65] Mathew Vekathanam, op.cit., 458.

[66] Ibid., 890.

as is clearly evident in this world, and man is also not fully a sinner, as there is goodness and love in him in this world.

vii. Christianity in its Western colonial forms is unacceptable and indigestible in India. Therefore, Christianity should be Indianized and should not carry with it the Western colonial elements. In this relation, one of the most important tasks of Christianity in India should be to incorporate the Gandhian insights about the ethics of Christ in its framework and explore the fuller meaning of the Sermon on the Mount in relation to the practical living and the present realities of India. Further, it also must give attention to the *Advaitic* emphasis on direct religious experience (*anubh*ūti), in Indian context, while holding its doctrinal dimensions.

viii. Above all, we need to develop a positive attitude towards the 'other'. As Gandhi said: "A religion has to be judged not by its worst specimens but by the best it might have produced."[67] Hence we need to approach each other, not "as a fault-finding critic but as a devotee hoping to find that like beauties in other religions and wishing to incorporate in my own, the good I may find in them and miss in mine."[68] Hence, we need to find the best in Hinduism as well as in Christianity.

ix. Another thing is the observation for a fruitful dialogue between *Advaitic* Hinduism and Indian Christianity, as we need a good-willed and non-confrontational approach between *Advaita Vedānta* and Christianity beyond colonialism and blame. A vision of reconciliation between Hindus and Christians should be the basis for such a dialogue. This motive prevents one from making a pre-judgment of the other, yet it does imply equilibrium between them. It envisions a new structure of society and a new mode of human existence after reconciliation is effected between these communities in the process of informal and formal dialogues between them.[69] Hence this dialogue should be seen as a necessary and adequate mode of relating themselves to each other in today's secular democratic India. This dialogical relationship does not need to be focused on mere 'intellectual debate' on the concept of reality in *Advaita* and Christianity, but it can also take a common concern for the economic and social well-being of the people of India.

x. As the colonial context of the past has been changed, mutual perception and response also must be changed today in the post-

---

[67] *Harijan*, 18.07.1936.

[68] *CWMG*. 55: 353.

[69] Nirmal Minz, op.cit., 153.

colonial context. So there should be a 'fusion of horizons'- a synthesis and philosophical reconciliation – between East and West, experience and reason, metaphysics and history, principle and person. Both should work in a complementary way in the spirit of love, dialogue and harmony.

6.7. Conclusion

This chapter has attempted to critically analyse the issues of comparative approach in Hindu-Christian relations in the colonial context and also in the reactionary response of Vivekananda and Gandhi. The colonial-superior attitude of missionaries and their subsequent criticisms of Hindu religion have caused an equally reactionary response from Hindus like Vivekananda and Gandhi, but that response was also superior, comparative and reductive. Hence mutual correction of the past perception and responses of each other is suggested, so that the Hindu-Christian relations of the present day secular democratic India would not commit or repeat the past mistakes. A vision of mutual reconciliation between *Advaitic* Hinduism and Christianity is suggested, so that both religions will move beyond from an attitude of mutual rejection to one of mutual-acceptance and dialogue in order to understand and enter into the depths of the other's experience and thereby contributing to the common wellbeing of India.

Chapter 7

Conclusion

Vivekananda and Gandhi encountered with the Western protestant missionary Christianity in the 19th century context of British India, which was closely associated with colonial structure and shared its assumptions and attitude towards India. Vivekananda and Gandhi were offended by the missionary preaching and the resultant denunciation of Indian tradition and Hindu religion. Missionaries and colonizers alike viewed India as a dark land, and as culturally and religiously 'inferior' to the West. This assumption of the superiority of the West over everything Indian had its philosophical basis in the philosophy of Aristotle, who, in his hierarchical system classified and justified the exploitation of the lower by the higher. Hence, the East/India was viewed as inferior to West/Europe. Therefore, the exploitation and denunciation of Indian economic and cultural resources had been justified and were viewed as a divine right by the Europeans, with their assumed superiority. Since, West, in its everything such as religion, culture, language, science, civilization, polity, etc. claimed to be superior; they thought to replace everything Indian with the Western. Hence, both Christianity and imperial power worked hand in hand in order to replace and destroy the age-old tradition and religion of India on the one hand, and for the spread of Western civilization and the permanency of British Raj in India on the other.

It was in this context, we see the formation and responses of Vivekananda and Gandhi. Although they were impacted by various influences, including Western, in the formation of their personality and viewpoints, we see a re-affirmation of the superiority and pride in Vivekananda and Gandhi in Indian tradition and in the *Advaitic* form of Hinduism. They firmly opted for the Indian and *Advaitic* philosophy of Hindu religion, in the context of threat to it by Western imperial power and Western Christianity. They did not accept the claims of the West or Christianity, as theirs is the superior civilization or the only true religion, etc. rather they viewed it suspiciously and defended the age-old religion and tradition of India.

Vivekananda and Gandhi, thus affirmed the superiority of Indian tradition over the Western Christianity and its colonial and materialistic civilization. The spiritual, tolerant, non-violent, pluralistic and inclusive tradition of India has been highlighted by them against the exclusive, colonial and domineering tradition of the Christian West, which was based on exploitation, violence and material pleasures. Vivekananda and Gandhi also did not accept the superior view over other religions by the Christian missionaries, and their remarks of them, as 'the work of the devil' 'false', 'darkness' or 'non-valid', etc. On the other hand, they affirmed the equality of all religions in accordance with Indian tradition and the pluralistic emphasis of *Advaita*.

Further they realised that, the Western Christian tradition, they encountered with, was colonial in nature, and the work of missionaries harmed India than benefitted it. Therefore they understood, the Western Christianity came to India, as a tainted form of Christianity, which had divorced itself from the teachings and spirituality of Christ. Hence, they separated Christ from this Western Christianity. As a result, even in the counter-attack and reactionary responses of Vivekananda and Gandhi, they admired Christ and realised that Christ is not present in Western Christianity, nor did He approve the colonial practices of Europe over Asia, or the way of missionary work carried on in India. Hence, Christ became the focal point of interaction between Hinduism and Christianity in colonial India.

They, thus perceived Christ in Indian terms and rejected the Western understanding of Christ, based on the epistemological tools of Aristotle. They rejected the doctrines, dogmas, rituals and interpretations of the Bible by the Western Christianity. They basically questioned the colonial epistemology of Christianity based on the thinking of Aristotle, in which reason was considered as the superior tool to understand the religious truths. Hence, Christian West interpreted Christ in terms of intellectual doctrines and placed the emphasis on historical Christ (empirical). In Western Christian thinking, Christ-experience thus meant, the customary belief in the unique incarnation of Christ in history and placed their belief in the death of Christ on the cross and His resurrection for the remissions of sins of humanity (atonement theory). In this teaching, man is perceived as sinner and God as above man and as 'the holy other', thus it meant dualism and inequality between God and humanity. These teachings were unacceptable for the Indian *Advaitic* minds like Vivekananda and Gandhi.

Hence, the differences between the Christ-experience of Vivekananda and Gandhi and the traditional Christianity. Vivekananda and Gandhi rejected the colonial Aristotelian philosophical framework of the West in their understanding of Christ and adopted the *Advaitic* epistemology of experience, metaphysics of oneness and non-violent love ethics in their Christ-experience. Rather than the rational understanding of Christ, they emphasised on the primacy of intuitive experience (*anubhūti*) in Christ-experience. Hence, theirs is experiential epistemology over the rational epistemology of the West. Moreover, they understood Christ as a meta-historical spiritual principle to be experienced in one's own context, an example of God-realisation, than as a 'unique' historical person. Hence as Christ realised God, we could also realise God and become another Christ. To follow Christ means to become Christ. Hence, there is metaphysical equality with Christ; as Christ is a son of God, we could also become sons of God. Therefore, the Christ-experience of Vivekananda and Gandhi transcends from sinner-saviour relationship to that of *Advaitic* equality and metaphysical oneness with Christ. That means there can be many Christs in Indian understanding, than the emphasis on the 'exclusive divinity' of the historic Christ in the West. Hence, their Christ-experience was metaphysical and ethical, rather than rational, doctrinal, historical or ritualistic.

Thus, they totally rejected the Aristotelian framework of the Western Christian understanding of Christ and stressed Him as one belonging to the East – Christ as an Oriental. Thus Christ was understood as an '*Advaitin*' by Vivekananda and as a '*Satyāgrahi*' by Gandhi. They gave importance to the teachings of Christ in the Sermon on Mount and understood Christ as a 'renouncer', who was selfless and suffered for others through non-violent love. Hence, their *Advaitic* Christology is the best example of inter-religious interaction and dialogue.

Hence, Vivekananda's and Gandhi's Christ-experience reveals new dimensions of Christ-experience, hitherto to unknown or negated in the Western Christian tradition. However, there are problematic elements in their understanding of Christ. This is mainly due to the colonial context of missionary criticisms and the *Advaita Vedāntic* reactionary response to Western Christianity. The colonial Christian spirit of superiority and domineering was challenged by *Advaita*, but in this process, *Advaita* also acquired the same spirit of domineering and superiority. Hence their understanding of Christ in terms of Indian tradition and *Advaita* has used the same comparative approach, which was used earlier by the missionaries to evaluate Hinduism in terms of Western Christianity. Thus in this process, they used selective and reductive methods, which do not do justice to the New Testament understanding of Christ or to the original context of many of Christ's sayings. Hence, in the Hindu-Christian understandings of Christ, there are many philosophical differences. Although, these conceptual differences come from the 19th century colonial context, it can still hurt and create tension and animosity between Christians and Hindus of today, in the present secular, democratic context of India, as Vivekananda's and Gandhi's views are influential and still form the Hindu views on Christ and Christianity. Therefore, there should be re-thinking and there is a need to develop a very positive view of the 'other' by both Hindus and Christians, which is empowering, and mutually acceptable. So, a correction of attitudes of both the Christian missionaries and *Advaita Vedāntins* are recommended for a better understanding and healthy dialogical relations of Christians and Hindus for a better future of their co-existence in a pluralistic India.

Therefore, a philosophical reconciliation is suggested in Hindu-Christian relations and in their perceptions of each other's traditions as well as Christ-experience; from the past colonial confrontation to a dialogical relationship in the present democratic and secular India; from thesis, anti-thesis tension to a viable synthesis and a mutual understanding and acceptance of the 'other' by recognizing the differences of each other. In this new relationship, there is no place for denunciation, offending, reaction, comparative approach, colonial attitude, superior-inferior complexes, reductionism, etc. "For he who does reverence to his own sect while disparaging the sects of others wholly from attachment to his own sect, in reality inflicts, by such conduct, the severest injury on his own sect."[1]

[1] From Edict XII of Ashoka, translated by Vincent A. Smith, *Asoka: The Buddhist Emperor of India* (Oxford: Clarendon Press, 1909), 170-171.

Bibliography

A. Primary Sources on Swami Vivekananda

The Complete Works of Swami Vivekananda, Vols. 1-9. Kolkata: Advaiata Ashrama, 2009.

Vivekananda, Swami. *My India, The India Eternal*. Calcutta: Ramakrishna Mission Institute of Culture, 7th Reprint, 1998.

B. Primary Sources on Mahatma Gandhi

Gandhi, M. K. *All Religions Are True*. Bombay: Pearl Publications, 1962.

__________. *An Autobiography OR The Story of My Experiments with Truth*. Ahmedabad: Navajivan Publishing House, First Edition - 1927, Reprint, 2011.

__________. *Christian Missions, their Place in India*. Ahmedabad: Navajivan Publishing House, 1940.

__________. *Ethical Religion*. Ahmedabad: Navajivan Publishing House, 1968.

__________. *Food for the Soul*. Mumbai: Bharatiya Vidya Bhavan, 1998.

__________. *From Yervada Mandir*. Ahmedabad: Navajivan Publishing House, 2011.

__________. *God is Truth*. Mumbai: Bharatiya Vidya Bhavan, 1998.

__________. *Harijan*. (1933-1942).

__________. *Hind Swaraj or Indian Home Rule*. Ahmedabad: Navajivan Publishing House, 20th Reprint, 2008.

__________. *Hindu Dharma*. New Delhi: Diamond Books, 2009.

__________. *In Search of the Supreme*. Vol. 3. Ahmedabad: Navajivan Publishing House, 1962.

__________. *India of My Dreams*. Ahmedabad: Navajivan Publishing House, 1959.

__________. *Indian Opinion*. (1904-1914).

__________. *Modern Vs. Ancient Civilization*. Mumbai: Bharatiya Vidya Bhavan, 1998.

__________. *My Dear Child*. Ahmedabad: Navajivan Publishing House, 1956.

__________. *My Religion*. Ahmedabad: Navajivan Publishing House, 1958.

__________. *On Myself*. Mumbai: Bharatiya Vidya Bhavan, 1998.

__________. *The Collected Works of Mahatma Gandhi*, Vols. 1-100. New Delhi: Publication Division, Ministry of Broadcasting, Government of India, 1958–1994.

__________. *The Law of Love*. Bombay: Bharatiya Vidya Bhavan, 1962.

__________. *The Message of Jesus Christ*. Mumbai: Bharatiya Vidya Bhavan, 1998.

__________. *The Selected Works of Mahatma Gandhi*. Vols. 4 & 5. Edited by Shriman Narayan. Ahmedabad: Navajivan Publishing House, 2006.

__________. *The Spirit of Hinduism*. New Delhi: Pankaj Publications, 1980.

__________. *The Way to Communal Harmony*. Ahmedabad: Navajivan Publishing House, 1994.

__________. *What Jesus Means to Me*. Ahmedabad: Navajivan Publishing House, 2009.

__________. *Young India*. (1919-1932).

C. Books

Abraham, C. E. "The Rise and Growth of Christianity in India." in *The Cultural Heritage of India*. Vol. 4. Edited by Haridas Bhattacharyya. Calcutta: The Ramakrishna Mission Institute of Culture, 2001.

Aleaz, K. P. *Harmony of Religions: The Relevance of Swami Vivekananda*. Calcutta: Punthi-Pustak, 1993.

__________. *Jesus in Neo-Vedanta: A Meeting of Hinduism and Christianity*. Delhi: Kant Publications, 1995.

Andrews, C. F. *Mahatma Gandhi's Ideas*. New York: The Macmillan Company, 1930.

Aravindakshan, K. *Gandhiyude Jeevitha Darsanam*. Kozhikode: Mathrubhumi Books, 2008.

Bali, Dev Raj. *Modern Indian Thought from Rammohun Roy to Jayaprakash Narayan*. New Delhi: Sterling Publishers, 1996.

Bharati, K. S. *Thoughts of Mahatma*. Vol. 1. Nagpur: Dattsons, 1995.

__________. *Encyclopaedia of Eminent Thinkers, The Political Thought of Vivekananda*. Vol. 8. New Delhi: Concept Publishing Company, 1998.

Bhuyan, P. R. *Swami Vivekananda Messiah of Resurgent India*. New Delhi: Atlantic Publishers and Distributors, 2003.

Bose, Nirmal Kumar. *My Days with Gandhi*. New Delhi: Orient Longman, 1987.

Burke, Marie Louise. *Swami Vivekananda in the West New Discoveries*. Vols. 1-6. Calcutta: Advaita Ashrama, 1st edition, 1986.

Chacko, K. C. *Metaphysical Implications of Gandhian Thought*. Delhi: Mittal Publications, 1986.

Chandra, Prakash. *Modern Indian Political Thought*. New Delhi: Vikas Publishing House, 2000.

Chatterjee, Margaret. *Gandhi's Religious Thought*. London: The Macmillan Press, 1983.

Chatterji, Suniti Kumar. "Reminiscences." In *Mahatma Gandhi 100 Years*. Edited by S. Radhakrishnan. New Delhi: Gandhi Peace Foundation, 2009.

Chattopadhyaya, Rajagopal. *Swami Vivekananda in the West*. Calcutta: K. P. Bagchi & Company, 1994.

Chaudhuri, Asim. *Swami Vivekananda in Chicago: New Findings*. Kolkata: Advaita Ashrama, 2005.

Chunder, Pratap Chandra. *On Understanding Gandhiji*. Mumbai: Bharatiya Vidya Bhavan, 2003.

Daniel, P. S. *Hindu Response to Religious Pluralism*. Delhi: Kant Publications, 2000.

Das, P. K. *Modern Vedanta Gandhi's Philosophy Compared with the Philosophies of Vivekananda, Raman Mahershi, Tagore, Aurobindo, Ramatirtha, Radhakrishnan and Deen Dayal Upadhyaya*. Meerut: Rahul Publishing House, 2004.

Das, Sisir Kumar. *The Shadow of the Cross Christianity and Hinduism in a Colonial Situation*. New Delhi: Munshiram Manoharlal Publishers, 1974.

Dasgupta, R. K. *Swami Vivekananda on Indian Philosophy and Literature*. Calcutta: The Ramakrishna Mission Institute of Culture, 1996.

Datta, Bhupendranath. *Swami Vivekananda Patriot-Prophet: A Study*. Calcutta: Navabharat Publishers, 1954.

Devanandan, P. D. *The Gospel and Renascent Hinduism*. London: SCM Press, 1959.

Devdas, Nalini. *Svāmī Vivekānanda*. Bangalore: CISRS, 1968.

Dhar, Sailendra Nath. *A Comprehensive Biography of Swami Vivekananda*. Parts 1-3. Chennai: Vivekananda Kendra Prakashan, Third Edition, 2005.

Dharmaraj, Jacob S. *Colonialism and Christian Mission: Postcolonial Reflections*. Delhi: ISPCK, 1993.

Dhawan, Gopinath. *The Political Philosophy of Mahatma Gandhi*. Ahmedabad: Navajivan Publishing House, 1962.

Diwaker, R. R. *Gandhi's Life, Thought and Philosophy*. Bombay: Bharatiya Vidya Bhavan, 1963.

Doke, Joseph J. *M. K. Gandhi: An Indian Patriot in South Africa*. New Delhi: n.p., 1967.

Dutta, D. M. *The Philosophy of Mahatma Gandhi*. Madison: The University of Wisconsin Press, 1953.

Eastern and Western Disciples. *The Life of Swami Vivekananda*. Vols. 1 & 2. Kolkata: Advaita Ashrama, Tenth Impression, 2010.

Ellsberg, Robert. *Gandhi on Christianity*. New York: Orbis Books, 1991.

George, P. V. *The Unique Christ and the Mystic Gandhi*. Thiruvalla: The Malabar Christian Office, 1934.

George, S. K. *Gandhi's Challenge to Christianity*. Ahmedabad: Navajivan Publishing House, 1947.

Halbfass, Wilhem. *India and Europe: An Essay in Philosophical Understanding*. Delhi: Motilal Banarsidass Publishers, 1990.

Hammer, Olav. *Alternative Christs*. Cambridge: Cambridge University Press, 2009.

Hunt, James D. *Gandhi and Nonconformists Encounters in South Africa*. New Delhi: Promilla & Co., Publishers, 1986.

Iserwood, Christopher. *Ramakrishna and His Disciples*. Calcutta: Advaita Ashrama, 1986.

Iyer, Raghavan N. *The Moral and Political Thought of Mahatma Gandhi*. Delhi: Oxford University Press, 1973.

__________. *The Essential Writings of Mahatma Gandhi*. Delhi: Oxford University Press, 1994.

Jawed, Ajeet. *Swami Vivekananda: An Iconoclastic Ascetic*. New Delhi: Ane Books India, 2007.

Jayapalan, N. *Aristotle*. New Delhi: Atlantic Publishers and Distributors, 1999.

Jesudasan, Ignatius. *A Gandhian Theology of Liberation*. Anand: Gujarat Sahitya Prakash, 1987.

Jones, E. Stanley. *Mahatma Gandhi: An Interpretation*. New York: Abingdon-Cokesbury Press, 1948.

Karandikar, V. R. *Ramakrishna and Vivekananda*. Bombay: Bharatiya Vidya Bhavan, 1991.

Kavungal, Devis. *The Philosophical Foundation of Mahatma Gandhi's Vision of Sarvodaya*. Bangalore: Dharmaram Publications, 2000.

Keer, Dhananjay. *Mahatma Gandhi*. Bombay: Popular Prakashan, 1973.

Kim, S. K. *The Philosophical Thoughts of Mahatma Gandhi*. New Delhi: Vikas Publishing House, 1996.

Kumari, Prem. *Comparative Ethics of Gandhi and Kant*. New Delhi: Classical Publishing Company, 1996.

Lal, Basant Kumar. *Contemporary Indian Philosophy*. Delhi: Motilal Banarsidass, 1995.

Lekshmikutty, N. *Swami Vivekananda on Indian Reconstruction*. Vadakara: Malabar Institute for Research and Development, 2009.

Mahadevan, T.M.P. "The Advaita of Mahatma Gandhi." In *Facets of Mahatma Gandhi*. Vol. 4. Edited by Subrata Mukherjee and Sushila Ramaswamy. New Delhi: Deep & Deep Publications, 1994.

Majumdar, R. C. *Swami Vivekananda: A Historical Review*. Kolkata: Advaita Ashrama, 2004.

Mangalath, Daniel. *A Challenge and a Promise Mahatma Gandhi's Philosophy of Man and Life*. Trivandrum: M S Publications, 1996.

Mannumel, Thomas. *The Advaita of Vivekananda: A Philosophical Appraisal*. Madras: T. R. / Satya Nilayam Publications, 1991.

Mathai, M. P. *Mahatma Gandhi's World-View*. New Delhi: Gandhi Peace Foundation, 2000.

Mathew, Tony. *Vivekananda Prasnothari*. Kottayam: Current Books, 2004.

Minz, Nirmal. *Mahatma Gandhi and Hindu-Christian Dialogue*. Madras: Christian Literature Society, 1970.

Mital, S. S. *The Social and Political Ideas of Swami Vivekananda*. New Delhi: Metropolitan Book, 1979.

Mukherji, Santi L. *The Philosophy of Man-Making: A Study in Social and Political Ideas of Swami Vivekananda*. Kolkata: New Central Book Agency, 2008.

Nair, Santhinikethanam Krishnan. *Gandhijiyum Adhunika Darsanikarum*. Kottayam: D. C. Books, 1998.

Nanda, B. R. *In Search of Gandhi: Essays and Reflections*. New Delhi: Oxford University Press, 2002.

Nikhilananda, Swami. *Vivekananda: A Biography*. New York: Ramakrishna-Vivekananda Center, 1953.

Nirvedananda, Swami. *Swami Vivekananda on India and Her Problems*. Almora: Advaita Ashrama, 4th edition, 1946.

Nivedita, Sister. *The Master As I Saw Him*. Calcutta: Udbodhan Office, Sixth Edition, 1948.

Pal, Jaladhar. *The Moral Philosophy of Gandhi*. New Delhi: Gyan Publishing House, 1998.

Panikkar, K. M. *Asia and Western Dominance*. Mumbai: Somaiya Publications, 1999.

Parameswaran, P. *Marx and Vivekananda: A Comparative Study*. New Delhi: Sterling Publishers, 1987.

Paranjape, Makarand. *The Penguin Swami Vivekananda Reader*. New Delhi: Penguin Books, 2005.

Parekh, Bhikhu. *Colonialism, Tradition and Reform: An Analysis of Gandhi's Political Discourse*. New Delhi: Sage Publications, 1989.

Pattery, George. *Gandhi – The Believer: An Indian Christian Perspective*. Delhi: ISPCK, 1996.

Paul, Lizy. *Dynamics of Personality Development: A Study Based on Mahatma Gandhi's Life and Writings*. Bangalore: Dharmaram Publication, 1997.

Philip, T. V. *Reflections on Christian Mission in Asia*. Delhi: ISPCK/CSS, 2000.

Pillai, K. V. Paul. *India's Search for the Unknown Christ*. New Delhi: Fazl Publishers, 1978.

Prabhu, R. K. and U. R. Rao. *The Mind of Mahatma Gandhi*. London: Oxford University Press, 1946.

Pulickan, Jacob. *Gandhiji Life and Philosophy*. Thiruvananthapuram: Centre for Gandhian Studies, University of Kerala, 1999.

Puri, Bindu. *Gandhi and the Moral Life*. New Delhi: Mittal Publications, 2004.

Pushparajan, A. *From Conversion to Fellowship: The Hindu-Christian Encounter in the Gandhian Perspective*. Allahabad: St. Paul Press, 1990.

Pyarelal. *Mahatma Gandhi: The Early Phase*. Vol. 1. Ahmedabad: Navajivan Publishing House, 1965.

Radhakrishnan, K. S. *Gandhijiyude Ramarajyadarsanam*. Kottayam: Sahithya Pravarthaka Co-operative Society, 2012.

__________. *Gandhi- Sree Narayana Guru*. Kottayam: D. C. Books, 2013.

Radhakrishnan, S. *Indian Philosophy*. Vol. 2. London: George Allen & Unwin, 1966.

__________. *Our Heritage*. Delhi: Orient Paperbacks, 1976.

Raju, P. T. *The Philosophical Traditions of India*. London: George Allen & Unwin, 1971.

Ramabadran, R. S. *Vivekananda Divinity on Earth*. Madras: Vivekananda Literature Society, 1991.

Ramachandran, G. and T. K. Mahadevan. *Quest for Gandhi*. New Delhi: Gandhi Peace Foundation, 1970.

Rambachan, Anantanand. *The Limits of Scripture: Vivekananda's Reinterpretation of the Vedas*. Delhi: Sri Satguru Publications, 1995.

Ranganathananda, Swami. *Eternal Values for a Changing Society*. Bombay: Bharatiya Vidya Bhavan, 1971.

Rao, K. L. Seshagiri. *Mahatma Gandhi and Comparative Religion*. Delhi: Motilal Banarsidass, 1978.

Rao, V.K.R.V. *Builders of Modern India, Swami Vivekananda*. New Delhi: Publications Division, Ministry of Information and Broadcasting, Government of India, 1979.

__________. *Swami Vivekananda: The Prophet of Vedantic Socialism*. New Delhi: Publications Division, Ministry of Information and Broadcasting, Government of India, 1979.

Reddy, A. V. Rathna. *The Political Philosophy of Swami Vivekananda*. New Delhi: Sterling Publishers, 1984.

Roy, Binoy K. *Socio-Political Views of Vivekananda*. New Delhi: People's Publishing House, Third Reprint, 1983.

Rynne, Terrence J. *Gandhi and Jesus: The Saving Power of Non-violence*. Bangalore: Asian Trading Corporation, 2009.

Samartha, S. J. *The Hindu Response to the Unbound Christ*. Madras: CLS, 1974.

Sarma, D. S. *Hinduism through the Ages*. Mumbai: Bharatiya Vidya Bhavan, 2000.

Satprakashananda, Swami. *Vivekananda: His Contribution to the Present Age*. Kolkata: Advaita Ashrma, 2011.

Sen, Amartya. *The Argumentative Indian Writings on Indian Culture, History and Identity*. London: Penguin Books, 2005.

Smith, Vincent A. *Asoka: The Buddhist Emperor of India*. Oxford: Clarendon Press, 1909.

Srivastava, Rama Shanker. *Contemporary Indian Philosophy*. New Delhi: Munshiram Manoharlal Publishers, 1983.

Stephen, Abraham. *The Social Philosophy of Swami Vivekananda: Its Relevance to Modern India*. Delhi: ISPCK, 2005.

Stephen, M. *Introducing Post Modernism and Post Colonialism*. New Delhi: Concept Publishing Company, 2013.

Sumithra, Sunand. *Christian Theologies from an Indian Perspective*. Bangalore: Theological Book Trust, 1995.

Sykes, Marjorie. "East Wind, West Wind." In *Facets of Mahatma Gandhi*. Vol. 4. Edited by Subrata Mukherjee and Sushila Ramaswamy. New Delhi: Deep & Deep Publications, 1994.

Tendulkar, D. G. *Mahatma Life of Mohandas Karamchand Gandhi*. Vols. 1-8. New Delhi: The Publications Division, Ministry of Information and Broadcasting, Government of India, 1988.

The Complete Works of Sister Nivedita. Vol. 1. Kolkata: Advaita Ashrama, Fifth Impression, 2006.

Thekkinedath, Joseph. *Love of Neighbour in Mahatma Gandhi*. Bangalore: St. Paul's Press Training School, 1971.

Thomas, M. M. *The Acknowledged Christ of the Indian Renaissance*. Madras: CLS, 1991.

Thomas, Santhosh. *Christianity and Culture*. New Delhi: Mittal Publications, 2005.

Thottakara, Augustine. *Spirituality of Dialogue: Indian Experiences*. Bangalore: Dharmaram Publications, 1994.

Tiwari, Ravi. *Reflections and Studies in Religion*. Delhi: ISPCK, 2008.

Vasudev, Kasthuri. "The Metaphysical Basis of Gandhian Political Philosophy." In *Indian Philosophical Annual*. Vol. 5. Edited by T.M.P. Mahadevan. University of Madras, 1969.

Veerraju, Gummadi. *Gandhian Philosophy Its Relevance Today*. New Delhi: Decent Books, 1999.

Vekathanam, Mathew. *Indian Christology: Perspectives and Challenges*. Bangalore: Asian Trading Corporation, 2004.

Verma, Surendra. *Metaphysical Foundation of Mahatma Gandhi's Thought*. Bombay: Orient Longman, 1970.

Wadhwa, Madhuri. *Gandhi between Tradition and Modernity*. New Delhi: Deep & Deep Publications, 1997.

Wilson, Boyd H. "Ultimacy as Unifier in Gandhi." In *Religion in Modern India*. Edited by Robert D. Baird. New Delhi: Manohar Publishers, 2001.

Wynne-Tyson, Esme. "Gandhi's Rediscovery of Christianity." In *Facets of Mahatma Gandhi*. Vol. 4. Edited by Subrata Mukherjee and Sushila Ramaswamy. New Delhi: Deep & Deep Publications, 1994.

D. Articles

Adams, Norman R. "Background of Some Hindu Influences in America – The Ramakrishna Movement." *Journal of Ecumenical Studies* 9/2 (Spring, 1972): 318-340.

Bain-Selbo, Eric. "Understanding the Other: The Challenge of Post-Colonial Theory to the Comparative Study of Religion." *Religious Studies and Theology* 18/1 (June, 1999): 60-108.

Bishop, Peter D. "Ahimsa and Satyagraha the interaction of Hindu and Christian Religious Ideas, and their Contribution to a Political Campaign." *The Indian Journal of Theology* 27/2 (April-June, 1978): 53-66.

Brown, Linda Keller. "Mission, A Cultural Confrontation: Swami Vivekananda and The American Missionary Movement." *Journal of Dharma* 6/2 (April-June, 1981): 167-189.

Clooney, Francis X. "Hindu Views of Religious Others: Implications for Christian Theology." *Theological Studies* 64/2 (June, 2003): 306-333.

Devanandan, P. D. "The Modern Hindu Attitude Toward Christian Evangelism." *Union Seminary Quarterly Review* 12/3 (March, 1957): 65-76.

Jesudasan, I. "Gandhian Perspectives on Missiology." *Indian Church History Review* 4/1 (June, 1970): 45-72.

Jha, Rama. "Gandhi's Encounter with Western Thought." *Gandhi Marg* 5/4 (July, 1983): 209-221.

Keller, Carl. "The Vedanta Philosophy and The Message of Christ." *The International Review of Missions* 42/168 (October, 1953): 377-389.

Malkovsky, Bradley. "Advaita Vedanta and Christian Faith." *Journal of Ecumenical Studies* 36/3-4 (Summer-Fall, 1999): 397-422.

Mampra, Thomas. "Encounter Between Hinduism and Christianity." *Journal of Dharma* 1/3 (January, 1976): 246-266.

Maynard, John A. "Christian Theology and Hindu Religious Thinking." *Anglican Theological Review* 1/2 (1918): 184-190.

Middleton, Vern. "Caste Issues in the Minds of McGavran and Gandhi." *Missiology: An International Review* 13/2 (April, 1985): 159-173.

Naik, J. P. "Development and Gandhian Tradition in India." *The Review of Politics*, 45/3 (July, 1983): 345-365.

Paradkar, Balwant A. M. "Hindu Interpretation of Christ from Vivekananda to Radhakrishnan." *The Indian Journal of Theology* 18/1 (January-March, 1969): 65-80.

Philip, T. V. "Christianity in India during Western Colonialism: Conflict, Reconciliation or Adjustment." *Indian Church History Review* 21/1 (June, 1987): 15-27.

Rambachan, Anantanand. "Interpreting Another Tradition: Vivekananda on Christ and Christianity." *Anima* 20/2 (September, 1994): 127-133.

Richards, Glyn. "Gandhi's Concept of Truth and the Advaita Tradition." *Religious Studies*, 22/1 (March, 1986): 1-14.

Streiker, Lowell D. "The Hindu Attitude Toward Other Religions." *The Journal of Religious Thought* 23/1 (1966-1967): 75-90.

Tinker, Hugh. "Nonviolence as a Political Strategy: Gandhi and Western Thinkers." *Gandhi Marg* 2/5 (August, 1980): 241-255.

Vrajaprana, Pravrajika. "What Do Hindus *Do?*—The Role of the Vedanta Societies in North America." *Cross Currents* 47/1 (Spring, 1997): 69-85.

E. Unpublished Thesis

Prasannakumary, B. "Vedanta Philosophy and Religion of Swami Vivekananda." Ph. D Thesis, University of Kerala, 1990.

Thomas, Mathew. "Christian Missions in the Pluralistic Context of India – The Relevance of Gandhian Approach." Ph. D Thesis, Mahatma Gandhi University, 2003.